D0643467

"ASPECT" GEOGRAPHIES

GEOGRAPHY OF THE EEC

"ASPECT" GEOGRAPHIES

GEOGRAPHY OF THE EEC

A Systematic Economic Approach

C. G. BAMFORD
BA, MCIT

Senior Lecturer in Geography, The Polytechnic, Huddersfield

H. ROBINSON
BA, MA, MEd, PhD

Formerly Head of the Department of Geography and Geology and Dean of the Faculty of Arts, The Polytechnic, Huddersfield

MACDONALD AND EVANS

MACDONALD & EVANS LTD
Estover, Plymouth PL6 7PZ

First published 1983

©
MACDONALD & EVANS LTD
1983

British Library CIP Data

Bamford, C. G.
Geography of the EEC.—(Aspect geographies)
I. Title   II. Robinson, H.   III. Series
914   D923
ISBN 0-7121-0745-2
ISBN 0-7121-0732- Pbk

Printed in Great Britain by
Butler & Tanner Ltd
Frome and London

Introduction to the Series

THE study of modern geography grew out of the medieval cosmography, a random collection of knowledge which included astronomy, astrology, geometry, political history, earthlore, etc. As a result of the scientific discoveries and developments of the seventeenth and eighteenth centuries many of the component parts of the old cosmography hived off and grew into distinctive disciplines in their own right as, for example, physiography, geology, geodesy and anthropology. The residual matter which was left behind formed the geography of the eighteenth and nineteenth centuries, a study which, apart from its mathematical side, was encyclopaedic in character and which was purely factual and descriptive.

Darwinian ideas stimulated a more scientific approach to learning, and geography, along with other subjects, was influenced by the new modes of thought. These had an increasing impact on geography, which during the present century has increasingly sought for causes and effects and has become more analytical. In its modern development geography has had to turn to many of its former offshoots—by now robust disciplines in themselves—and borrow from them: geography does not attempt to usurp their functions, but it does use the material to illuminate itself. Largely for this reason geography is a wide-ranging discipline with mathematical, physical, human and historical aspects: this width is at once a source of strength and weakness, but it does make geography a fascinating study and it helps to justify Sir Halford Mackinder's contention that geography is at once an art, a science and a philosophy.

Naturally the modern geographer, with increasing knowledge at his disposal and a more mature outlook, has had to specialise, and these days the academic geographer tends to be, for example, a geomorphologist or climatologist or economic geographer or urban geographer. This is an inevitable development since no one person could possibly master the vast wealth of material or ideas encompassed in modern geography.

This modern specialisation has tended to emphasise the importance of systematic geography at the expense of regional geography, although it should be recognised that each approach to geography is incomplete without the other. The general trend, both in the universities and in the school examinations, is towards systematic studies.

This series has been designed to meet some of the needs of students pursuing systematic studies. The main aim has been to provide introductory texts which can be used by sixth-formers and first-year university students. The intention has been to produce readable books which will provide sound introductions to various aspects of geography, books which will introduce the students to new ideas and concepts as well as more detailed factual information. While one must employ precise scientific terms, the writers have eschewed jargon for jargon's sake; moreover, they have aimed at lucid exposition. While, these days, there is no shortage of specialised books on most branches of geographical knowledge, there is, we believe, room for texts of a more introductory nature.

The aim of the series is to include studies of many aspects of geography embracing the geography of agriculture, the geography of manufacturing industry, biogeography, the geography of transport and tourism, the geography of settlement and tropical geography. Other new titles will be added from time to time as seems desirable.

H. ROBINSON
Geographical Editor

Preface

SINCE the Second World War, the most important influence on the economic geography of Europe has been the realisation and spread of integration. Although arising out of necessity, the processes of integration have continued and developed so that modern Europe is dominated by two formidable economic units, the European Economic Community (EEC) and the Council for Mutual Economic Assistance (COMECON). Any contemporary geographical study cannot ignore the fact that these units have had a tremendous economic impact upon the space economy of the continent.

This new addition to the "Aspect" Geographies series provides a systematic study of the economic geography of the EEC. Although the geography of individual member states cannot be completely ignored, the emphasis of the text is to view their economic geography within the context of EEC policies and in particular to look at the impact and problems of such policies upon their recent economic performance and well-being. The book is divided into three parts. Part One provides an introduction to the modern economic geography of the EEC through an analysis of the resource base of Western Europe and an account of economic integration up to the signing of the Treaty of Rome. The emphasis of the text in Part Two is upon present day economic problems and policies of the EEC. Trade, the first stage towards the realisation of integration, is discussed in Chapter III while Chapter IV analyses in detail one of the major problem areas of integration, that of agriculture and fishing. Other chapters of this part analyse further areas of the systematic economic geography of the EEC while the final chapter looks at some important future issues including geographical enlargement and economic and monetary union. Part Three deals with regional issues of integration. Recognising that geographically the benefits of integration have not been spread evenly between the regions of the EEC, Chapter XI provides an up-to-date analysis of variations in living standards in the EEC while Chapter XII outlines and appraises the regional policies of member states and the Community. The final chapter of the book gives a series of contrasting examples of problem regions of the EEC.

Both authors have had a longstanding interest in the economic geography of the EEC. Harry Robinson has written widely on the subject and this text complements and updates his regional geography of Western Europe (University Tutorial Press, Cambridge). Colin Bamford, who since 1972 has taught a third-year course at

Huddersfield Polytechnic on "Aspects of European Integration", has used this experience as a basis for the text. The partnership has been a particularly fruitful one since one author is a longstanding geographer, the other an economist turned geographer. The nature of the subject lends itself well to this combined approach.

This book, like others in the series, has been designed for use by sixth-formers and first-year university students. As well as being of value to students of Geography, the book will also provide useful material for those studying for qualifications in European Studies, Economics and Politics. The authors also hope that it may reach an even wider market, providing up-to-date information on a most important subject. More specifically, the book will be of relevance as a course text for new revised G C E "A" level syllabuses on the E E C such as Syllabus C of the Joint Matriculation Board.

The authors have endeavoured to provide up-to-date statistics, although in a few instances this has been not possible due to data limitations. In general, most tables in the text relate to 1979 and, in some cases, 1980. Readers seeking more detailed sources of statistics and a pathway through the maze of E E C publications may find it useful to consult J. Jeffries, *A Guide to the Official Publications of the European Community*, 2nd edition, Mansell, 1981.

All chapters in Part Two include some reference to the accession of Greece to the E E C and Chapter X, in discussing the problems of geographical enlargement, has a full analysis of the issues involved in Greek membership. The authors did not feel it appropriate to include Greece in tables and figures relating to the E E C economy in the late 1970s, and in any case there were many statistical problems in seeking to do this.

The authors would like to record their thanks to the London office of the Commission of the European Communities for a regular supply of publications and advice on statistical problems. Readers seeking information on aspects of Community affairs are well advised to contact the Commission at 20, Kensington Palace Gardens, London W8 4QQ. Given the ever-changing nature of E E C affairs, readers may wish to keep in touch with day-to-day developments by reading a good newspaper. The authors, as recognised in the text, have gained much information from Alan Osborn's regular reports in *The Daily Telegraph.*

We wish to thank all those publishers who gave their permission for quotations from books published by them. Our thanks also go to Steve Pratt and Margaret Brooke for help and advice on certain figures, to Judith Ayre for typing parts of the manuscript and to Jacqueline MacDonald and the editorial staff of Macdonald and Evans Ltd. Finally, we must record thanks to our respective wives

for their patience and understanding during the course of preparation
of this book.

1982   C. G. B.
                                                                 H. R.

Contents

List of Illustrations

List of Tables

Part One

INTRODUCTION

Chapter I

The Geographical Framework and Characteristics of Europe

Europe: Its Location, Size, Shape and Configuration

M A N Y advantages have accrued to the continent of Europe through its location, size, shape and configuration. Location is a fundamental geographical concept but it implies two things: absolute location and relative position. Absolute location is geographical position defined in terms of latitude and longitude: it is mathematically determined, fixed and unalterable. Thus Europe is said to lie between approximately 35° and 70° latitude north, and to extend from 6° longitude west to about 45° east. There is, however, the other aspect of geographical location which may be termed relative position and such a situation refers to the location of an area with respect to other areas (either land or sea) and, especially, its accessibility.

Though the absolute geographical position of the continent of Europe has remained constant and never changed, at least for several thousands of years, its relative position has changed: it has been variable throughout the historical period. Europe's importance has grown in relation to the extent of the known world and its accessibility. In antiquity the only part of Europe that was really known and really mattered was the territory bordering the Mediterranean Sea which formed part of the literate world and in which technology and urbanisation were of a relatively high order. Even after the Roman conquest of Gaul, the British Isles lay on the very edge of the vaguely known world. *Ultima Thule*, which means "the ends of the earth", was the name given to the lands of North–West Europe.

The Mediterranean remained the heart of the known world throughout classical and medieval times, and it was not until the great navigations of the fifteenth and sixteenth centuries revealed the presence of the "New" World that the centre of gravity, as it were, moved from the Mediterranean to the marginal lands and seas of North–West Europe. Thus the European countries on the Atlantic seaboard came to be in a much more favourable position to undertake oceanic exploration and to engage in overseas trade and colonisation; thus power and wealth accrued to Portugal, Spain, France, the Netherlands and Britain in turn.

Two special advantages arise out of Europe's location: first, it lies in the centre of the "land hemisphere" of the world, a fact which has accentuated Europe's focal position in the world; and, second, its position in mid-latitudes has ensured that the western portion of it enjoys a temperate climate which is especially advantageous from the point of view of man's physical and mental well-being.

Europe, Australia excepted, is the smallest of the continents having an area of rather more than 10m km^2 or approximately 3.8m sq. m. In many respects smallness of size may be a drawback but in others it may bring distinct advantages as, in fact, it does in the case of Europe which is sufficiently small to possess a relatively high degree of unity. The continent is small enough for its various regions to have influenced one another: physical divides, for example, are nowhere so high nor so difficult as to separate and isolate the various parts of the continent as happens in Asia. Moreover, peoples and ideas have been able to circulate with relative freedom, hence Europe has enjoyed a considerable measure of interchange and bears a common stamp largely of a cultural character. Although this common stamp is, perhaps, rather intangible, Europe has a quality, character, personality, however it may be identified, which is clearly recognisable as European. This "Europeanness" pervades the continent as a whole and is distinguishable notwithstanding the political fragmentation, the varied economic conditions and ethnic and cultural differences.

On a world map, Europe appears to be merely a peninsula of Asia with no greater claim to continental status than either the Indian peninsula or the peninsula of South-East Asia. The Ural Mountains in terms of relief are of slight consequence and do not form a physical barrier but, along with the Caspian Sea, they have traditionally been accepted as marking the eastern boundary of Europe. Traditionally, ethnically and culturally, Europe has always been perceived as distinct from Asia and been differentiated as a separate continent. This, however, does not alter the basic fact that physically Europe is merely a prolongation of Asia and does not qualify as a continent in the sense that it is a separate physical entity. The notion that Europe is a distinct entity has long persisted, notwithstanding its physical shortcomings, principally because it is a culture area distinguished by its Graeco-Roman base and its Christian heritage. As Jordan has commented: "Europe is a human entity rather than a physical one, and its distinctiveness is to be sought in the character of the peoples who occupy it rather than in its physical environment."[1]

In more recent decades the traditional concept of Europe has become modified, since the Soviet Union, bestriding Eurasia like a colossus, is now, by virtue of its political, economic and social distinctiveness, generally looked upon as a separate unit. Thus the traditional Europe has been shorn of much of its "continental" part and the new "Europe" is confined to that portion of the continent lying west of the Soviet Union. If this latter interpretation be accepted, then the European continent becomes even more pronouncedly peninsular in its character. From the main peninsula, which has formed the core of Europe, a series of smaller peninsulas extend from it; hence Europe has been very aptly described as a "peninsula of peninsulas". Europe's very irregular coastal configuration has meant that, in relation to its size, it has a longer coastline than any other continent; altogether, the total length of coast approximates 32,000 km (20,000 m). Two important advantages accrue from this pronounced irregularity of coastline:

(i) large areas of the continent are affected by maritime influences resulting from the deeply penetrating arms of the sea (the North Sea–Baltic extension in the north and the Mediterranean–Black Sea extension in the south) and so enjoy some of the benefits of the mild oceanic climate of the western fringes of Europe; and

(ii) just as these sea extensions carry oceanic influences deeply inland so, too, they provide the greater part of Europe with easy access to the great ocean highways permitting many countries to develop shipping and to participate in sea trade; moreover, the irregularity of the coast has offered an abundance of excellent harbours which have greatly facilitated sea trade.

Peninsular and Trunk Europe

The late Professor L. W. Lyde claimed that peninsularity was the differentiating feature of Europe as a continent and that it had exerted profound effects upon the human life of the continent, especially upon its political, economic and social development. Lyde claimed, with much justification, that it was possible to draw a distinction between the continental or "Asiatic" portion of the continent and the peninsular or truly European part.[2] Professor J. F. Unstead carried this concept a stage further: he gave the names "Trunk" and "Peninsular" Europe to these two distinctive parts of the continent defining them as follows:

We may regard Peninsular Europe as that part of the continent which adjoins the Atlantic Ocean and has been given peninsular form by the penetration of the North and Baltic Seas on the north and the Mediterranean on the south. It may be broadly limited eastwards by a line drawn through the Gulf of Bothnia and the Baltic Sea to near the mouth of the Nieman (Memel) River ... and thence ... to near the delta of the Danube. By such a division, both Peninsular and Trunk Europe include portions of several

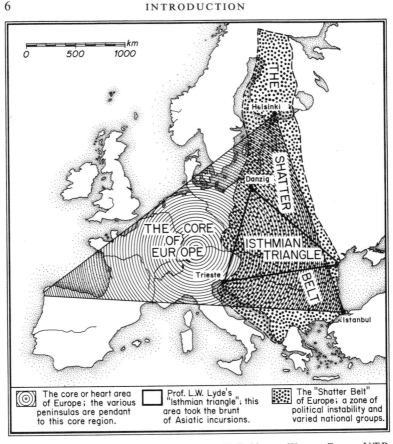

km
0   500   1000

THE

SHATTER

Helsinki

Danzig

THE CORE
OF
EUROPE

ISTHMIAN
TRIANGLE

Trieste

BELT

Istanbul

| ◎ The core or heart area of Europe; the various peninsulas are pendant to this core region. | ▢ Prof. L.W. Lyde's "Isthmian triangle"; this area took the brunt of Asiatic incursions. | ▦ The "Shatter Belt" of Europe; a zone of political instability and varied national groups. |

[*Source*: H. Robinson, *Western Europe*, UTP.

FIG. 1.—Peninsular and trunk Europe.

geographical regions, but the former is more open to maritime and western influences, while the latter has a continental and eastern orientation.[3]

To the west of a line running roughly from Leningrad to Istanbul no point in Europe is more than 720 km (450 m) from the sea; east of it places may be 1,287 km (800 m) distant; hence, the sea and maritime influences have tended to play an important role in the lives of many peoples in Peninsular Europe while, in contrast, at least until very recent times, the peoples of Trunk Europe have displayed little interest in, and have shown little understanding of, the sea and its influences. Whereas Peninsular Europe has an extremely varied relief of mountains and plateaux, valleys and plains, Trunk Europe physically is a vast platform of level or rolling relief with limitless horizons and a monotonous aspect. West of the Leningrad-Istanbul line climatic conditions generally are less extreme and along the Atlantic margins extremely equable conditions with generally abundant and well-distributed rainfall occur; east of the line, conditions are characteristically extreme, precipitation is much less, and the rainfall is more pronouncedly seasonal in its incidence.

Racially and culturally there are also marked differences between west and east. In the west, there are Nordic, Alpine and Mediterranean racial components although there has been considerable intermixing, whereas the peoples to the east are mainly Alpine in racial type with a Mongoloid admixture. In the west the peoples principally speak languages belonging to the Germanic and Romance families and are members of the Roman Catholic and Protestant Churches, while in the east the peoples speak mainly Slavic tongues and, formerly, were adherents to the Greek Orthodox Church or national modifications to that Church. The western portion, too, differs from the east in that its culture and civilisation have an essentially Graeco-Roman origin; one of the more obvious distinguishing characteristics of Western European civilisation is its close link with the early Mediterranean civilisations and its absorption of Greek and Roman cultural features manifest in, for example, the alphabet, law, democracy and civic life.[4]

The Revolution in Russia in 1917 and the establishment of a Communist regime led to profound changes in the political, economic and social life of that country. The traditional differences existing between Europe west and east of the Leningrad-Istanbul line were accordingly heightened and a distinct cleavage between the two areas, epitomised in the term "the Iron Curtain", developed, although the Leningrad-Istanbul line and the Iron Curtain do not coincide. After the Second World War Soviet influence extended westwards and a number of Communist regimes were set up in the states marginal to western Russia which, it should be recalled, had already occupied and integrated the former independent Baltic States of Estonia, Latvia and Lithuania. The new Communist states—Poland, East Germany, Czechoslovakia, Hungary, Romania, Bulgaria, Yugoslavia and Albania—lie in what has been called the "shatter belt", i.e. that transitional zone or marchland belt between west and east which historically has always been politically unstable and has been subjected to varying pressures from both east and west. More significant is the inclusion of Eastern Germany (the German Democratic Republic) which really lies outside the shatter belt but which, because of its occupation by the Soviet Union after the Second World

War, had a Communist Government imposed upon it. Today, therefore, an irregular line between Lübeck and Trieste, separates the Soviet Union and its eastern European satellites from Western Europe.[5]

Europe: Its Major Geographical Regions

The Leningrad-Istanbul line, it has been argued, provides a fairly clear-cut division of Europe into two quite distinctive parts: the extensive continental and the broken peninsular areas of the continent. The Alps and their associated ranges of young fold mountains trend roughly west-east across Europe, more or less cutting off the three southern peninsulas of the continent—Iberia, Italy and the Balkans—from the rest of the land mass (*see* Fig. 2). By using these two broad lines for division, a simple but effective and geographically

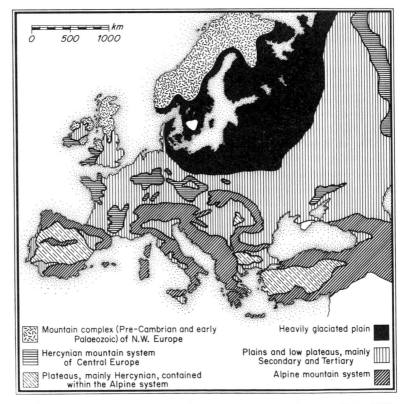

Mountain complex (Pre-Cambrian and early Palaeozoic) of N.W. Europe

Hercynian mountain system of Central Europe

Plateaus, mainly Hercynian, contained within the Alpine system

Heavily glaciated plain

Plains and low plateaus, mainly Secondary and Tertiary

Alpine mountain system

[*Source*: N. J. G. Pounds, *Europe and the Soviet Union*, 1966.

FIG. 2.—The physical background of Europe.

sound primary division into three major areas or regions can be distinguished:

(*i*) the north-western portion focusing upon the narrow seas;
(*ii*) the eastern essentially continental portion; and
(*iii*) the southern part oriented towards the Mediterranean.

Within these tripartite divisions there are areas where the characteristic features are developed *par excellence*, e.g. the Atlantic margins of the first, the Soviet Republic of the second, and the southern parts of the Mediterranean peninsulas of the third.

Away from these characterising areas the typifying conditions become modified and in the "frontier" zones there is a merging of one region with another. There is, in fact, a central transitional area whose physical features and characteristics, and even aspects of its human geography, go far to warrant the area being considered as a separate region. German geographers, indeed, have always subscribed to the concept of *Mitteleuropa*, i.e. Middle or Central Europe.

Formerly, this central region was often considered to coincide broadly with that part of Europe where the German language was spoken, i.e. pre-war Germany, Austria, and most of Switzerland, although parts of Czechoslovakia and Poland were, also, often considered to be part of this central region. The Germans living in the central part of Europe have always stressed that a central European region did exist and that it was a geographical and cultural entity. The Nazis, indeed, in the 1930s invoked the idea of *Mitteleuropa* to justify their aggressive and expansive actions; in other words, they believed that *Mitteleuropa* was synonymous with, or should be synonymous with, Germany. Non-German scholars often found difficulty in defining Central Europe and were not convinced of its reality. A Committee of Cultural Experts of the Council of Europe came to the conclusion that: "The characteristics of Central Europe are of such variety as to obscure the notion or even obliterate it. Until now it has not been possible to define this regional entity with accuracy. Nevertheless, it is well established that Central Europe exists precisely in that area which is the meeting place of great diversities and deep inter-penetrations."[6] The Committee therefore considered that from this standpoint Central Europe appeared as a true geographical entity.

The aftermath of the Second World War led to this central region being divided into two: the eastern parts fell within the orbit of the Soviet Union, while the western parts, most of the German-speaking area that is, lay outside the Iron Curtain and, significantly enough, were those parts of the central region which are more characteristically European and less "continental" in their make-up. Most of the western portion felt the influence of, even if it lay outside, the Roman Empire and it is still fundamentally "Western" in its civilisation, its economic pattern, and its way of life. Thus this west-central area may be considered with the rest of north-western Europe. ⊬

The Growth in Importance of Western Europe

It is our intention to examine and analyse the growth in importance economically and politically of Western Europe during the nineteenth century and the beginning of the present century up to the First World War, then to elicit and explain the problems which beset Western Europe in the inter-war period, and finally to trace the efforts and the stages since the Second World War in the economic rehabilitation of Western Europe and its struggle for some form of political unity, taking cognisance of the various pressures both internally and externally which have gone far to altering its whole political and economic structure. Let us begin this investigation by looking at the factors or reasons which helped, initially, to make Western Europe important and powerful.

Although Western Europe has a relatively restricted land area, it has a complexity of structure which has given it a physical diversity almost unmatched elsewhere in the world. Mountain building, volcanic eruptions, seismic activity, extensive glaciation, marine invasion and land emergence have all contributed to the shaping and diversifying of the region's physiography. Peak and plateau, basin, valley and plain often lie in close juxtaposition, while deep penetrations into the land by an encroaching sea has produced a wealth of peninsular and insular forms. The compartmentalisation of the land surface by mountain ranges gave rise to basins and plateaus which became core areas for national growth and helped to foment nationalism. Indeed, it was here in Western Europe that the concept of the nation-state emerged which, for good or ill, has proved to be such a powerful force in the modern world. Many nation-states, separated by linguistic and religious differences as well as physical barriers, developed early on.

Austria, Switzerland and Luxembourg excepted, every country in Western Europe possesses a sea coast and most have had fairly close relations with the sea. Some, such as the UK, France, Portugal, Spain, the Netherlands, Denmark and Norway in particular, have been maritime-minded and all, at one time or another, have been interested in, and concerned with, oceanic exploration, overseas colonisation, deepsea fishing, maritime trade and naval power. Even Germany, more pronouncedly continental than the rest, has not been entirely uninfluenced by the attractions of the sea. Thus an oceanic marginal location, a maritime outlook, and overseas connections are features which have helped to distinguish Western Europe from much of the remainder of the continent and which historically from time to time have brought power, wealth and influence to many of the seaboard countries.

The UK was the home of the agricultural and industrial revolutions of the eighteenth and nineteenth centuries, although these economic changes were soon adopted by other West European countries. The revolution in farming introduced crop rotation schemes, the gradual growth of mechanisation, and a more scientific approach to crop cultivation and animal husbandry; the industrial revolution brought powered mechanisation to industrial manufacture and factory organisation in production. As a consequence of these changes, Western Europe came to lead the world in the production of agricultural produce and industrial manufactures. The use of coal, the adoption of steam power together with iron and steel products provided the industrial base which enabled the West European countries to become world powers. The development of new forms of mechanised transport by both land and sea created greater mobility facilitating the import of raw materials and the export of manufactured goods. The UK had pioneered industrial production and by the middle of the nineteenth century had become "the workshop of the world" with, at that time, few or no competitors. A generation later she was producing nearly three-quarters of the world's ships and was exporting coal, steel and textiles in massive quantities to many parts of the world. By the end of the nineteenth century industrialisation had spread to many other West European countries, notably Belgium, France and Germany, and Western Europe dominated world industrial production. In the early years of the present century Western Europe was enjoying outstanding productivity in terms of output of industrial raw materials, power supplies and manufactured goods. The world's finest transportation network, an unrivalled foreign trade, and a high degree of business enterprise were concomitants of this productivity.

The Dominance of Western Europe

From the sixteenth century onwards the countries of Western Europe gradually assumed a dominance in world affairs politically, economically and culturally, which was unchallenged and which reached its peak between approximately 1850 and 1913. This dominance manifested itself in three principal ways.

First, as a result of its military and naval prowess, Western Europe or, more precisely, some of the countries of Western Europe, were able to carve out for themselves overseas imperial possessions which, in total, covered more than a quarter of the world's area. Portugual and Spain, though politically in decline, still held on to their colonial territories; the former, though losing Brazil in 1889, continued to hold substantial areas in Africa and minor outposts in South-East Asia; the latter had lost its extensive possessions in Latin America but still had territories in north Africa and continued to control the Philippine Islands until the Spanish-American War when, following the Battle of Manila Bay, in 1898, the archipelago came under the control of the United States. The other important countries of Western Europe—the UK, France and the Netherlands first, and subsequently Belgium, Germany and, finally, Italy—all acquired substantial overseas territories which, with the exception of Germany which lost its African possessions at the end of the First World War, they continued to hold on to until the Second World War or after. The UK, with its vast scattered Empire and innumerable Imperial Outposts and its unchallenged naval might, virtually policed the world for half a century or more.

Secondly, Western Europe, as the home of the industrial and technical revolution, dominated the world in terms of energy production, manufactured goods and international trade. Many of the world's great dams, irrigation projects, bridges and railway systems (e.g. those in India, Argentina and Chile) were built with British capital, manufactured products and expertise. After the unification of Germany and the Franco-Prussian War of 1871, the German Empire was created and Bismarck became Chancellor (1871–90). Under his direction German industrialisation was speeded up and the country's political and military power greatly enhanced with the result that Germany quickly came to rival the UK. France, as the former leading power in Europe, now lagged well behind as number three. However, as Minshull has commented: "At the end of the nineteenth century Western Europe as a whole accounted for approximately ninety per cent of world industrial production."[7]

Thirdly, Western European civilisation and culture were widely spread throughout the world. The British people largely colonised Canada, Australia and New Zealand, while substantial numbers emigrated to the British colonies in Africa and elsewhere, taking with them the English language, culture and institutions. In much the same way, French settlers in Quebec, the Caribbean and North Africa carried the French language, culture and institutions to these areas, while French control of Indo-China left a strong French imprint in that region. Apart from the indelible Dutch (Boer) influence in South Africa, Dutch influence was less significant. As a whole, however, Western European influence has been profound in most parts of the world and European ideas of democracy, nationalism, industrialism, co-operative farming, as well as language, religion, legal institutions and architecture, have found wide acceptance in many parts of the world.

The Decline in World Power Status

National rivalries and ambitions from about 1870 onwards led to two major wars between the main protagonists which came to have worldwide ramifications. The First World War brought dreadful slaughter to Germany, France and the UK and the four years of attrition seriously dislocated the economies of all the European participants. After the war Germany suffered hyper-inflation and the collapse of the mark which became worthless; the Dawes Plan, a scheme to stabilise the German currency and reparations payments, was set up in 1923 and presided over by General C. G. Dawes, an American soldier and politician. The UK and France, though victors, suffered economic difficulties and acute unemployment. Conditions were just beginning to turn for the better when the Wall Street crash occurred in the United States which precipitated the Great Depression bringing worldwide repercussions.

The economic difficulties of the post-war period fostered right wing Fascist movements in Italy and Germany and led to the Spanish Civil War. In Italy, from 1922 onwards, Mussolini created a centralised Nationalist State and sought to increase the country's economic power by reviving industry and its political power by developing the armed and naval forces. In the 1930s Mussolini adopted an aggressive policy attacking and annexing Ethiopia in 1935-6 and invading Albania in 1939. Meanwhile Hitler and his Nazis, bent on creating a German Mitteleuropa, invaded Czechoslovakia, then Austria and, finally, Poland which plunged Europe into the Second World War.

The war, 1939-45, left much of Western and Central Europe devastated and economically exhausted. As Parker has said: "Years of concentration on armaments followed by the havoc of total war had dislocated the economies of all but the few neutrals."[8] Moreover, the demands of the war had drained Europe of much of its natural resources—coal, iron ore, lead, zinc, timber—and completely disrupted its trade and communications. For three years after the cessation of hostilities industrial production merely limped along and it was not until the establishment of the Organisation for European Economic Cooperation (OEEC) in 1948, which brought massive United States aid to Europe, that the slow process of economic recovery began to be effected.

Even before the Second World War it was becoming apparent to many that the more important countries of Western Europe had certain built-in weaknesses. Individually they were not large enough, populous enough, nor productive enough to match up with the United States which had already become politically and economically the most important country in the world. The Western European nations were becoming increasingly inward-looking and were fostering economic nationalism by erecting tariffs, imposing quotas, controlling trade relations and restricting the movement of capital abroad. The contraction of international trade led the countries which had overseas possessions to look to them for their economic salvation; for example, The UK developed Imperial preference, France turned to her overseas colonies, Italy exploited her African colonies, Belgium the Belgian Congo, and the Netherlands the Dutch East Indies. Germany, which had no colonies, developed a different strategy: she commenced the economic infiltration of the Danubian countries and by the beginning of the Second World War was exercising economic hegemony in the Danubian basin. Such measures were intended to breathe new life into the economically stagnating countries. But, as Parker commented, "in many cases the economic significance of colonies was exaggerated, (though) they indubitably possessed a psychological value which considerably influenced national policies. Besides suggesting a way out of difficulties they increased the national self-esteem and encouraged the imperial neighbours in their European semi-detacheds to 'go it alone' and cut their mutual contacts to a minimum." The emergence in the post-war years of nationalist movements within the colonial territories of Britain, France, Belgium, the Netherlands and Portugal and the attainment, one after another, of political independence, completely sabotaged the pre-war policies of the imperialist countries. However, the loss of colonies was by no means as economically disastrous as many had surmised; nevertheless the notion of economic salvation through imperialism foundered completely and other solutions to Western Europe's nationalist problems had to be explored.)

The Second World War had also drastically upset the balance of power. The power and importance of Western Europe was at a discount and power and influence in the post-war world tested in the hands of the two new super-powers, the United States and the Soviet Union, with their great territorial size, rich natural resources and substantial populations. Politically and economically the super-powers wield a dominating influence. While a hundred years ago vast size could be, and was, a political drawback, since it was liable to militate against national cohesion and unity, the development of modern systems of transport—railways, arterial motorways and airways—have provided linkages which have bound even distant regions together and helped to consolidate the United States and the Soviet Union (though less so) politically.

At this point we may recall Sir Halford Mackinder's prognostication in 1919[10] that

> Who rules East Europe commands the Heartland:
> Who rules the Heartland commands the World-Island:
> Who rules the World-Island commands the World.

Soviet space, excepting its eastern Asiatic territory, is virtually co-incident with Mackinder's "heartland" and the USSR has exploited its considerable potentialities; e.g. she has come to dominate the countries along her western margins and begun to exert her influence along her southern margin, e.g. in Afghanistan and, it would seem, in Iran too. The United States is less well placed in relation to the world at large than the Soviet Union but she has long looked upon the Western Hemisphere as her preserve and, because of her tradi-

TABLE 1

Comparative economic resources of EEC, USA and USSR, 1979

	EEC 9	USA	USSR
Area and population			
Area ('000 sq. km)	1,526	9,363	22,402
Population (m)	260.4	220.6	264.1
National accounts			
Gross Domestic Product at			
market prices (mrd ECU)[1]	1,753.6	1,714.5	na
Energy production			
Crude petroleum (m toe)[2]	89.0	488.1	601.9
Coal production (m toe)	174.6	431.8	357.3
Natural gas production (m toe)	137.5	467.5	338.6
Selected industrial and agricultural production			
Crude steel ('000 t)[3]	140.2	126.1	151.4
Motor vehicles (m)[4]	11.9	12.9	2.2
Cereals[5] (m t)[6]	113.4	299.3	208.8
Meat (m t)[4]	27.7	25.6	15.3
Trade			
Total exports (mrd ECU)	418.8	132.7	47.4
Total imports (mrd ECU)	439.6	151.1	42.3

NOTES
1. mrd ECU = '000 million European currency unit.
2. m toe = million tonne of oil equivalent.
3. '000 t = thousand tons.
4. 1978.
5. Average production 1976-8.
6. m t = million tons.
na Not available.

tional links with Peninsular Europe, has twice within the present century come to its aid when its security was threatened. The North Atlantic Treaty Organisation (NATO) is a measure of the United States' continuing concern for Western European security.

Economically, also, the two super-powers enjoy almost a world dominance and this on two main counts: first, because of their great size they possess a plenitude of natural resources in terms of energy supplies, mineral wealth, agricultural produce, etc., and, secondly, they benefit from the economies of scale which large economic units can effect as a result of the freedom of movement of power supplies, raw materials, labour and capital and the distribution of finished goods to every part of the country. Table 1 gives the comparative economic resources of the European Economic Community, the United States and the Soviet Union.

It is a moot point as to whether the individual countries of Western Europe could have remained economically viable and relatively prosperous if they had not joined together to form the EEC since none of them had a large enough population nor a large enough economic base to enable them to compete with any real success under the rigorous conditions of present-day international trade. Jointly, they have been able to survive, and even to prosper, until the energy crisis of 1973, inflation, and an economic recession with substantial unemployment problems afflicted them.[7]

As we have attempted to show, integration does have a sound and logical geographical base to it and, as Chapter II will further show, the moves towards unity were by no means as sudden and impulsive as they might first seem. Neither is it a coincidence that those countries which make up the core of peninsular Europe should be the first to integrate within the European Economic Community.[9]

NOTES

1. Jordan, T. G., *The European Culture Area*, Harper & Row, 1973, p. 6.

2. Lyde, L. W., *Peninsular Europe*, Longmans, Green & Co., 1930, p. 2.

3. Unstead, J. F., *A Systematic Regional Geography: Europe*, University of London Press, 1939, p. 75.

4. Robinson, H., *Western Europe*, 5th edition, University Tutorial Press Ltd., 1977, pp. 6–7.

5. Robinson, H., *op. cit.*, p. 7.

6. *Report of the Committee of Cultural Experts of the Council of Europe*, 1961, p. 7.

7. Minshull, G. N., *The New Europe*, Hodder & Stoughton, 1978, p. 3.

8. Parker, G., *The Logic of Unity*, 2nd edition, Longmans, 1975, p. 3.

9. *Ibid.*, p. 4.

10. Mackinder, Sir Halford, J., *Democratic Ideals and Reality*, Constable, 1919 (re-issued, Pelican Books, 1944).

Chapter II

A Historical Perspective of European Integration to 1958

Integration and Economic Geography

A CONVENTIONAL political map of contemporary Europe gives little indication of the most significant feature of its post-war economic geography, that of growing economic integration. Although the boundaries of Europe have been re-drawn in the wake of political settlements following two devastating world wars, it could equally be argued that they need to be re-drawn yet again to take economic integration into account (*see* Fig. 3). Present-day Europe is dominated by two formidable integrated units, the European Economic

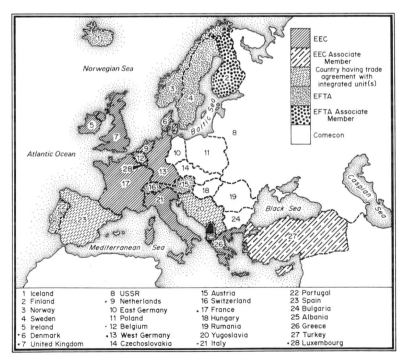

1 Iceland	8 USSR	15 Austria	22 Portugal
2 Finland	9 Netherlands	16 Switzerland	23 Spain
3 Norway	10 East Germany	17 France	24 Bulgaria
4 Sweden	11 Poland	18 Hungary	25 Albania
5 Ireland	12 Belgium	19 Rumania	26 Greece
6 Denmark	13 West Germany	20 Yugoslavia	27 Turkey
7 United Kingdom	14 Czechoslovakia	21 Italy	28 Luxembourg

FIG. 3.—Economic integration in Europe.

Community (EEC) with ten member states and the Council for Mutual Economic Assistance (COMECON) with seven full European members. In addition, six nations are members of the European Free Trade Area (EFTA) and Finland has associate member status. Of the remaining major countries of Europe, Turkey is an associate member of the EEC while Yugoslavia, an observer member of COMECON, and Spain have developed less formal trade links with the Community. Albania withdrew from COMECON in 1962 but remains a member of the Warsaw Pact; it is the only major country to have no economic ties within Europe. Additionally, as Chapter III indicates, there are also various trading agreements between the various groupings and countries. This all adds up to a closely integrated, though at times divided, Europe.

In its simplest form, a standard dictionary definition can be used as a starting point for our discussion of integration. Integration is defined as "the act of making the parts into the whole". Geographically, it is a process by which the national barriers of Europe have been broken down, formally and informally. It can take a variety of forms, involving purely economic or both economic and political elements. Whatever its form, integration has strong links with economic geography as the following definitional quotations indicate:

> It is a movement to fuse markets and economies into one (Hallstein, W., *Europe in the Making*, 1961).

> The counter-action of national weaknesses with positive benefits (Parker, G., *The Logic of Unity*, 1975).

> A process set in motion by institutions concerned to break down national limits to the articulation of the goods and factor markets on a European scale (Lee, R., *Economy and Society in the EEC*, 1976).

The processes of integration are closely tied up with the growth of trade and trading relationships. Europe has a natural resource weakness (*see* Chapter I), so it seems logical to foster links not only outside the continent but also within so as to derive maximum benefit from existing scarce resources. These links have been progressively, although not smoothly, developed over hundreds of years, the greatest advance being made since the time of the Industrial Revolution. Through trade, a country is no longer restricted by its own resources and specialisation is encouraged. Lee takes the concept of integration a stage further, by including the interchange of ideas, labour and capital. While this aspect of integration has accelerated over the last twenty years there are ample earlier examples. Parker's definition implicitly links such types of movement to Europe's economic geography, although he understates its true significance. Political integration may develop simultaneously or as a consequence of economic integration. In Western Europe, the former has been the case, but in Eastern Europe, political pressure has been exerted to achieve economic objectives.

In studying the contemporary economic geography of Western Europe, integration can be seen in varying degrees in most sectors of the economic system. It is best developed in the primary sector, reflecting a natural resource weakness. In the secondary sector, integration is not as obvious at first sight. There has, however, been a significant movement of industrial capital and labour as a consequence of integration. Transport and trade are necessary tertiary links with integration, and there is also evidence in retailing and banking services. So, the economic geography of Western Europe is inextricably linked with integration. The historical development of this relationship will be outlined in the remainder of this chapter.

Integration and Disintegration Before 1950

Economic co-operation arose out of necessity in the few years following the Second World War and this brief period laid the foundation for the establishment of the EEC. The pioneer work of fostering integration, however, has its roots in the nineteenth century and the various attempts which were made to liberalise intra-European trade. To fully appreciate its significance, it is necessary to understand the prevailing economic climate of those early days. International trade in the late eighteenth and early nineteenth centuries was severely restricted by high tariffs and physical problems of movement. Economic nationalism prevailed amongst the nations of Europe, although some trade did cross international frontiers.

The first significant attempt to liberalise trade was the Anglo-French commercial treaty of 1786, but this experiment was short-lived due to the French Revolution and the rise of Napoleon. The initiative for breaking down barriers came from Prussia with the creation of the Zollverein (1834). This customs union was joined by most of the German states and there were even suggestions for its geographical extension. Enthusiasm for this type of co-operation was closely linked to the trade cycle, upturns of the cycle coinciding with favourable integrative tendencies. The UK (ironically in some respects) played a leading part in the free trade movement. A second commercial treaty with France in 1860 was followed by a liberal policy towards the rest of Western Europe. The Zollverein negotiated a treaty with France in 1862, and like the one between the UK and France, import duties on manufactured goods were reduced. Other treaties were signed involving Belgium, Italy, Austria, the Netherlands, Spain, Sweden and Norway and for a brief time in the 1860s, Western Europe became a low tariff area. As Pollard discusses in detail, this "liberal interlude" was only brief.[1] By 1870, Europe had reached the parting of the ways. "In one direction, progress towards the economic integration of the whole of Europe could continue ... in the other direction, the political *raison d'état* continued the traditional division of Europe into warring and jealous units".[2] Unfortunately, Europe turned in the second direction. The Franco-Prussian War was a setback both economically and politically to relations between European neighbours. Partly as a consequence, the middle 1870s saw a severe downturn in the trade cycle and industrial production suffered. The outcome was the re-erection of trade barriers in order to avoid dumping, so that in a very short time, the traditional protectionist system had returned to Western Europe.

Beneath the clamour of nineteenth century European politics, there were other less publicised factors promoting integration within the European economy. The most significant of these were the new modes of transportation and the establishment of a comprehensive European network. The lack of transportation infrastructure can hamper trade links, while conversely, the growth of a network to move goods can promote trade. Initially, it was the inland waterways followed by the railways which did much to physically strengthen links between the countries of Europe. Unlike the UK, and as Chapter I has indicated, the rivers of Europe are important natural highways. This remains as true today as in the time of industrial advance in the early half of the nineteenth century. As Pollard indicates, the Rhine, Seine, Oder, Vistula and Nieman river systems were all important in linking continental Europe.[3] The Rhine was of greatest significance but the many tolls and other duties hindered the growth of trade. Once these barriers were dismantled, around the middle of the century, trade flourished especially to the free port of Frankfurt. Canalisation also played its part. Once again in contrast to Britain, canals were designed to link natural waterways and provide connections between commercial centres. Two of the most important were the Rhine–Rhône and Rhine–Marne Canals.

Water transport, by river or canal, is best suited for the carriage of bulky, heavy, imperishable loads. It is a slow means of transport and can only adequately serve those areas directly served by the network. The railway in contrast does not have these inherent functional weaknesses. Rail transport is quick and efficient for most types of load and contributed tremendously to the growth of European trade. Pollard once again contrasts the British and European experience.[4] In the UK railways came towards the end of the Industrial Revolution, on the continent, they were a significant part of it, with most

railways being constructed for economic motives. The earliest railways, as expected, served the main centres of population in Belgium,
France, Germany and Austria, but in time, links were forged with
Italy. Geographically, the several great valleys and natural gaps
provided convenient avenues. The Alps and Pyrenees were formidable natural obstacles for the engineers, as were sea gaps like the
English Channel. The broken terrain of southern and south-eastern
Europe also militated against railway development. Such basic
geographical factors are reflected in the density of the railway network of Europe, both in the late nineteenth century and at the
present time. They are also salient factors in explaining economic
integration.

In spite of the political fragmentation of nineteenth century
Europe, the adoption of a standard gauge facilitated international
travel and traffic. Only at the Spanish and Russian frontiers was
transhipment necessary. London (with its rail links to the packet
ports), Paris, Cologne, Berlin, Regensburg, Verona and Belgrade
were all important international rail centres. Moreover, long-dis-
tance travel could take place in the comfort of services operated by the
Compagnie des Wagons-Lit and goods were able to reach their destination safely. Geographically, today's trans-European express routes
have much in common with the continental system of the 1870s.

Politically, the railway did much to unify Germany and Italy.
Economically, it helped to create intra-European trade—fruit and
grain were exported from France and Italy, manufactured goods
from Germany and the UK and there was even trade in grain between
Russia and the rest of Europe. Economic inter-dependence was growing, although on the surface the politicians saw a protectionist set-up
more desirable.

Simultaneously with transport development and interchange,
there was a second type of spatial integration, the movement of men,
ideas and capital. Of particular significance was the spread of industrial capital from the UK and North-West Europe to the core continental areas. Pollard gives ample evidence of their being a single
international capital market in the nineteenth century.[5] As in England, railway construction required vast amounts of capital, and
often it was the small saver who provided the finance. British funds
proved to be very important in some early ventures in Belgium and
France. Finance from the major European countries followed this
lead, with German capital particularly fostering the eastwards push
of the network. Managers, engineers and labourers invariably
accompanied the hard capital. Financial integration was not confined just to railway construction and there are many examples of
international finance being provided for the European coal, metals

and textile industries. As Pollard concludes, "Everywhere it became increasingly clear that, economically speaking, there existed only a single European community".[6] Politically, however, there were many divisions and it was these forces which, as we have shown, proved to be the major stumbling block to greater integration.

The political settlement following the First World War did nothing to promote integration. Natural economic units were broken up and the new international boundaries paid little attention to established trade and transportation links. Almost immediately, governments began to pursue policies of self-sufficiency. The return of Alsace and Lorraine to France deprived Germany of valuable mineral resources and her problems were further exaggerated by the French occupation of the Ruhr in 1923. War had left a severe financial toll in Europe and the recognised systems were in disarray. This was hardly the stage for promoting greater integration and the distinct threat of disintegration increased with the Wall Street crash of 1929. Germany and Austria were worst affected and suffered total economic collapse. For the other countries of Europe, the depression was a deep one— prices fell sharply, yet unemployment continued to grow. The dominant economic philosophy was that self-sufficiency was the key to recovery and one by one, the leading industrial nations re-erected trade barriers. At the same time, restrictions on labour and capital movements were intensified. Nationalism rather than co-operation was the order of the day with Germany and Italy in particular pursuing vigorous policies of economic nationalism.

The immediate post-Second World War years provide a remarkable contrast to the inter-war period. Integration became a reality and was forced upon Europe through economic necessity. The main motivating factor was the profound effect that the war had left on the European economy. First, the physical loss in terms of resources was both serious and frightening. Henderson states that "the war of 1939–45 shattered the delicate mechanism of the West European economy. Important industrial centres and ports had been razed to the ground. Great cities like Rotterdam, Hamburg, Essen and Cologne were almost unrecognisable. Transport was hopelessly disorganised".[7] He then looks at these losses in detail. Industrial output of the nations of central Europe was only 30–40 per cent of its prewar level, agricultural production was about half of normal and international trade was stagnant. Secondly, the cost of war had destroyed the international financial payments system. Western Europe was heavily in debt to the United States and did not have the goods or contacts to sell in traditional export markets. Food and other raw materials were urgently required for survival and to promote economic recovery, but the countries most in need did not have the means to pay for such resources. As Henderson concludes, "Only international co-operation could prevent Europe from falling into decay".[8]

In June 1947, the United States made its famous offer of help through their Secretary of State, General Marshall. Without this assistance the European economy would have suffered serious economic and political consequences. It was a condition of the aid that the European states should agree on allocation issues, so establishing the principle of economic co-operation. A new agency, the Organisation for European Economic Co-operation (OEEC) was set up, with headquarters in Paris, to supervise all aspects of Marshall Aid. The American offer of help was made to all countries of Europe, including the Eastern bloc. It was accepted by sixteen: the ten current members of the EEC, five subsequent EFTA nations plus Turkey. Over its four-year lifespan, the American-financed recovery programme amounted to over $23,000 m, two-thirds of which was for economic assistance. The UK was the single largest recipient, followed by France and Italy. An offshoot of the Marshall Aid programme was the American contribution given to set up the European Payments Union. This body, as its name suggests, was established in an attempt to revive the established pattern of intra-European trade.

The Benelux union was also significant in the context of intra-European trade. Even before the Second World War had ended, the three small continental nations of Belgium, the Netherlands and Luxembourg had decided to follow the example of the nineteenth century German states by setting up their own customs union. As such it was a geographical extension of a previous agreement made in 1922 between Belgium and Luxembourg and came into operation in October 1947. The task of removing the various trade barriers was not easy, and initially only around one-third of their trade was free of restrictions. It was however another agent in the fostering of European integration.

As a result of Marshall Aid, the economic recovery of Western Europe was achieved and by 1952, European trade had expanded beyond its pre-war levels. Above all, out of economic necessity, it proved that the countries involved could co-operate effectively in peacetime as well as war. From Marshall Aid, there emerged a movement of statesmen determined to continue with economic co-operation once the programme had been completed. To this extent, it succeeded, where all previous attempts had failed, in asserting the underlying geographical logic of European integration. On the other hand, it represented a negative form of watershed—Marshall Aid became an instrument of the Cold War and divided Europe into two hostile camps, each with their rival protectors. The over-whelming economic and political power of the USSR with regard to the smaller states of Eastern Europe was manifest in the setting up of COMECON (1949) and the Warsaw Pact (1953). Henceforth, the two parts of Europe have gone their own ways. The term "European integration" no longer covers the over-all unification of a continent—it now refers to a division between two significant aggregated units.

The Genesis of the European Economic Community 1950–1957

The formative years of present day integration in Europe were those immediately following the Second World War. The creation of the OEEC and to a lesser extent, the Benelux union, were only the beginnings of a much stronger movement. Although the will to integrate was hardly in dispute, there were significant differences between Western European statesmen as to what form it should take and how it should proceed. The major division was between a federal or functional approach. The federalists favoured the idea of a single European state on the lines of the United States, Australia and Switzerland. Churchill was a great admirer of this approach and the idea was first mentioned by him in a speech made in Zurich in 1946. Under a federation, the countries of Western Europe would retain their identities but be required to transfer certain powers to a con-trolling supranational organisation. Churchill argued that as there were attitudinal differences between countries, a federation would provide the best chance of success. Above all, he wanted such an organisation to be quickly created so that it could stand as an effective bloc in world affairs. What was not obvious at this time was that he did not want Britain to become involved. The question of timing was the fundamental difference between this and the function-alist approaches. The latter group were in favour of a more cautious process, with integration being developed step by step. Under their system, each European state would retain its basic independence, but little by little each would hand over some powers to supranational institutions. These bodies, unlike their equivalent within a federation, would have limited functions and be controlled directly by member states. There would be a gradual hand-over of certain powers while other functions were retained by members. This second approach was the model chosen for the EEC.

The initiative to create a functionally integrated Western Europe was first taken up by the French Foreign Minister, M. Robert Schu-man. In May 1950 he proposed that the entire production of the French and German coal and steel industries should be placed under a common High Authority. He saw this as the first step towards the more far-reaching objective of a European federation and an essential buffer to further hostilities between the two countries. As control of German activities in the Ruhr was under temporary Allied control, his plan also served as a longer-term solution to this particular problem. The two other major coalfield areas, the Saar and the Moselle field in Lorraine, were both sensitive areas, having changed political hands twice in the present century. He invited all other countries of Western Europe to participate in the plan and saw it as a means of achieving a level of integration "always prescribed by geography yet prevented by history". Four other countries, the Benelux nations and Italy, as well as West Germany, responded to his proposal. In April 1951 they signed a treaty in Paris creating the European Coal and Steel Community (ECSC).

As with other proposals for integration, the UK, and to a lesser extent the Scandinavian countries, took no action. The UK was concerned not to damage her "special relationship" with the United States and was also intent on protecting the interests of her Commonwealth. This was the stand which had earlier blocked the possibility of the Council of Europe promoting an integrated Europe. A further British worry was the problem of sacrificing some of her sovereignty, i.e. the ability to fully control her own internal affairs. It was a genuine fear at the time of the setting up of the ECSC and has persistently explained the British fear of European supranational institutions. Like her neighbours in North-West Europe, the UK would have been quite happy to have been part of a general European free trade area, but at the time did not wish integration to proceed any further than this.

The ECSC was in retrospect a blueprint for the functionalist approach towards integration. The Treaty of Paris made provision for the establishment of a "common market" in coal and steel products through the abolition of tariffs, quotas, subsidies and various restrictive practices. The regulation of this system was to be undertaken by the High Authority, an independent body but one which was required to submit proposals to a Council of Ministers representing member governments. A Court of Justice was set up for any appeals that were to be made and the High Authority was finally responsible to a Parliamentary Assembly which had ultimate powers of dismissal. The High Authority had nine members elected by national governments and under the vigorous direction of its first President, Jean Monnet, made arrangements for the early creation of common markets for coal and steel (February and May 1953). Both products were vital for the effective recovery of the Western European economy, and through the ECSC the logic of the industrial collaboration which had appeared briefly in the middle of the nineteenth century was given a new chance to reassert itself.

In these early years, the ECSC was a success and the handing over of powers went smoothly. The world economy was experiencing a period of boom for steel products in the early 1950s and production of the ECSC members rose by almost 50 per cent to 60 m tons in 1957. Coal production, however, was not in such a healthy state and it was necessary to import heavily from the USA. Certain geographical areas of production, e.g. the Borinage coalfield, were in need of modernisation, but the full need to rationalise was not realised until surpluses accrued due to the switch-over to oil in the late 1950s. In short, the ECSC provided proof that economic integration could successfully foster and increase the well-being of Western Europe, without creating too many political difficulties. The scene was now set for further penetrative moves to be made.

In June 1955, following a meeting of Foreign Ministers at Messina, it was agreed to set up an intergovernmental committee to discuss ways of increasing co-operation between the nations of Western Europe. In many ways this was a compromise solution following the abortive attempts to set up the European Defence Community and the European Political Community and the considerable disagreement which existed over the further functional basis of economic integration. This committee was chaired by the Belgian Foreign Minister Spaak, who like Monnet, Schuman and Adenauer, was a fervent believer in increased European Unity. Three areas were to be investigated—the possibility of a common market for all goods and services, the development of common institutions and the progressive fusion of national economies. In retrospect, the first two in particular were to form the basis of the Treaty of Rome. The UK had been an observer at the Messina Conference, but it now became abundantly clear that British ideas on European integration were not as forthright or committed as those of the Six. Consequently, the UK became instrumental in setting up the European Free Trade Area (EFTA), along with six fellow Western European countries.

The Spaak report was accepted by the Foreign Ministers of the Six in April 1956 and a draft treaty was to be prepared. Nevertheless, differences between the Six still existed, the major split being between France and West Germany. Traditionally, French industry had relied upon a high tariff level to remain competitive. There were strong French fears that her home market would be swamped with German products under a common market situation. Using her substantial diplomatic weight, France was able to negotiate various provisions to safeguard her industrial sector, and at the same time was successful in getting a firm commitment on the adoption of a common agricultural policy and a special policy for former colonies. This late compromise guaranteed the successful completion of negotiations, and on the 27th March 1957 the Foreign Ministers of the Six signed the treaties establishing the European Economic Community (EEC) and the European Atomic Energy Community (Euratom).

An Appendix to this book outlines the principal provisions of the Treaty of Rome.[9] Article 2 states that the objective of the Community is "to promote throughout the Community a harmonious development of economic activities, a continuous and balanced expansion, an increase in stability, an accelerated raising of the standard of living and closer relations between the States belonging to it". Article 3 details how this will be achieved. Functionally, the provisions of Article 3 can be subdivided into four main groups, each of which has been of significance in the contemporary economic geography of Western Europe. They are:

(*i*) The customs union—the progressive creation of a common market for goods between the Six and the establishment of a common external tariff on trade with third party countries.

(*ii*) Free factor mobility—the progressive abolition of barriers to the free movement of labour, industrial capital and services between the Six.

(*iii*) Common policies—provision for the establishment of common policies governing agriculture, transport, the rules of competition, taxation, commercial relations and social aspects.

(*iv*) Relations with less-developed countries—provision for the association of certain developing economies which previously had colonial ties with member states.

Structurally, the EEC is very much more than a "common market". It may be better described as a "customs union with certain common policies", although as yet, not fully developed. The Treaty of Rome specified that the customs union would be created in a series of stages over a ten-year period and this has been successfully achieved (*see* Chapter III). A good deal of progress has also been made to complete the free movement of factors of production—many restrictions on labour and capital were removed by the late 1960s although the same progress has not been made on service mobility. These provisions have had a profound impact on the recent space economy of the Community, as Chapters VI, VII and IX indicate. There is a comprehensive policy towards LDCs (*see* Chapter III) but the progress in setting up common policies has been painfully slow and difficult. Apart from the Common Agricultural Policy (*see* Chapter IV), other Community policies are either disappointingly small and weak, e.g.

Regional Policy, or almost non-existent, e.g. Transport Policy (*see* Chapters V III and XII).

Nevertheless, integration in Western Europe is now a reality—it is no longer merely a pipe-dream. It may have been prompted out of necessity in the few years following the Second World War, but it was by no means a sudden, impulsive decision.

NOTES

1. Pollard, S., *European Integration 1815–1970*, Thames & Hudson, 1974, p. 117.

2. *Ibid.*, p. 119.

3. *Ibid.*, pp. 39–42.

4. *Ibid.*, p. 43.

5. *Ibid.*, Chapter I II.

6. *Ibid.*, p. 97.

7. Henderson, W. O., *The Genesis of the Common Market*, Frank Cass & Co. Ltd, 1962, p. 125.

8. *Ibid.*, p. 127.

9. For details, see Cmnd. 4864, H M S O, 1972; Cmnd. 5179-II, H M S O, 1973.

Part Two

ASPECTS OF INTEGRATION AFTER 1958

Trade

T R A D E is a central feature of E E C affairs as laid down in the Treaty of Rome. Article 9 states that "the Community shall be based upon a customs union which shall cover all trade in goods ... and the adoption of a common customs tariff in their relations with third countries".[1] In retrospect, the completion of the customs union in 1968 and its subsequent substantial impact have been outstanding achievements and the first step towards the integration of individual economies of member states. Amidst the turmoil of E E C politics, there is a danger that this solid foundation is underrated.

The first part of this chapter will analyse some of the theoretical arguments which have been advanced both for the breaking down of trade barriers and for their subsequent modification within the framework of a customs union. This is followed by an appraisal of the impact of the E E C's customs union on both internal and external trade. The links between the Community and developing nations, an important aspect of external trading relations, are discussed in detail in the final section.

Trade and the Customs Union

The virtues of trade stem from arguments put forward over a century ago by classical economists such as John Stuart Mill and David Ricardo. Mill wrote "The benefit of international trade is a more efficient employment of the productive forces of the world."[2] Accordingly, countries should aim to specialise in those goods in which they possess a comparative advantage *vis-à-vis* each other. From a geographical viewpoint, comparative advantage reflects the resource endowment of a particular country, with trade taking place in those goods which countries are not able to produce efficiently for themselves. A simple model can be used to illustrate this principle (*see* Table 2).

Table 2 shows the hypothetical situation of two countries each able to produce two products, food and clothing. It is assumed that half of each country's total resources is devoted to each product and that no transport costs exist in trade between them. The table shows the corresponding levels of output, given these assumptions. As can be seen, Country A produces more food than Country B, but B is the more efficient producer of clothing. Country A, therefore, possesses

TABLE 2

The impact of trade between two countries

| | Before trade | | After trade | |
	Food	Clothing	Food	Clothing
Country A	32	8	64	0
Country B	28	12	0	24
Total production	60	20	64	24

Net increase in production is 4 units of food, 4 units of clothing.

a comparative advantage in food production, Country B in clothing production. If there is no trade between them, each will produce both products. Once trade takes place, it is more beneficial for Country A to put all of its resources into food production. The reverse applies to Country B. Mill's previous comment on international trade is substantiated by the fact that after trade the total production of both products has increased—the fixed resources involved have so been allocated in a more efficient manner.

Ideally, in the real world, to reap maximum benefit from international trade, a multilateral free trade situation should exist. In view of the "regional" economic groupings referred to in Chapter II, these benefits are only partially realised. The General Agreement on Tariffs and Trade (GATT) has done much to break down barriers to trade, but significant obstacles still exist. Kindleberger argues the case for multilateral free trade, while pointing out that, in certain situations, some degree of protection may even be desirable.[3] A customs union, he argues, can very much be seen as a case of "second best", given that free trade cannot be achieved.[4] These views are based upon the authoritative work of Viner who, in looking at the consequences of integration, introduced the concepts of trade creation and trade diversion.[5] A customs union, by definition, involves the setting up of a common external tariff on trade with nonmembers. As a consequence, imports from such countries may be replaced by goods from relatively less efficient suppliers within the union. The shift in the sources of supply is known as trade diversion. Trade creation, on the other hand, occurs where previously inefficient production is replaced by imports from another more efficient source within the union. As no trade existed, trade has been created as a result of integration. This aspect of a customs union is consistent with the simple model of Table 2. Kindleberger regards a customs union as being second best in so far as the benefits of trade creation have to be offset against the effects of trade diversion. The theoretical message is a clear one—to gain from membership of a customs union, a country must seek to obtain the opportunities presented through the existence of a larger free trade area since trade diversion could be detrimental.

The impact on trade and trading patterns is the most important aspect of a customs union.[6] The full impact is much wider and is set out on *a priori* grounds in Table 3.

TABLE 3

The theoretical effects of a customs union

	Member countries	Non-member countries
A. Static effects	(*i*) Trade creation	(*i*) Trade diversion
	(*ii*) Increased consumption	
	(*iii*) Improved terms of trade	(*ii*) Worsened terms of trade
B. Dynamic effects	(*i*) An opportunity to gain economies of scale in industrial production	(*i*) Retardation of exports to customs union
	(*ii*) Increased competition	
	(*iii*) Investment creation	(*ii*) Investment diversion
	(*iv*) Impact of other common policies	(*iii*) Spillover effects of common policies

Source: Adapted from Kreinin, M. E., *Trade Relations of the EEC: an empirical investigation*, 1974, p. 19.

The static effects, so called because they involve the reallocation of existing resources, cover trade creation and diversion along with other trading issues. The dynamic effects, in contrast, are rather wider and more obtuse. These are the indirect effects of an expansion in size of the market within a customs union and in particular, can accrue as a result of an enhanced economic growth rate. Equally, a poorer member of a customs union may gain little (and could even suffer) from these effects. From a geographical viewpoint, they can be particularly significant in exaggerating the problem of regional imbalance within the customs union (*see* Chapter XI). The remainder of this chapter will be concerned with a basic investigation of these static effects.

The Impact of the Customs Union and External Trade Policy

Following the Treaty of Rome, it was agreed that the EEC customs union should be fashioned over a period of ten years. This transition period would involve the progressive annual reduction of internal tariff barriers and the approximation of national tariffs to a Common External Tariff (CET) in three phases. Such a programme was necessary due to the substantial tariff differences existing between member states before 1958 and was further desirable since it safeguarded the weaker economies from being flooded by imports from more competitive members. The programme of internal tariff dismantling went smoothly and was twice accelerated, resulting in free trade between members in the summer of 1966. The CET was completed on schedule, so that by 1968 the customs union was fully operational.

Various studies have attempted to assess the impact of the customs union on Community trade and trade patterns. They invariably involve a complex form of analysis, so at this stage, only a crude appraisal will be attempted. The message from empirical investigations is a clear one—the customs union has been extremely beneficial to member states. As Taber says, "Throughout a decade and a half of crises, boycotts and all-night marathon conferences, the Community's one consistently brilliant prodigy has been intra-Common Market trade. ... Community trade has developed far beyond the most optimistic predictions of statesmen and economists."[7] Table 4 shows the foundation of such claims in value terms. Excluding the effects of inflation, intra-Community trade from 1958 to 1972 grew over sixfold at an average annual rate of increase of 15.1 per cent. As Taber emphasises, the yearly growth rate for world trade as a whole over the same period was 8.4 per cent per annum. In a crude way, therefore, there would seem to be a substantial trade creation impact. It is also interesting to note that extra-Community trade grew at an average annual rate of 8.4 per cent per annum, exactly the same rate of increase as for world trade as a whole.

TABLE 4

Growth in value of intra-EEC trade, 1958–80 ($ U Sm)

1958	1965	1972	1975[1] EEC-6	1975 EEC-9	1980[2] EEC-6	1980 EEC-9
6,790	20,442	60,792	120,944	145,586	283,552	347,613

NOTES
1. Based upon a conversion rate of 1 ECU = $1.24077.
2. Based upon a conversion rate of 1 ECU = $1.39233.

Sources: Taber, G. M., *Patterns and Prospects of Common Market Trade, 1974*, Table 5, and *Basic Statistics of the Community*, Eurostat, 1982, Table 102.

There was a further boom in intra-EEC trade following the 1973 enlargement, but a period of stagnation quickly followed between 1974 and 1975 when all economies of the Nine were affected by the impact of escalating fuel costs. Since 1975, as Table 4 shows, the value of trade between member states has continued to grow at around 16 per cent per annum although, in volume terms, growth has only been around half this level. Even so, it is still a solid achievement, given the economic problems of some member states in this period. National experiences over these troubled times have differed, with the lowest growth rates being experienced by the U K, Denmark and Belgium. For the future, the key to further growth in intra-EEC trade must depend upon a sustained upturn in the world economy along with a determined bid by businessmen to seek new trade outlets in other member states.

The substantial growth in intra-Community trade has furthered the dependence of the economies of member states as Table 5 crudely indicates. In all cases except the U K, imports and exports between trading partners are approaching or greater than half the value of each member's total trade. This degree of dependence has increased progressively since 1966 when all internal barriers to trade were finally removed and is consistent with the theoretical arguments previously suggested. The Benelux countries and Ireland exhibit the highest levels of dependence on fellow member states, although this partly reflects the limited base of their domestic economies. The U K, as Table 5 clearly shows, is the major exception. Although trade with the rest of the Community is growing, almost two-thirds of the U K's total trade is with countries outside the E E C partners but in 1980, due to the sale of oil products, there was a positive balance of 1,960 m E C U. For the U K to benefit from the customs union, it is essential that trade with the rest of the Community is further developed, particularly in non-oil products.

Internally, therefore, the impact of the customs union has been for trade between members to increase substantially and for their econ-

TABLE 5

Trade dependence of E E C member states, 1980

Country	Imports from member countries (%)	Exports to member countries (%)
West Germany	47.8	49.1
France	46.3	51.9
Italy	44.3	49.0
Netherlands	53.7	72.2
Belgium/Luxembourg	63.1	71.8
UK	38.7	42.7
Ireland	74.5	74.9
Denmark	49.2	50.5

Source: Basic Statistics of the Community, Eurostat, 1982, Tables 100 and 101.

omies to become more dependent upon each other. In view of this, it may be thought that the C E T has had a prohibitive effect upon trade with the rest of the world. Taber showed that this was not true (*see* above) and furthermore, in practice, the E E C has placed a liberal interpretation upon its C E T. The motive for this attitude is locked away in Article 110 of the Treaty of Rome, which states that "By establishing a customs union between themselves, Member States aim to contribute, in the common interest, to the harmonious development of world trade, the progressive abolition of restrictions on international trade and the lowering of customs barriers".[8] This approach to the C E T, although at times contradictory, is shown in a variety of ways including a low average rate of duty and special trading arrangements with groups of third party countries.

The common external tariff was established as the mathematical average of the tariffs previously existing in the Six. France and Italy had been high tariff countries, while the other members were rather more liberal in their attitude to imported goods. For industrial goods, the average is quite low at around 6 per cent and incidentally tends to be much lower than that of the United States. The C E T is much higher for the import of agricultural goods, and as Chapter I V indicates, is designed to foster home production for those products which the E E C can produce itself. On the other hand, given that the Community lacks many raw materials, these are often zero-rated or subject to a very low tariff. In accordance with the G A T T recommendations, quantitative restrictions are not applied apart from in sensitive areas like textiles and clothing. The logic behind this policy is shown by Table 6 which analyses E E C imports and exports by broad commodity groups.

Crudely speaking, trade with the rest of the world has traditionally involved the import of raw materials, their processing in the Community, and the subsequent export of manufactured products.

TABLE 6

External trade of the E E C by product group, January 1978 (m E C U)

Imports		Exports
2,056	Food, beverages and tobacco	814
4,046	Fuel products	502
1,776	Raw materials and chemicals	270
2,023	Machinery and transport equipment	5,516
4,064	Other manufactured goods	5,346
13,965	Monthly total	12,448

Source: Monthly General Statistics Bulletin, 4/6 1978, Eurostat, 1978.

Over the last few years, the EEC has had a continual deficit on trade with the rest of the world, entirely accounted for by the vast cost of importing oil. By 1980 this deficit had reached 48,000 m ECU, but seems likely to decrease as more of the Community's fuel needs are met from the UK.

Geographically, the United States is the EEC's leading trading partner—in 1980, Community imports amounted to over 16 per cent of total imports into the USA, with the USA exporting over 21 per cent of her total exports to the Nine. Other traditional export markets are the neighbouring industrialised countries of Western Europe (*see* Table 7). In early 1972 the Community successfully negotiated agreements for tariff-free trade in industrial products with the six remaining members of EFTA. Tariffs were cut in five equal stages so that from 1st July 1977 there were no longer any barriers to trade in such products between the two trading blocs. Sensitive products like paper products, textiles and special steels have a longer transitional period before free trade is established.[9] The agreements with the EFTA countries largely exclude agricultural goods for obvious reasons. Even so, the result is that there is now an industrial free trade area amongst the major economies of Western Europe.

Greece and Turkey, both developing Mediterranean economies, have expanded their trade links with the EEC as a consequence of their associate member status. The agreement with Greece was signed as early as 1961 when it was specified that by 1974 a customs union should be established in the trade of industrial goods. Greek agriculture was the biggest stumbling block towards further commitment, but in May 1979 it was formally agreed that Greece should become the tenth Community member with effect from the 1st January 1981. The association treaty with Turkey was signed in 1963, but the customs union timetable was looser than the one agreed with Greece. Further trade agreements have been signed between the Community and Morocco, Tunisa and Algeria, Malta, Israel, Yugoslavia, Cyprus, Lebanon and Spain.[10] In this way, a common external policy towards the Mediterranean has developed with the creation of a large free trade area for raw materials and manufactured goods. As in the case of Greece, it will prove to be extremely difficult to modify such agreements to encompass the field of agriculture.

Finally, reference should also be made to the EEC's trade links with Eastern Europe and China. For political reasons, there are quite significant differences in attitude. France, Italy and the UK have been successful in making their own trade agreements with COMECON countries, but in November 1976 proposals to establish a more general trade link were rejected by the EEC's Council of Foreign Ministers. The grounds were political, with the Ministers

TABLE 7

External trade of the E E C with selected European countries, 1980

Imports from E E C			*Exports to E E C*	
Value (m ECU)	%[1]	*EFTA countries*	*Value* (m ECU)	%[2]
10,914	62.6	Austria	6,980	56.0
3,775	33.7	Finland (E F T A associate)	4,044	39.8
na	na	Iceland	na	na
5,851	48.1	Norway	9,559	72.0
1,979	42.1	Portugal	1,446	57.8
11,912	49.6	Sweden	11,079	49.9
17,543	67.2	Switzerland	10,944	51.5
		Associates		
3,030	39.7	Greece	1,775	47.6
1,528	34.0	Turkey	822	41.6

NOTES
1. Percentage share of total imports of importing country.
2. Percentage share of total exports of exporting country.
na Not available.

Source: Basic Statistics of the Community, Eurostat, 1982, Tables 100 and 101.

rejecting the idea that C O M E C O N was a proper body to undertake trade negotiations. It therefore remains for member states to negotiate their own bilateral agreements with individual C O M E C O N countries. The more general co-operation with C O M E C O N is confined to technical fields such as agriculture, waterways and electricity generation. In contrast, Community links with Peking have advanced rapidly with the signing of a five-year trade agreement in April 1978. Unlike C O M E C O N, the Chinese have always supported the idea of a united Europe and this latest agreement should open up trade between the world's most densely populated nation and its largest individual trading partner.

Along with the special agreements for developing nations (*see* below), the external trade policy of the E E C has been much more liberal than may seem to be the case at first sight. As Coffey concludes in detail, the package of trading agreements and concessions is a unique advance and in the future, will undoubtedly be intensified.[11] Coupled with the spectacular increase in intra-Community trade, the present state of the customs union is the most significant economic achievement of the European Economic Community.

The EEC and Developing Economies

During the 1960s the Community started to develop a common personality and display a considerable degree of unity *vis-à-vis* third parties.[12] The special relationship with developing countries, progressively built up over the last fifteen years, has been particularly significant and is regarded as a unique programme of co-operation between developed and Third World economies. The origins of this relationship were one of the hardest-fought issues of the negotiations leading to the Treaty of Rome. Although Belgium, France, Italy and the Netherlands all had colonial links, there were divisions between them as to the future status of their territories. France demanded a continuation of the trading links with its colonies and also the establishment of a joint Community fund of development aid.[13] The other countries, along with West Germany, were in favour of a more open yet generous policy towards the Third World. The compromise, as set out in Articles 131-6 of the Treaty of Rome, was for the "association" of these former countries and territories. The purpose of this was "to promote the economic and social development of the countries and territories and to establish close economic relations between them and the Community as a whole".[14] After these countries became independent, a convention governing their association was signed in 1963 (The First Yaoundé Convention). This agreement has since been renewed and was revised in 1975 to accommodate the UK's accession.

The Yaoundé Convention, named after its signature in the capital of Cameroon, established the EEC-AASM (Associated African States and Madagascar) Association. It was followed by a second convention of the same name which entered into force in July 1969 and expired at the end of January 1975. Eighteen developing countries were included in the conventions, Mauritius joining in 1971. The main features of the agreements were:

(i) the establishment of a free trade area between the EEC and AASM Association;
(ii) the provision of financial and technical aid;
(iii) the setting up of joint institutions.

Generally speaking, customs duties were eliminated between the Community and the AASM Association. Food and agricultural raw materials from the developing economies received tariff-free access to the Six in return for the same allowance for EEC manufactured goods. There were some exceptions to this general principle—certain agricultural products produced by EEC farmers did not have free access since the Community was keen to protect the interests of its own farmers (*see* Chapter IV), while in some instances the A A S M countries could erect selective import tariffs and quotas in order to protect their own developing economies. Even so, A A S M agricultural imports received more preferential treatment than those from third parties. Direct aid to support the economic development of the Associated States was given by the E E C in exchange for this reciprocity. The financial help was channelled through the European Development Fund (E D F) and supplemented by loans from the European Investment Bank (E I B). Table 8 breaks down this aid programme for the two Conventions.

TABLE 8

Aid to A A S M countries, 1963–75 (million u.a.)*

		Yaoundé I	Yaoundé II
EDF	Grants	620	748
	Special loans	46	80
		666	828
EIB	Loans	64	90
	Five-year Total	730	918

* One unit of account was equivalent to one U S dollar until 1971. By the completion of Yaoundé II, it was worth approximately 1.1 U S dollars.

The E E C also cultivated links with other developing economies outside the A A S M group. A partial free trade area was negotiated between the Community and the Commonwealth states of Kenya, Uganda and Tanzania (the Arusha Agreement) in 1969, but no direct financial aid was included. The two Yaoundé Agreements, on balance, would seem to have benefited both the E E C and the A A S M Association. Coffey provides evidence of trade creation in agricultural imports to the Community along with some diversions from non-Yaoundé to Yaoundé sources.[15] There is also evidence that industrialisation has taken place within the A A S M group. There have been criticisms of the Agreements, which will be reviewed later, but the preferential system developed has formed an important identity between the Community and its former colonies.

With the U K's accession to the Community in 1973, it seemed logical that former British colonies should be given an opportunity to join in a new agreement. Negotiations commenced in July 1973 and were concluded in February 1975 by the signing of the Lomé Convention between forty-six A C P (African, Caribbean and Pacific) countries and the Community of Nine. Fig. 4 shows the initial sig-

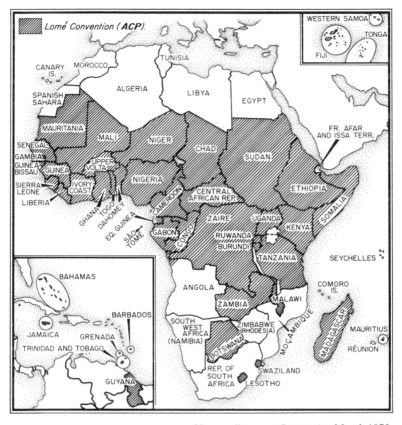

[*Source: European Community*, March 1975.
FIG. 4.—Initial signatories of the Lomé Convention.

natories. Due to the "open" nature of the agreement, a further eleven
ACP countries have subsequently joined. Coffey lists the major
issues in detail, but in innovative terms, the Lomé agreement had two
major new departures from its Yaoundé predecessors.[16] Firstly, the
EEC relinquished its right of reciprocity. Although 95 per cent of
exports of the ACP group enter the Community free of duty, reciprocity is no longer a condition. The ACP countries have only to
guarantee no discrimination against the EEC *vis-à-vis* other trading
countries. This general trading agreement has been supported by
three special agreements covering sugar, rum and bananas. The
former is particularly significant since the EEC has agreed to purchase an annual quantity of 1.3m tons of sugar at a price related to

the internal price within the Community. For sensitive agricultural products not covered (e.g. Botswanan beef and certain cereal products), the ACP countries still receive preferential access. A second innovative aspect of the Lomé Convention, that of the creation of the STABEX fund, has created enormous interest since it is a unique feature in relations between developed and developing economies. As its name suggests, the STABEX fund is designed to guarantee a developing country's export revenue from primary products:

> The mechanics of the STABEX system are that where an ACP country's export proceeds from one product represent 7.5% of total export earnings, and where the proceeds from the export of the product to the Community fall below 7.5% of the negotiated reference level of earnings, then that state may ask for financial assistance from the STABEX fund. In the case of the poorest twenty four ACP states, the reference level is 2.5%. The very poorest countries will be eligible for help, irrespective of the destination of their exports. Twelve principal products and a group of sub-products were originally chosen to be eligible for this treatment.[17]

The STABEX fund provides loans to the richer members of the group and these have to be repaid if export earnings subsequently rise. The very poorest countries in contrast do not have to pay back into the fund. STABEX is an attempt to overcome the natural fluctuations in commodity markets and so provide the ACP countries with a better basis for planning their internal economic development.

Although STABEX has captured a lot of publicity, its financial significance is not very great as Table 9 shows. It is nevertheless a useful addition to the project finance available from the EEC to its associated less developed countries, and it does of course, further guarantee the supplies of essential primary resources into the Community. The Lomé Convention has been "hailed as a 'new model' for relations between industrialised and developing countries"[18] and as seen above, has produced benefits for both parties. It does, however, have its critics. For example, developing nations outside the ACP group (particularly those in Asia and South America) suffer a form of discrimination in so far as they may experience some degree of trade diversion as a result of the setting up of the large tariff-free area between the EEC and ACP countries. More significantly, some of these other developing nations could in time demand a similar guaranteed-price access agreement for the sale of their primary products not only into the EEC, but into other developed economies. If this were to happen, then the traditional structure of world commodity markets would be dramatically changed.

TABLE 9

Aid to the ACP group under the Lomé Conventions (million u.a.)

		Lomé I	*Lomé II*
EDF	Grants	2,155	2,928
	Special loans	444	504
	Risk capital	94	280
	STABEX	382	550
	Minerals facility	—	280
EIB	Loans	390	685
	Total (5 years)	3,466	5,227[1]

NOTE
1. Excludes 380 m.u.a. aid from outside the Convention.

Source: "The Second Lomé Convention", Hewitt, A. and Stevens, C., in *The EEC and the Third World: A Survey*, Stevens, C., ed., 1981, p. 51.

Negotiations for a new agreement began in September 1978. Their main objective was to consolidate the progress made under the Lomé Convention; at the same time they could ensure that the ACP countries receive further help to ease their worries over increased payments for oil imports. The EEC Commission were seeking more consultation over certain sensitive areas relating to industrialisation and the protection of EEC investments in the ACP countries. On this latter aspect the Commission were concerned that investment in the exploitation of minerals should be protected in order to guarantee the vital raw materials needed by member states in the 1980s. The talks were protracted and difficult, breaking up in disagreement in May 1979. The ACP Group were disappointed at the EEC's offer of loans and grants, feeling that it was inadequate in relation to the guarantees sought. For a time the future of the EEC's development policy seemed in doubt, but a compromise was agreed on the 31st October 1979 with the signing of a second Lomé Agreement.

At first sight, Lomé II closely resembles the 1975 Agreement. Hewitt and Stevens describe the new trade package in terms of "a little more of the same".[19] This is quite true given the increase in the number of ACP states and classes of product covered by the STABEX scheme (*see* Table 10). In particular, the ACP states negotiated new concessions for the out-of-season export of certain vegetables to the Community and the retention of the special arrangements for sugar. The beef quota, so keenly contested by Botswana, has been increased and there have been minor improvements to the other special agreements for rum and bananas. The threshold variation for export revenue, crucial to the operation of STABEX, has been reduced from the

TABLE 10

Products covered by the Lomé Conventions and new ACP states

	STABEX I	STABEX II
Products covered	groundnuts & groundnut oil	as STABEX I *plus*
	cocoa beans, paste & butter	vanilla
	raw or roasted coffee & extracts	cloves
	cotton & cotton linters	wool & animal hair
	coconuts, copra & coconut oil	gum arabic
	palm oil, nuts & kernels	pyrethrum
	various types of skin & leather	essential oils
	wood	sesame seeds & cashew nuts
	fresh bananas	pepper
	tea	prawns, shrimps & squid
	raw sisal	cotton seeds & oil cake
	iron ore	rubber
		peas, beans, lentils
New ACP States (Additional to Fig. 4)	Benin (Dahomey), Cape Verde, Comoros, Djibouti, Dominica, Kiribati (Gilbert Is.), Papua New Guinea, St Lucia, São Tomé and Principe, Seychelles, Solomon Islands, Surinam and Zimbabwe	

Source: *South Magazine*, December 1980, p. 61.

7.5 per cent of Lomé I (*see* above) to 6.5 per cent of total export earnings.

On Aid, as Table 9 indicates, the total finance available from the European Development Fund (EDF) and the European Investment Bank (EIB) has risen by over 60 per cent. In real terms, though, the value of the package is rather less once the effects of inflation have been taken into account.

The most important new provision of Lomé II is the inclusion of a minerals package, known as "MINEX".[20] The main element concerns a STABEX-type scheme to stabilise the export earnings of ACP states in the field of copper, phosphates, manganese, bauxite/alumina, tin and iron ore production. Unlike the STABEX scheme, the compensatory payments are not automatic and give the Community a certain degree of discretion in allowing a transfer of funds. A code to protect the investments of member states in the mining industries of ACP states has also been agreed. A third new area of

Lomé II is an agreement to guarantee the pay and social security rights of ACP migrant workers within the Community.

Despite its shortcomings and critics, the 1975 Lomé experiment has been renewed, reinforcing the over-all development policy which the Community has been keen to foster over the last twenty years or so. In a world economy dominated by resource issues, the EEC has managed to secure important resource imports while at the same time helping the economic development of a significant group of less developed economies.

NOTES

1. *Treaty establishing the European Economic Community*, Cmnd. 4864, HMSO, 1972, p. 6.

2. Mill, J. S., *Principles of Political Economy*, 1848.

3. Kindleberger, C. P., *International Economics*, R. D. Irwin, 1971, Ch. 12.

4. *Ibid.*, p. 183.

5. Viner, J., *The Customs Union Issue*, Carnegie Endowment for International Peace, 1953.

6. *See*, for example, Kreinin, M. E., *Trade Relations of the EEC : an empirical investigation*, Praeger Publishers, 1974, Ch. 3.

7. Taber, G. M., *Patterns and Prospects of Common Market Trade*, Peter Owen, 1974, p. 17.

8. *Treaty establishing the European Economic Community*, Cmnd. 4864, HMSO, 1972, p. 41.

9. For details *see* Taber, G. M., *op cit.*, p. 100.

10. For details *see* Coffey, P., *The External Economic Relations of the EEC*, Macmillan, 1976, pp. 14–19.

11. *Ibid.*, pp. 89–96.

12. *Ibid.*, p. ix.

13. Taber, G. M., *op. cit.*, p. 137.

14. *Treaty establishing the European Economic Community*, Cmnd. 4864, HMSO, 1972, p. 48.

15. Coffey, P., *op. cit.*, pp. 4–8.

16. *Ibid.*, p. 74.

17. *Ibid.*, p. 79.

18. *European Community*, No. 9, October 1978, p. 8.

19. Hewitt, A. and Stevens, C., "The Second Lomé Convention", in *The EEC and the Third World: A Survey*, Stevens, C., ed., p. 47.

20. For details *see Ibid.*, pp. 137–43.

Chapter IV

Agriculture and Fishing

AGRICULTURE occupies a central place in EEC affairs and has been a notable area in which the process of integration has occurred through a common Community policy as laid down in the Treaty of Rome. The Common Agricultural Policy (CAP) was established in 1965 and holds the distinction of being both the first and best developed of all. It has consistently accounted for around three-quarters of the EEC Budget and been quite rightly labelled "the cornerstone" of the Community.

The CAP strives to marry the economics of agricultural markets with the geographical realities of production. In practice this is both a difficult and complex task; consequently, the CAP is the most comprehensive of all managed market farm policies. To fully understand the background to CAP some knowledge of the agricultural geography of the EEC is required along with an understanding of the basic economics of agricultural markets. Both these topics are covered in this chapter, along with the mechanics and present day problems of CAP.

CAP has also been an agent of disintegration, leading to many national conflicts between the member states of the EEC. Moreover, the second geographical enlargement of the Community presents both an obstacle and a challenge, not only to CAP, but also to the whole concept of economic integration in Western Europe (*see* Chapter X).

An overview of Agriculture in the EEC

Just as diversity is the keynote of the physical environment, so it is the keynote of the agricultural economy of Western Europe. Much variety occurs between country and country, and between region and region within each country, not only in the relative importance of agriculture but in the relative intensity of its development. In a broad way there is a correlation between the kind of farming practised and the major physical regions: in the northern highlands pastoral farming with the cultivation of hardy cereals and fodder crops is dominant; in the lowlands of the North European Plain farming is mainly concerned with dairying in the cooler, moister northern parts, and grain and livestock in the southern parts; the hill country of central Europe, together with the intervening valleys and basins, has a more mixed agricultural economy; while the Mediterranean coastlands of France and much of Italy are characteristically under "Mediterranean" type crops (*see* Fig. 5).

The growing demands of agriculture have resulted in many

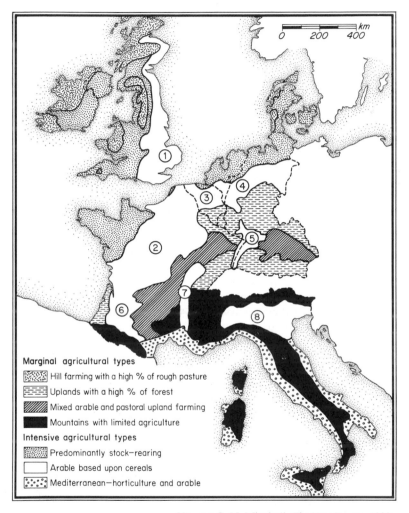

Marginal agricultural types

[Hill farming with a high % of rough pasture]

[Uplands with a high % of forest]

[Mixed arable and pastoral upland farming]

[Mountains with limited agriculture]

Intensive agricultural types

[Predominantly stock-rearing]

[Arable based upon cereals]

[Mediterranean—horticulture and arable]

[*Source*: G. N. Minshull, *The New Europe*, 1980.

FIG. 5.—Agricultural regions of the EEC. Principal agricultural regions (based on macro-climatic and relief criteria). 1. East Anglia and the lowlands of eastern England. 2. Paris Basin and scarplands. 3. Flanders and high plain of Belgium. 4. Börde of Westphalia and Saxony. 5. Rhine–Main valley. 6. Basin of Aquitaine. 7. Rhône valley. 8. Plain of Lombardy.

changes in the natural landscape over wide areas which have been transformed into a humanised or cultural landscape manifest in its growing crops, segregated animals, hedgerows and walls, clumps of trees and its over-all checkerboard of fields. Except in the industrialised urban areas, nowhere is the impress of man upon his environment more obvious than in the ordered pattern of his farmlands. But the demands of agriculture have led to other landscape changes; for example, the need of additional cropland or pastureland has produced the terracing of steep hillslopes as in the Rhinelands and in Mediterranean France, to the draining of marsh and fen as in parts of eastern England and in the French Landes district, to the empoldering of land below sea-level in the Netherlands, and to the regulation of rivers to prevent flooding in land fit for agriculture. Again, if the pressure of population and the demand for food is sufficiently strong, man will go to great lengths to use the land at his disposal; for instance, the heathlands of Belgium, the Netherlands, West Germany and Denmark, though ill-suited to tillage, have been mixed, limed, and fertilised to render them usable while in southern France and parts of Italy there has been much investment in irrigation to make more adequate use of the land.

A variety of factors influence the agricultural development of any area and the relative intensity of its development. The elements of climate—temperature, occurrence of frost, precipitation and sunshine—may be said to be *the* main factors influencing the type of agriculture that can be carried on in a given area. Temperature determines the northern limits of the various cereals, the occurrence of frost sets a limit to certain fruit crops, while the annual total rainfall determines whether cereal cultivation, or grass and fodder crops will dominate. Soils vary widely in their quality and fertility but the best, the alluvial, loessal, and fine clay soils, are the most favourable for arable farming and form the richest farming areas in Western Europe. Heavy, wet clays are unsuitable for arable and so are usually laid down to grass. Areas of light sandy soils, which warm up quickly, are commonly devoted to market-gardening. Surface topography exerts an obvious control: areas of large-scale cultivation are confined to low-lying plains since upland areas are often unsuited to it, militating against the use of machinery. Again, where the terrain is hilly, terracing must often be resorted to if the land is to be used at all. Mountainous country, too, is likely to favour the practice of transhumance, e.g. the French Alps. In the EEC farming methods generally are advanced but considerable variations do occur as, for example, between Scottish crofters, French peasant farmers and Dutch horticulturalists. Differences in methods are related, amongst other things, to size of landholdings, crop rotation systems, the degree of mechanisation and the use of fertilisers. The method of landholding and the organisation of labour are also factors affecting the character of agriculture. Farming organisation varies from the peasant smallholding, through the individually owned farm of a few hundred acres, to the large estate worked by hired labour. There are also varying degrees of co-operative farming. The type of organisation influences land improvement and the efficiency of farming. Except where agriculture is almost solely for subsistence purposes, it is largely geared to market demands. Since living standards on average are high in the E E C, there is a large demand for a wide and sophisticated variety of foodstuffs. The large and dependable markets have exercised a strong influence upon farming, notably so since producing areas are frequently in close proximity to highly urbanised areas. The factor of market demand has tended to override all other factors and many commodities are produced where they are, not because the natural conditions are ideally suited to them, but because of economic demand. The E E C's Common Agricultural Policy to be discussed later, has exerted profound influences upon many aspects of Western European agriculture.

Although, as indicated above, the sizes of farms and holdings in any country are likely to vary quite widely, it is instructive to look at Table 11 which gives the average farm size in the nine member states. Over much of peninsular Italy peasant holdings are very small

TABLE 11

Number of agricultural holdings and average size, 1979

	No. of holdings of of 1 ha and over ('000)	Average size[1] (ha)
West Germany	807	10
France	1,103	19
Italy[2]	2,192	7
Netherlands	132	11
Belgium[3]	97	10
Luxembourg	5	17
U K	260	33
Ireland[4]	260	16
Denmark	120	19
E E C	4,976	16

NOTES
1. Based upon mid-point calculations from class interval data.
2. 1977.
3. 1978.
4. 1975.

(*minifundia*), though some of the traditional *latifundia* or large estates continue to persist.

A number of features characterise Western European agriculture:

(*i*) the production of food crops, such as cereals, vegetables, sugar-beet, potatoes and fruit, is important and the region is not far off being self-supporting; industrial crops, such as flax and tobacco, play only a minor role in the farming;

(*ii*) pastoral farming for beef and veal but more especially for milk production and dairy produce is particularly important in the cooler, moister parts of northern Europe where it is based upon pasture and fodder crops;

(*iii*) although some areas are more especially concerned with arable farming, and even in the production of specific crops, and others are more particularly concerned with livestock, there is much mixed farming, though this is more characteristic of the Hercynian upland areas. Monoculture, such as that frequently found in some of the "newer lands" of the world, is, except perhaps in parts of the Iberian Plateau, foreign to Western European farming practice;

(*iv*) except in some marginal areas, such as Celtic Britain, Brittany, south-west France and southern Italy, farming is, in general, intensive in its nature, and output per capita is fairly high, and in south-east England, north-east France, Belgium, the Netherlands and Denmark very high, a fact supported by the great production surpluses which have accrued in recent years;

(*v*) although, as in England and northern France, there are

TABLE 12

Subdivision of the agricultural used area, 1979

(in '000 hectares)

Land use	EEC	West Germany	France	Italy	Neth.	Belg.	Lux.	UK	Ireland	Den.
Agricultural used area	93,108	12,314	32,151	17,865	2,040	1,461	130	18,467	na	2,920
Arable land	46,222	7,285	17,449	9,383	826	751	58	6,837	na	2,644
Permanent grassland	41,358	4,797	12,912	5,150	1,172	673	71	11,543	na	263
Land under permanent crops (e.g. fruit and vines)	5,125	180	1,553	3,269	38	15	1	72	na	14
Kitchen gardens	na	52	256	62	5	22	0	16	na	na

na Not available

Source: *Basic Statistics of the Community*, Eurostat, 1982, Table 25.

some farms up to 250 ha, or even more, in size, medium- to small-scale farm units are fairly characteristic; in some areas such as Belgium and the Netherlands intensively-worked smallholdings are often only 1 or 2 ha in size (*see* Table 12).

The Problem of Agriculture in the EEC

Agriculture, as in most developed economies, is a problem activity. Although production has increased in absolute terms since 1958, there has been a progressive reduction in the agricultural labour force and a more general problem of inefficiency in comparison with other sectors of the economy. What has happened to the EEC is by no means unique—it is merely part of the process of structural change within an economy. The impact of this change is such that it inevitably requires attention outside the normal market mechanism. In the case of the EEC the Common Agricultural Policy has been a forceful instrument of integration while at the same time providing essential protection for the farming community.

Four important background economic factors should be recognised. First, agricultural productivity in the EEC has advanced rapidly due to the increased mechanisation of production, the intensive use of fertilisers, the improved methods of stock-rearing and the better selection of seeds. Although the pattern of improvement has been by no means uniform throughout the agricultural space economy, it has resulted in total production moving ahead of effective demand. Secondly, in developed economies like the EEC, there is a low income elasticity of demand for agricultural products. In other words, as living standards rise through economic growth, the proportion of a household's income spent on food decreases. This is in contrast to the market for most other consumer goods and services, where a rise in income leads to an increase in effective demand. The quality rather than the quantity of food consumed becomes the most important consideration once income reaches a certain level. Thirdly, and very much a result of these two earlier factors, the price level of agricultural goods has not increased as quickly as the price of industrial goods. Farmers are having to pay higher prices for essential inputs from other sectors, but the real price which they are receiving for their products is facing a long-term decline. Finally, the prices of agricultural goods are subject to violent fluctuations, unlike most manufactured items. This is inherent in the nature of farming since the producer is unable to control the supply of his products. Weather conditions have an important bearing on production and yields. If prices are high due to a poor harvest, the farmer may not necessarily prosper. Conversely, at a time of bumper harvests, prices may fall so low that it is not economic for the farmer to put his crops on the market. It is very difficult for farmers to plan and change production in anticipation of prices. So, in economic language, the supply of their products is price inelastic.[1] For the above reasons, therefore, agriculture requires protection; but there are other good reasons which are more peculiar to the EEC situation.

Table 13 shows that in all countries, agriculture's contribution to Gross Domestic Produce (GDP) is less than its equivalent manpower input. The member states are listed in descending order according to their percentage of working population in agriculture in 1978. As this table indicates, agriculture is relatively more efficient in some countries than in others. The UK, Netherlands and Denmark would seem to have the most efficient farming sectors, while France, Italy and West Germany have most problem farming regions. There are also marked internal geographical variations within the member states. These are most acute in France, the major food producer, and in Italy, where two thirds of all agricultural holdings are less than five hectares in size. In contrast, the UK has around 30 per cent of its farms over 50 hectares in size, and absolutely within the EEC, this total is exceeded only in France. So, within the EEC, there is a situation of agricultural duality—large, efficient, mechanised farms operating alongside small, inefficient, under-capitalised units. This is largely a consequence of geography, as the last section indicated, but it provides further evidence of the complex problems to be accommodated by the CAP.

As well as too many farms, the EEC also has too many farmers. The agricultural labour force has declined by around 5 per cent per

TABLE 13

Agriculture as a percentage of GDP and the working population in 1978

% working population		% contribution to GDP[1]
22.1	Ireland	15.9
15.4	Italy	7.0
9.1	France	4.9
8.7	Denmark	5.5
6.5	West Germany	2.5
6.5	Netherlands	2.6
6.2	Luxembourg	4.4
3.2	Belgium	2.5
2.6	UK	2.2

NOTE
1. Measured in terms of gross value added.

Source: Basic Statistics of the Community, 1979, Tables 9 and 18, Eurostat, 1979.

annum since 1958, but most would argue that this has not been fast enough. In 1958 there were over 16m agricultural workers in the Six, equivalent to around one in every five workers employed. In the enlarged Community of Nine there were 7.8m persons employed in agriculture, less than 8 per cent of the total workforce, in 1979. Tables 14 and 15 show the full extent of this significant change. The biggest movement from the land has been in Italy. In the 1960s, the Italian economy experienced fundamental structural change as a consequence of the "economic miracle". Industrialisation, particularly in the north, was rapid and many jobs in agriculture were lost. The largest fall, however, was in the *Mezzogiorno* and by no means compensated for by new job opportunities (*see* Chapter XIII). France and West Germany have also experienced large absolute and proportionate falls in their farming populations. The accession of Denmark and Ireland to the EEC in 1973 has added two important producer nations, both of whom had strong agricultural motives for membership and relatively significant agricultural workforces. The second geographical enlargement of the EEC will add a further 4.5m workers to the agricultural population and significantly raise the proportion of the population dependent upon agriculture.

The UK is the most efficient farming member of the EEC and has the smallest proportion of working population in agriculture. It is, on the other hand, a heavy food importer and so indirectly pays to support less efficient producers in other countries. This provides yet

TABLE 14

Working population employed in agriculture ('000)

	1958	1961	1967	1970	1975	1979
Belgium	324	288	209	174	136	118[1]
France	4,455	4,044	3,216	2,821	2,104	1,867
Italy	6,974	6,207	4,480	3,878	3,274	3,012
Luxembourg	24	21	18	13	11	10
Netherlands	495	449	366	329	299	235
West Germany	3,978	3,449	2,638	2,262	1,823	1,544
Denmark	(380)	(356)	(305)	(266)	228	208
Ireland	(407)	(379)	(320)	(283)	252	220
UK	(1,057)	(972)	(792)	(784)	664	632
EEC Total	16,250[2]	14,458[2]	10,927[2]	9,477[2]	8,791	7,890

NOTES
1. Figure for 1978.
2. EEC–6.

Sources: Farming Facts—the New Common Market, Barclays Bank Ltd, 1972, and *Review, 1970–1979*, Eurostat, 1980.

TABLE 15
Percentage working population in agriculture

	1961	1970	1975	1979
Belgium	8.3	4.7	3.6	3.1[1]
France	21.6	13.9	10.2	8.8
Italy	31.0	20.2	16.7	14.8
Luxembourg	15.7	9.5	6.8	6.1
Netherlands	10.9	7.2	6.6	4.8
West Germany	13.1	8.6	7.4	6.2
Denmark	(17.1)	(11.5)	9.8	8.3
Ireland	(36.3)	(27.1)	24.2	21.0
UK	(4.0)	(3.2)	2.7	2.6
EEC Average	19.0[2]	12.0[2]	8.7	7.7

NOTES
1. Figure for 1978.
2. Estimate for EEC-6.

Sources: Farming Facts—the New Common Market, Barclays Bank Ltd, 1972, and
Review, 1970–1979, Eurostat, 1980.

another problem area of EEC agriculture—some member states are net producers, whereas others are large importers of food. As well as the UK, West Germany and the Benelux nations rely on the others for food imports. Italy tends to be both a large producer and importer due to geographical factors.

As this analysis has indicated, agriculture is a problem activity in the EEC. Against a background of economic weakness and general inefficiency, there is a complex geographical problem of duality both between and within member states. At the same time, the EEC must have adequate supplies of food to meet the needs of its 260m consumers. For these reasons, therefore, some form of Agricultural Policy is essential.

The Common Agricultural Policy

Prior to 1958, for the reasons described above, each of the Six had their own managed market policy for agriculture. It was therefore essential in the Treaty of Rome to replace these differing policy devices with a single common policy so that the principle of free trade between members could apply to agricultural products. Article 39 of the Treaty of Rome sets out five objectives for a common agricultural policy. These are:

(*i*) to increase agricultural productivity by promoting technical progress, rationalising agricultural production and the optimum utilisation of factors of production, especially labour;

(*ii*) to ensure a fair standard of living for the agricultural community, in particular by increasing the individual earnings of persons engaged in agriculture;

(*iii*) to stabilise markets;

(*iv*) to assure availability of supplies;

(*v*) to ensure supplies to consumers at reasonable prices.

The wide range of objectives is a reflection of the diverse nature of EEC agriculture. Taken together, they attempt to create the protection of a managed market situation, where competition between member states is at agreed uniform price levels. This is in contrast to the market for industrial and manufactured goods, where price competition is a vital element of intra-Community free trade.

Articles 40 and 41 of the Rome Treaty provide for the common organisation of markets (COM) by means of common rules on competition and the compulsory co-ordination of national marketing organisations. The COMs operate on a product basis, e.g. cereals, sugar, wine, beef and dairy products. In particular they aim to regulate prices, control aids to producers and introduce measures for the stabilisation of exports and imports within their own product markets.[2] Most of the individual COMs were set up between 1966 and 1968 through the abolition of quantitative restrictions and custom duties on trade between member states. Market stabilisation involves the fixing of a series of common prices within each product group. To do this effectively, it is essential to have a common measure of value, known as the "agricultural unit of account". The exchange rate between the national currency of a member and its unit of account is nicknamed "green currency". So, the unit of account is not a currency as such—it is merely an accounting device. Converted into national currencies, the following rates applied on 25th July 1975—1 u.a. = £0.536569, = DM 3.578726, = FF 5.633168. By this conversion, the prices fixed in the individual product markets can be easily expressed in national currencies. The fluctuation of individual currencies, e.g. the devaluation of the French franc in the late 1960s and the pound sterling in the mid-1970s, has caused many problems for this system. The green currencies used tend to differ from official parities and Monetary Compensation Amounts (MCAs) have been created to maintain the value of price guarantees during periods of monetary instability. In the absence of this special system, the free movement of goods at fixed prices would break down. France was the first member state to experience an export levy and import subsidy in 1969. More recently, the UK and other member countries have been cushioned from rising food import prices by this MCA system.

The general over-all financial aspects of the C A P are administered by the European Agricultural Guidance and Guarantee Fund (EAGGF or FEOGA). Since 1971 it has had control over its own financial resources, which in turn come from the Community Budget. Financially, EAGGF accounted for a massive 80 per cent of the Budget in 1971. Today, its percentage allocation is nearer 75 per cent, although absolutely, its finances have increased. EAGGF's

TABLE 16

Expenditure of the E A G G F for 1979

A. *Guarantee: 6,959.1 million u.a.*

Sectors	Refunds (m.u.a.)	Interventions, production aid (m.u.a.)	Other types of aid (m.u.a.)
Cereals	1,493.4	434.8	—
Rice	38.5	2.9	—
Milk products	1,572.9	2,144.7	—
Olive oil	1.1	320.6	—
Oil seeds	6.0	195.2	—
Sugar	751.8	252.9	—
Beef and veal	122.7	365.6	—
Pigmeat	68.6	16.3	—
Eggs and poultry	41.2	—	—
Fruit and vegetables	35.6	290.9	—
Wine	5.6	97.7	26.1
Tobacco	5.4	256.6	—
Miscellaneous	—	112.5	—
Processed products	—	176.2	—
Compens. amounts —monetary	—	—	809.2

B. *Guidance : 432.3 million u.a.*

Joint schemes	Million u.a.
Reform of agricultural structures	146.4
Marketing and processing of agricultural products	18.1
Particular sectors:	
fisheries	36.1
beef and veal	4.5
fruit and vegetables	4.0
wine	31.5
milk	73.4
cattle health and improvement	20.0
Special measures (fruit and vegetables)	3.5
Individual projects for the improvement of agricultural structures	40.0
Others	54.8
TOTAL	432.3

Source: Europe Today, The European Parliament, 1979, Table 3.34.

resources are divided between two sections, the Guarantee Section and the Guidance Section. Table 16 indicates how E A G G F's total expenditure was divided between the two sections in 1979. The accounting units used are the agricultural units of account referred to earlier. The Guarantee Section, which subsumed over 90 per cent of E A G G F's total budget, finances the market support and trade policies of the product C O Ms. The value of these functions for each product group is given in the second and first columns respectively. Refunds to exporters are based upon the difference between Community prices and the generally lower prices on world markets. Figure 6 shows how the levy system operates within the C O M for

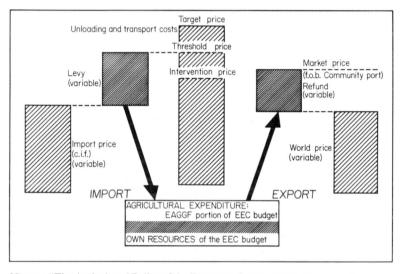

[*Source*: "The Agricultural Policy of the European Community", *European Documentation Periodical* 2/79.

F I G. 6.—Levy and refund system for wheat.

cereal products. Export refunds on dairy products constitute the single largest refund item. Through this system surplus production is sold off to third party countries like the U S S R and Poland. The value of the market intervention function is given in the second column of Table 16. In all product markets, intervention occurs when the internal market price in the E E C falls below an agreed level, the intervention price. The system is a complex one—there are many different types of price and each product market operates in its own peculiar way.[3] The basic principle in each C O M, however, is the same, and the following example explains in a simple way how the intervention system operates in the cereals market.

Example—The Common Organisation of the Market for Cereal Products

As in all COMs, the protection of farm incomes is achieved through the application of uniform prices throughout the Community. These are fixed annually at the meeting of EEC Agricultural Ministers, held in January or February. The COM for cereal products covers common wheat, durum wheat (for pasta products), rye, barley and maize. It has been operational since July 1967. Prices are fixed for the period the 1st August to the 31st July of the following year and are wholesale rather than retail prices. Table 17 gives details of the type and level of cereal prices set for 1975–76. These are diagrammatically related in Fig. 6, referred to earlier.

There are three basic types of price:

(*i*) *Target Price* applicable for all the above cereal products. It is an agreed price considered to be a fair market price, balancing both the needs of the farming community and consumers. It is not guaranteed, but offers protection against fluctuations in world market prices through the introduction of a variable levy;

(*ii*) *Intervention price* for common wheat, this takes the form of a basic intervention price, fixed for Duisberg in West Germany. This producing region in the Ruhr Valley was chosen since it is the area of shortest supply within the Community. This price is up to 8 per cent below the Target price and is the point where national intervention agencies buy up supplies. For the other cereal products, this is referred to as a single or uniform intervention price;

(*iii*) *Threshold price* used in conjunction with a variable levy and is the minimum price at which imports can be delivered at EEC ports. It is fixed at a level where, once transport costs are added, the price of wheat at Duisberg would be above the target price. The variable levy, calculated on a daily basis, is paid by the importer and is charged on all consignments entering the Community, on that particular day (*see* Fig. 6).

The total value of the intervention function in 1979 was over 5000m units of account (Table 16). The largest sum paid out was for dairy products, where the Community has the highest degree of surplus production. Within the above framework, the COMs operate a managed, as distinct from a controlled, market. Prices still fluctuate as a result of supply and demand forces, but only above the intervention price level. A product shortage will force the price above this level and farmers ought to gain. On the other hand, consumers are protected from the wider fluctuations on world product markets. The remaining expenditure of the Guarantee Section of EAGGF supports the MCA system referred to earlier.

TABLE 17
Cereal prices 1975–76

Products	Type of price or amount	Amounts set 1974-5 (u.a./tonne)	Amounts set in February 1975		
			Absolute value (u.a./tonne)	Percentage increase in 1975-6 over 1974-5	Period of application
Durum wheat	Target price	191.97	207.33	8.0	1.8.75–31.7.76
	Single intervention price	175.17	190.53	8.8	
	Minimum price (wholesale) guaranteed to producer	205.17	215.45	5.0	
	Aid	30.00	24.92	—	
Common wheat	Target price	127.93	139.44	9.0	1.8.75–31.7.76
	Basic intervention price	115.53	125.93	9.0	
Barley	Target price	116.08	126.99	9.4	1.8.75–31.7.76
	Single intervention price	101.43	110.96	9.4	
Rye	Target price	124.99	138.74	11.0	1.8.75–31.7.76
	Single intervention price	106.93	119.76	12.0	
Maize	Target price	114.92	126.41	10.0	1.8.75–31.7.76
	Single intervention price	94.03	103.43	10.0	

NOTE: For the pound sterling, 1 u.a. = £0.536569.

Source: Europe Today, The European Parliament, 1976, Table 3.431.

The Guidance Section has a fixed annual expenditure and is concerned with implementing the first agricultural objective of the Rome Treaty, i.e. improving the level of agricultural productivity in the EEC. It is therefore dealing with the over-all structural, rather than the day-to-day problems of agriculture in the Community. Its functions are varied, as its expenditure pattern indicates (*see* Table 16). To improve productivity it has contributed to the cost of farm consolidation programmes, particularly in parts of France and Italy where production units are small. It has also assisted in the marketing of certain types of product and in helping farmers to switch production. These structural aspects of agriculture are analysed in the next section. The balance of funds has been always heavily weighted in favour of the Guarantee Section. In more recent years there have been definitive moves to increase the funds of the Guidance Section and to modify the uniform price intervention function of the Guarantee Section. It is only in this way that the root of the EEC's agricultural problem can be tackled more effectively.

An integral aspect of CAP is its policy of dependence on third party suppliers. In particular, the EEC needs agricultural raw materials and tropical products which for geographical reasons cannot be produced in quantity in Western Europe. This need has had

TABLE 18

Geographical source of EEC agricultural imports 1973-6

Source	% total EEC agricultural imports				% change 1973-76
	1973	1974	1975	1976	
ACP (Lomé) Countries	10.8	12.0	12.8	13.1	+21.8
United States	17.1	18.9	20.9	19.9	+15.8
Latin America	15.6	15.1	15.0	16.1	+5.1
Various	9.9	10.3	10.6	9.8	−1.0
Centrally Planned	8.9	8.5	8.3	8.2	−7.8
Mediterranean[1]	11.6	11.3	10.8	10.6	−8.6
Western Europe[2]	10.2	9.9	8.2	8.8	−13.7
Japan	0.7	0.7	0.6	0.6	−14.3
Industrial Commonwealth[3]	13.8	12.4	11.9	11.6	−15.9
Yugoslavia	1.4	0.9	0.9	1.1	−21.4
EEC Total	100	100	100	100	

NOTES
1. Algeria, Cyprus, Egypt, Spain, Greece, Israel, Jordan, Malta, Morocco, Portugal, Syria and Tunisia.
2. Austria, Finland, Iceland, Norway, Sweden, Switzerland.
3. South Africa, Australia, Canada, New Zealand.

Source: Ceres, July–August 1978, p. 9.

an important bearing on Community relations with less developed economies (*see* Chapter III). The changing geographical origin of agricultural imports is shown in Table 18. For those commodities which the EEC can produce for itself, the attitude to outside suppliers is by no means as liberal as it is for industrial goods. The reasons for this are obvious from the previous discussion of the problem of agriculture. Selective bilateral agreements have been drawn up, although progress has been slow. With the major exception of the ACP (Lomé) countries, there is an import levy system in operation for most products (Fig. 6 shows how this operates for wheat imports). The other exceptions are the separate sugar agreement with 13 ACP producers and the UK's special dairy products agreement with New Zealand.

As we have shown, the Common Agricultural Policy is a massive, complex, managed market farm policy. Its success should be judged in terms of its objectives as laid down by the Treaty of Rome. On balance, its greatest achievement is that it has secured and guaranteed supplies to the EEC's 260m consumers. Table 19 shows that the Community is self-sufficient in most products which it is able to produce for itself. The main imports are tropical products plus citrus fruits, vegetable oils, maize, rice and lamb. Many of these items, however, are covered by the Lomé Convention and other bilateral agreements. So, even in the event of a severe dislocation of supplies, the EEC could feed its population although the quality of diet would suffer. This success, however, has only been achieved at a cost. Without a shadow of doubt, CAP is a "dear food" farm policy—the consumer has to pay high prices in order to guarantee supplies. So,

TABLE 19

Degree of self-sufficiency of major products in EEC agriculture (%)

Cereals (1978/79)		Meat (1979)		Other Crops (1978/79)		Dairy Products (1979)	
Overall	100	Overall	98				
Wheat	116	Beef	99	Potatoes	100	Cheese	105
Rye	114	Veal	105	Sugar[1]	124	Butter	119
Barley	113	Pork	101	Vegetables	94		
Oats	100	Poultry	105	Fresh fruit	77		
Maize	59			Citrus fruit	41		
				Wine	102		
Also Rice	81					Oils & fats	38

NOTE
1. Includes overseas departments.

Source: Basic Statistics of the Community, Eurostat, 1982, Table 39.

the final objective laid down in the Treaty of Rome cannot be met as long as it is necessary to pay inefficient farmers to keep in production. This in turn conflicts with the first objective of increasing the quality of EEC agriculture. So, success gained in setting up a managed market with secure supplies has to be offset against the structural problems of CAP discussed in detail below.

Present-Day Problems of CAP and Structural Issues

Through its development and importance, the CAP has become a forceful agent of economic integration in the EEC and, as we have noted, has to a considerable degree guaranteed the supplies of food to the Community's 260m consumers. Simultaneously, no single area of EEC affairs has taken up so much time or been the source of so much political wrangling as the CAP. The cause of these problems is both deep and longstanding, a function of the financing arrangements for EEC common policies.

The EEC Budget, three-quarters of which is spent upon CAP, is financed by contributions from member states who in turn receive payments from the various Community Funds (*see* diagram on p. 290). The net contribution of member states is most unbalanced and herein lies many of the present-day problems of CAP. Figure 7 shows this imbalance in 1973. As can be seen, the financing arrangements favour the producer nations at the expense of consumer nations, notably the UK. This state of affairs persisted in 1979, despite vigorous efforts to reform CAP from within, when the UK paid almost £600m more into EEC agriculture than her farmers received from EAGGF. West Germany was the other major contributor while the remaining member states were all beneficiaries. As in 1973, Denmark and the Republic of Ireland were the highest in terms of benefits per head. Clearly this is an intolerable situation, particularly for the UK, one of the poorer EEC members. Given the reluctant development of the remaining common policies, it would seem essential for a better balance of resources to be achieved.

A second financial criticism of CAP is that the high level of prices fixed for agricultural products do not provide enough encouragement for farmers to switch production away from those areas where there is over-production. Consequently food surpluses arise. The extent of food surpluses in 1976 is shown in Figure 8. The major surpluses are in dairy products. For skimmed milk powder, the EEC has the equivalent of over five years consumption in hand! The other surpluses, in retrospect, are not as extensive. For example, the much publicised "butter mountain" represents only around two months' supply and for other products, the surpluses are much less. It is not EEC policy to sell their surpluses to internal consumers at cheap

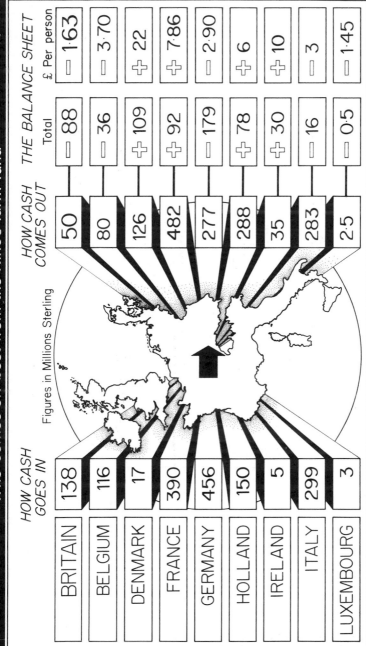

Who comes off best from the Nine's farm fund

Figures in Millions Sterling

	HOW CASH GOES IN	HOW CASH COMES OUT	THE BALANCE SHEET Total	£ Per person
BRITAIN	138	50	− 88	− 1·63
BELGIUM	116	80	− 36	− 3·70
DENMARK	17	126	+ 109	+ 22
FRANCE	390	482	+ 92	+ 7·86
GERMANY	456	277	− 179	− 2·90
HOLLAND	150	288	+ 78	+ 6
IRELAND	5	35	+ 30	+ 10
ITALY	299	283	− 16	− 3
LUXEMBOURG	3	2·5	− 0·5	− 1·45

[Source: The Sunday Times, September 29, 1974.

Fig. 7.—Geographical distribution of E A G G F funds in 1973. The E E C spends over 75 per cent of its budget on agricultural aid. The chart shows approximately how much each country contributed to the farm fund and how much it got out in 1973. Countries which do worst may console themselves with the tariff-free access they have to a market of over 250 million people for their manufactured goods.

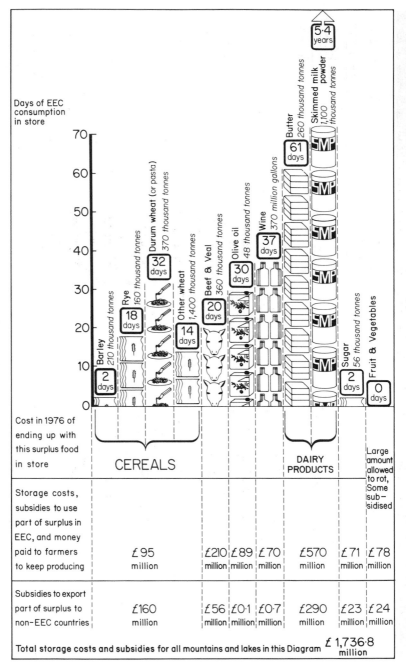

[*Source: Undercurrents*, 31, June 1978.

FIG. 8.—EEC food surpluses, storage costs and export subsidies, 1976.

prices. Instead, particularly for dairy products, subsidies are paid to export to non-EEC countries like the USSR. To some commentators, this policy is illogical and unfair. The Commission's attitude, however, is that internal prices could only be reduced slightly and there is a danger that a position of surplus could quickly be converted into one of shortages. The answer, they argue, is to encourage a reorientation of output in the desired direction, e.g. some dairy farmers should be encouraged to produce meat and poor quality wine producers should move into fruit and vegetable production. In this way, the root rather than the sign of the problem will be tackled and is in keeping with the more general process of the structural reform of agriculture discussed in detail below.

A final financial criticism, related to the problem of surpluses, is that the farm prices themselves are too high. In relation to EEC prices, the world price for many products is predominantly cheaper. If a world price for a product were rated as 100, in the year 1975–76 prices for the equivalent EEC food would be: butter 320, skimmed milk powder 226, olive oil 207, beef and veal 156, eggs 131 and barley 124.[4] Generally speaking, as indicated earlier, the EEC farm prices are uniform throughout the Community and based on the least efficient regions of production. Consequently, the efficient farmers receive high incomes. A special report on CAP published in January 1979 states that present farm prices afford an income of about three times the national average wage even to only moderately efficient farmers.[5] It suggests that real price cuts of at least 30 per cent would have to be made before there would be any reduction in farm output. It concludes that the political make-up of the EEC, coupled with a further decline in the agricultural workforce, are likely to force radical changes in the CAP in the 1980s.

This does not mean to say that the EEC is unaware of the structural problems of agriculture. In fact, for the last ten years or so there have been attempts to improve the CAP from within. In effect, these give a growing recognition to the spatial dimensions of the agricultural economy as outlined earlier. The negotiation of a realignment of the CAP took five years to complete. It started in 1968, with the publication of the radical Mansholt Plan, *Agriculture 1980*. Mansholt, who was the Commissioner responsible for Agriculture, recommended the withdrawal of 5 m farmers and workers from agriculture by 1980. Half would receive pensions, while the others would be found industrial jobs. His other major proposal was that over 5 m hectares would be removed from agricultural use and used for afforestation, national parks and recreation. In particular, he was recognising that the Community average farm size of 12 hectares was too low to provide an adequate income for farmers. The alternative to the structural reforms he proposed was the undoubted continuation of high food prices. Mansholt's proposals caused considerable disagreement amongst the Six—France and Italy, who would be most affected by the Plan were opposed to the level of reform proposed in view of its social and cultural impact on certain traditional farming regions; West Germany, on the other hand, was keen to see reform get under way.

Some proposals similar to those suggested by the Mansholt Plan were finally accepted by the Council Ministers in May 1971 and the directives were formally adopted in March 1972. These were additional to national structural policies, which operated independently of EAGGF. The reforms had three objectives—to prevent structural surpluses, to normalise price policy and to create modern farms. To achieve these objectives, a series of voluntary common measures were agreed. The most important ones were as follows.

(i) Modernisation aid—this is a programme of selective assistance for aiding farms capable of development. It is designed to turn inefficient farmers into efficient producers, but is only available in regions where farming is the main occupation. Farmers receive 25 per cent of their capital outlay from the Guidance Section of EAGGF and the planned expenditure of the ten-year programme to 1982 was 432m units of account (u.a.).

(ii) Aid to encourage farmers to cease farming—this may be granted to farmers or employees between 55 and 65 years of age. The recognised scale of annuities is 900 u.a. for married persons and 600 u.a. for single persons. Additional premiums may be given by member states, but this will not be reimbursed by EAGGF. Denmark and Italy have so far been excluded from this directive, for which a ten-year fund of 288m u.a. has been allocated.

(iii) Improved guidance and training—such measures are designed to increase the general efficiency of agriculture and aid of 110m u.a. has been provided.

The progress since 1972 has been slow. By 1976, only seven member states had fully or partially implemented the three measures outlined above, even though there had been agreement on a regional differentiation of the financial incentive and measures provided. France and Italy, the two member states with greatest structural problems, had failed to agree to their implementation.

There have been other common measures which have tried to further promote the structural reform of CAP. These have taken various forms, including special aid to vegetable and fruit producers, a slaughtering premium for dairy herds and aid for the reorganisation of citrus fruit production in Italy. A particularly significant step forward was the special help for mountain and hill farmers announced in 1974. This introduced the idea of a variable compensatory allowance of at least 15 u.a. per head of livestock. It was a recognition that price and structural policies were incapable of giving farmers in areas like the Alps, the Massif Central and the Pennines an adequate income. The short growing season and the steep terrain make farming a difficult life and farmers are not able to have a high rate of livestock per acre. The special payment is also available in other less favoured areas like Galway, the Ardennes and the Scottish Highlands, where agricultural productivities are similarly low. In such regions rural depopulation has been commonplace, and it is hoped that the compensatory payments will help farmers to stay in business.

Towards the end of the 1970s further pressure was exerted for the reform of CAP. Britain and other consumer member states have been keen to restrict the level of increase of guaranteed farm prices, arguing that this provides a built-in means of structural reform. France in particular has strongly resisted such moves and even given her farmers considerable financial support above the EEC limits. The European Parliament has also expressed its concern at the escalating cost of CAP, seeking to restrict its importance within the over-all Budget. In June 1981 this body passed its own plan for the reform of CAP based upon the setting of production targets (rather than guaranteed prices) for the main farm commodities. Price penalties were proposed for those farmers exceeding these limits. It remains to be seen whether or not this scheme has any more success than its predecessors.

In conclusion, therefore, it can be seen that plans to reform CAP have been discussed for many years, yet on the surface little would seem to have been achieved. The second geographical enlargement of the EEC may have posed less of an obstacle had progress been more encouraging. As events have turned out, the structural reform of CAP presents a fundamental challenge to the workings of the Community and the spread of integration in the 1980s.

Fishing

Most of the member countries of the Community have had, traditionally, well-developed and efficient fishing industries. The marginal seas of north-western Europe, in particular, lie, for the most part, on the continental shelf and the cool, shallow waters charged with fish food for long provided good conditions for organic production. Countries with many centuries of maritime tradition border these marginal seas. "Prosperous fisheries, indeed," wrote R. Morgan, "were an essential basis of their early mercantile and naval prowess, providing the training ground and reservoir of man-power."[6] Long exploitation of the fishing grounds together with vastly improved fishing technology have led to gross over-fishing in some areas, more especially in the North Sea. A number of other factors, apart from the shallow seas rich in minute marine organisms, have conspired to make North-West European fisheries among the more important in the world. First, in many areas of North-West Europe the land was niggardly in its resources and sometimes hostile to farming, hence man was urged to make use of the harvest of the sea and fishing still often augments farming in coastal localities. Secondly, the indented coastline with its wealth of sheltered harbours greatly assisted the development of the industry; the estuaries, rias and fiords provided maritime nurseries in the early days, tempting man to take to the sea and offering excellent training grounds. Thirdly, in earlier times religious practices, such as the proscription by the Roman Catholic Church against eating flesh on certain days, helped to stimulate the industry and a very considerable export trade in processed fish to Catholic countries grew up. Fourthly, the large demand for food from the densely populated industrial countries of Western Europe, together with the gradually increasing standards of living and the desire for a more varied and balanced diet helped greatly to stimulate the fishing industry.

The Traditional Fishing Grounds

The heart of the North-West European shelf is the North Sea, and for many centuries the Dogger Bank was the most productive area; the submerged plateau with its "pits" or channels grooving its margins has been a prolific source of fish, attracting fishermen from very early times. Fish in great variety inhabit the Bank, but especially cod from the Silver Pits and hake, plaice, sole and whiting. Herring, which formerly accounted for nearly half of the total North Sea catch, and which appeared regularly in large shoals in summer, have declined seriously in both their numbers and importance. Around the Lofoten Islands, off the coast of northern Norway, cod has long been extremely prolific, while in summer large catches of mackerel are made in the seas off south-western Norway. In the warmer waters of the English Channel and the Bay of Biscay different species of fish begin to occur, for example, pilchards are caught in the Channel and shoals of anchovy frequent Biscay. Albacore or tunny (tuna fish) are caught in the deeper offshore waters beyond the shelf. Anchovy, pilchard and tunny are not really typical of the north-western shelf; they belong rather to the warmer waters of more southerly latitudes.

The Baltic, in comparison with the North Sea, is of very minor significance as a fishing area and yet, during the medieval period it was of great importance for its herring which contributed to the fortunes of the Hanseatic merchants. Precisely why the herring forsook the Baltic has never been satisfactorily explained but it may well have been linked with the decreasing salinity of the sea. As a fishing area the Baltic has the great disadvantage that it does not support many marine species since its waters are too fresh (fish enter the sea but are unable to breed there successfully) while its waters are too salt to enable freshwater species to flourish. Furthermore, as a semi-isolated sea, it is not organically rich. The only fishing of real importance is that in the Kattegat where some cod, plaice and whiting occur. In the Baltic proper the chief fish types are the Baltic herring and the flounder, with some eel and salmon.

The Iceland and the Faeroës fisheries are comparable with the North Sea in the variety of their species and in the richness of their fish yields. Herring are abundant in summer but demersal fish, found on the sea-bed, especially cod, haddock and halibut, constitute the chief catch. Iceland, which is so poverty-stricken in land resources, depends principally on the sea for its support; indeed, of all the countries of Europe, fishing is of the greatest relative importance to Iceland. Other countries used to send their fishing vessels to the rich trawling grounds around Iceland but their activity has been curtailed as a result of the Icelandic government's action in extending the country's territorial waters.

The Barents Sea, lying between the north of Scandinavia and Novaya Zemlya, is an extensive fishing area rich in cold-water species, notably cod, haddock, halibut, redfish and saithe. Many countries have sent vessels to fish in these northern waters.

The Mediterranean Sea is not a rich fishing ground but anchovy, pilchard, mackerel, mullet, hake and tunny are caught. Fishing vessels and techniques are still largely traditional and the average production per fisherman is low; moreover, although the Mediterranean is probably fished to its maximum capacity, the fish production of its bordering countries is modest.[7]

Dwindling Fish Resources

In 1976, according to estimates made by the Food and Agriculture Organisation (FAO) of the United Nations, the world harvest of marine products had increased to a new record total of 72m tonnes.[8] Even so, in some areas, notably the North Sea and parts of the North Atlantic, stocks of many species of fish have fallen to crisis level and catches have, generally speaking, dwindled during the 1970s. Like any other living things, fish are a potentially renewable resource, but only if stocks are carefully husbanded at all stages of their growth.

In the marginal seas around Western Europe attempts at caring for these stocks have failed lamentably:

> An analysis of stocks drawn up by the European Commission in conjunction with scientists from member countries shows how critical the situation has become with many species. In the North Sea, for instance, herring and sole are "highly over-exploited". The spawning stock is "dangerously depleted", at one-tenth of its post-war level; catches are declining. Cod and haddock are "over-exploited", with a moderate spawning stock level. Plaice is "fully over-exploited", with spawning stock declining. It is a similar picture in the English Channel, with plaice "highly over-exploited", sole and mackerel "fully exploited" and herring "over-exploited". Off the west of Scotland herring, haddock and cod are "fully or over-exploited".[9]

The decline in fish stocks results primarily from increasingly intensive fishing which exceeds the sea's capacity to replace them. But a number of factors or conditions contribute to this situation. First, in order to offset diminishing returns. increasing marine capital has been employed and the result of this has been for catches to increase beyond the point at which yields can be sustained by natural regeneration. Secondly, over-fishing has resulted from fast-moving fleets, fitted with sophisticated sounding and catching equipment and able to almost sweep clear one area of fish and move swiftly on to the next.[10] Thirdly, many species of fish migrate over great distances in their life cycle, spawning in one area, feeding in another and finally maturing in another, but it is in the breeding grounds that the effects of over-fishing are most serious. Fourthly, industrial fishing for fish meal and fish oil creates special problems since it takes fish needed for human consumption and it also takes species which are important as food for the more valuable commercial species, thereby upsetting the marine ecology.[11]

Berendt has commented:

> All Community fishermen are feeling the impact of change. During the difficult period from the summer of 1973 to the summer of 1974, overall operating costs for the British, Irish, French, and Italian fishing industries all rose by 30 per cent. Costs have continued to go up since. Between 1974 and 1975, moreover, landings of fish in the UK dropped by 11 per cent, in Ireland by 9 per cent, in France by $9\frac{1}{2}$ per cent, and in West Germany by 14 per cent. Employment in the fishing industry has been affected as well. It has fallen in most Community member states, but particularly in West Germany, the Netherlands, and the United Kingdom. Ice-

land's action in unilaterally extending fishing limits has affected the West German as well as the British industry. The small rural communities which depend so heavily on fishing—for example, Brittany, Ireland, South-West England, and Scotland—are particularly vulnerable to the changes confronting the fishing industry. The Italian fishing fleet, too, which is one of the largest in the Community, has many boats that are too small or too old to provide adequate income.[12]

Problems and Politics of Community Fisheries Policy

The changes which the fishing industry is undergoing clearly affect fishermen in most member states. As with agriculture, there would seem to be a good case for tackling the problems on a Community basis, particularly as both activities have common characteristics. Structurally, there is a duality in the fishing industry similar to that in agriculture—there are Community fishermen who fish the waters around their own shores and those who fish farther afield in larger vessels. As Lambert comments. "There was no common measure between the Brittany fisherman owning a couple of tiny fishing vessels, leaving at dusk and sailing in at dawn, and the big trawler fleets of Bremen, equipped with refrigerated storage and fishing for days or weeks on end, far from their home ports, before landing their catch."[13] Secondly, both fishing and agriculture are facing long-term decline, although for different reasons. Thirdly, like agriculture, it would seem desirable to have a common Community market, with regulations to ensure fair competition. As with the product COM referred to earlier, there could be a system of common fish prices in operation, including essential market support from Community funds. For these and other reasons, there would seem to be a strong case for a common fisheries policy.

The growing problems of the EEC's fishing industry have emerged since the Treaty of Rome was signed. In fact, there did not seem to be too many difficulties ahead when the French began to press for a common policy in the late 1960s. Consequently, in June 1970 the Council of Ministers adopted the basic framework of a common fisheries policy. "This established the principle that all EEC fishermen should have equal access to the waters of member states. It also introduced a market organisation with reference prices to control imports and it encouraged the setting up of producer organisations to improve marketing."[14] The only exceptions to this general system were to be exclusive three-mile limits in certain parts of the Community where the local population was dependent on fishing for its livelihood. The regulation was implemented in early 1971, at a time when negotiations on enlargement were taking place with the UK,

Ireland, Denmark and Norway. But as Lambert points out, "know-ing that fisheries policy mattered to Britain, too, the French could strengthen their hand for the negotiations and for the future in the enlarged Community, by putting the British (and secondarily, the Norwegians) in the position of *demandeurs*—those asking for favours or concessions."[15] In retrospect, this has certainly turned out to be a major stumbling block.

In the enlarged Community of Nine, the UK controls 60 per cent of the fishing area and, if Ireland is added, twice as much sea as the rest of the EEC combined. For internal political reasons at the time of entry negotiations, the UK did not want to make too much of an issue of fisheries, although the common fisheries policy as it stood was totally unacceptable. Transitional arrangements for the UK and Ireland avoided an immediate confrontation—an exclusive six-mile limit, extended to twelve miles in certain important fishing areas (e.g. off South-West England, East Yorkshire and eastern Scotland) was agreed although it was only to operate during the first ten years of membership (*see* Fig, 9(*a*)). For Norway, the longer term impli-cations of a temporary twelve-mile limit were crucial as there were grave fears about the future of their fishing industry once waters were open to all EEC fishermen. Politically, the uncertainty over fishing had an important bearing on the Norwegian people's deci-

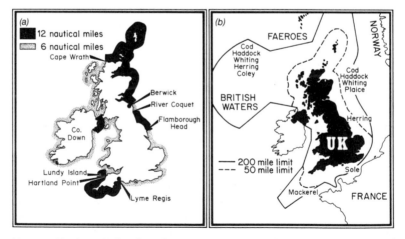

[*Source*: The Open University, *The European Economic Community: Economics and Agriculture*, 1974, p. 147.
(*a*) Limits negotiated at time of entry into EEC.
    [*Source*: *The Sunday Times*, December 31, 1976.
(*b*) 200 mile EEZ and 50 mile limit.
FIG. 9.—Fish stocks and fishing limits applying to the UK.

sion to reject the negotiated terms of entry and hence, Community membership.

Since the U K's accession to the E E C, attempts to find a permanent solution to the fisheries problem have failed and fisheries policy has been an important pawn in the political arena. Negotiations have been complicated by the E E C's acceptance of the 200-mile Exclusive Economic Zone (E E Z) recommendation of the United Nations Conference on the Law of the Sea, under which coastal states have control over the resources of both the sea and seabed within this limit of their shores (*see* Fig. 9(*b*)). The introduction of E E Zs will restrict catches by the longer distance fishing fleets of member states as countries like Norway and Iceland claim their new economic zones. This "will oblige the distant-water fleets to move closer to home in their search for fish, putting increased pressure on the middle-water and inshore fisheries, at a time when fish stocks seem to be declining."[16] The only compensation is that the catches of third party fishermen (e.g. from the U S S R, Poland, Rumania and East Germany) can be severely cut down through the same control. Table 20 shows the problem facing E E C member states and also illustrates the unique position of U K fishermen in the Community.

TABLE 20

Fishing catches of member states, 1973

	Total catch ('000 tonnes)	% Catch in own territorial waters & adjacent national zone[1]	% Catch in other members zones[1]	% Catch in zones of third party countries[1]
Belgium	49.1	52.7	31.4	15.9
Denmark	1,453.4	68.2	18.1	13.7
West Germany	418.2	5.1	27.1	67.8
France	593.9	26.8	46.3	26.9
Republic of Ireland	80.1	89.9	10.1	—
Netherlands	220.4	35.7	61.2	3.1
U K	1,048.7	63.6	0.3	36.1
Italy[2]	289.9	65.9	—	34.1
E E C Total	4,153.7	53.1	19.6	27.3

NOTES
1. Based upon 200-mile E E Z.
2. Predominantly, catch is of Mediterranean origin.

Source: Financial Times, 24th September 1976.

In November 1976 it was agreed by the foreign ministers of the EEC that the 200-mile EEZ should apply from the 1st January 1977. The UK and Ireland further proposed, as they had done previously, that there should be an exclusive fifty-mile limit for their domestic fishermen around their own coastal waters. The other member states and the EEC Commission thought that the proposals were far too excessive. A twelve-mile exclusive strip for member states was seen as more acceptable, so it was against this background that no over-all agreement was forthcoming. In the following month the lack of agreement remained, although it was agreed to serve notice on six third party countries that their catches in EEC waters must be cut substantially. A three-month quota was approved pending full agreement. Finally, in late December 1976, talks between the EEC and Iceland collapsed—Community vessels, British in particular, were banned from Icelandic waters from 1977 and in retaliation, the EEC omitted Iceland from the list of countries designated to fish inside the new EEZ. These events served only to strengthen the British insistence for a fifty-mile exclusive limit.

The dispute between the UK and the rest of the EEC has continued, with little sign of agreement. The UK has offered to abandon its earlier call for a fifty-mile exclusive limit in exchange for an exclusive twelve-mile limit and other areas between twelve and fifty miles where UK fishermen would enjoy a preferential share of the total catch. Having been forced out of distant waters, the UK is seeking to retain a dominant share of the catches in its richest fishing grounds. It has been estimated that this new UK suggestion would give 46 per cent of the total catch in EEC waters, although it is still well above the level envisaged by its fellow member states.

In February 1978 the eight other members of the EEC agreed to the introduction of a mini-fisheries policy to be operated independently as national programmes but in a co-ordinated way. Later the UK announced that new conservation measures were to be taken to protect stocks in the new 200-mile limit, including the so-called "pout box" off the east coast of Scotland. So, although EEC members have agreed on the need to drastically restrict the access of third party fishermen to Community waters, there is still no common agreement on how to allocate catches between themselves.

1980 was a bad year for both the Community's fishermen and the Commission's hope for agreement on a common policy. The UK fishing industry was cruelly affected by the extension of fishing limits by Iceland, Norway and the USSR, coupled with a further decline in fish stocks resulting from overfishing of North Sea and North Atlantic grounds. The Humberside port of Hull, for example, recorded fish landings of less than 50,000 tons—one-fifth of its 1976 level. As the number of fresh and freezer trawlers operating from the port fell then, so the number of jobs fell, not only on the vessels, but also on the quayside and in processing industries. Similar, if less spectacular, tales were reported from other UK ports and there was general unease about fish landings from non-UK vessels. In France, also, fishermen voiced their protests, culminating in a blockade of cross-Channel ferry services. Clearly there was an even more pressing need for an effective conservation programme to be set within a common fisheries policy.

One piece of agreement to be reached was on a Total Allowable Catch (TAC) for the EEC as a whole and on a method for the recording of catches. The practical application of these schemes is, however, dependent on the allocation of the TAC into quotas for each member state. In the 1980 talks the UK maintained its stand for a quota of 45 per cent of the total catch by value compared with the Commission's offer of no more than 31 per cent. To other big fishing member states, notably France and Denmark, even the Commission's suggestion was too high.

The transitional arrangements for the UK and the Republic of Ireland finished at the end of 1982, when fleets from the rest of the Nine were able to fish right up to their beaches. Free access, even allowing for a generous domestic quota, remains totally unacceptable to the UK. The fishing industry still favours a fifty-mile limit for the exclusive use of UK fishermen, although as mentioned earlier, politicians may be prepared to compromise for a twelve-mile exclusive limit with preferential access between twelve and fifty miles.

Access has clearly been a key issue in the long-drawn-out negotiations to settle a Common Fisheries Policy (CFP). Two related issues, which have been major stumbling blocks for the UK, have been the total catch allowed and its proposed distribution among member states. These problems have still to be resolved.

In Autumn 1981 the Community began a new initiative towards a CFP when agreement was reached on a "mini-package" of measures, the most important of which related to conservation.[17] The UK in particular was pleased to see an indefinite extension of conservation arrangements to protect fish stocks; in fact these were broadly based on those already introduced unilaterally by the UK. A second area of agreement was the introduction of marketing schemes to protect UK fishermen against the dumping of cheap fish imports in domestic markets. The UK was one of the countries most interested in this aspect of a CFP. Agreement on these protective measures has enabled the UK to lift the block it has been maintaining on EEC deals with third party countries such as Canada, Sweden and the Faeroë Islands.

New proposals to end the bitter six-year wrangle over fisheries were put to member states in June 1982. In a complex package of measures, the Commission sought to resolve two outstanding areas, the rights of access of EEC fishermen in the coastal waters of other member states and the distribution of the total catch. Free access, as previously stated, is an obligation of the Treaty of Rome but the latest plan provides for a possible twenty year transition on this sensitive issue. In short, the proposals seek to reserve an exclusive six mile coastal zone for member states and a further six to twelve mile band where local fishermen will have preferential access. For the UK, the twelve mile zone is unbroken around the coast of Scotland but only small exclusive zone sections are proposed around the coasts of England and Wales. If accepted the plan marginally increases the UK share of the total catch to about 35 per cent, still below the minimum level the British fishing industry is seeking. An area of the new plan acceptable to the UK is the proposal for the appointment of a team of fisheries inspectors to police vessels and monitor catches landed. For the first time, the UK sees the package as being broadly acceptable although Denmark has strongly opposed the quotas allocated to its fishermen.

Denmark's opposition to the proposed Common Fisheries Policy remained when the plan was put before the Council of Ministers. No serious negotiations were possible due to her unbending demands for greatly increased fishing quotas. With the transition arrangements expiring at the end of 1982, the Community has been under great pressure to reach agreement on a CFP. Indeed, it may well face a constitutional crisis, with the distinct prospects of a partial policy being implemented amongst nine member states. Important though the issue is to fishing regions, it hardly seems to warrant throwing the Community into turmoil at a time when it has far weightier issues to struggle with.

NOTES

1. For details, see Lipsey R. G., *Introduction to Positive Economics*, Weidenfeld & Nicolson, 1971, pp. 124–34.

2. For details of current state of integration see *Europe Today*, The European Parliament, 1976, section 3.6.

3. For details of prices and terminology, see *Europe Today*, The European Parliament, 1976, section 3.43.

4. "Undercurrents", 31, June 1978, p. 20.

5. *Political Change in the European Community: Implications for the CAP*, Agra Europe Ltd., 1979.

6. Morgan, R., *World Sea Fisheries*, Methuen & Co. Ltd., 1956, p. 184.

7. *Ibid.*, p. 210.

8. Hjul. P., "World Fish Stocks in a delicate balance", *Geographical Magazine*, October 1977, p. 27.

9. Berendt, M., "Fewer Fish in the Sea", *European Community*, No. 8, October 1976, p. 13.

10. Hughes, M., Report to The European Parliament, 1976.

11. *Ibid.*

12. Berendt, M., "Troubled Waters", *European Community*, No. 3, March–April 1976, p. 7.

13. Lambert, J., "The Politics of Fisheries in the Community", in *The European Economic Community: Economics and Agriculture*, The Open University, Unit P933 3-4, 1974, p. 141.

14. Berendt, M., *op. cit.*

15. Lambert, J., *op. cit.*, p. 139.

16. Berendt, M., *op. cit.*

17. See *The Daily Telegraph*, 1st October, 1981.

Chapter V

ENERGY

In the highly developed and highly industrialised countries of the world energy is of paramount importance. For example, the United States, for several decades the world's greatest user of energy, has been prodigal in its consumption of energy; with only about 5 per cent of the world's population, it has been consuming one-third of the energy resources produced every year in the world. It has been said: "Americans use more than 8 trillion horsepower hours of energy every year. .... Each American has at his finger-tips, on the average, the equivalent of the energy expended by 500 human slaves."[1] Although the EEC has only about one-third of this energy, its economy, which is primarily based upon manufacturing industry, requires very large amounts of energy. Moreover, as Minshull says, "energy needs to be available on a long-term, substantial and low-cost basis if industry is to plan and compete effectively".[2]

Coal, oil, natural gas, hydro-electric power and nuclear energy are the principal sources of energy. All are used to generate heat but much is converted into electrical energy which is much used in industry because it can be readily distributed by power line, thereby greatly freeing the location of industry. Since the Second World War, however, oil increasingly has come to be used as the primary source of energy and the countries of the EEC, possessing very small indigenous supplies until the North Sea discoveries, had to import vast quantities of oil from overseas.

The industrialised world has suddenly come under increasing pressure due to the dwindling supply of the traditional energy resources. The action of OPEC (Organisation of Petroleum Exporting Countries) in 1973 precipitated the oil crisis; not only has the output of petroleum been more or less stabilised but its price has escalated dramatically causing balance of payments problems to the big importers of oil. This growing energy crisis is compelling scientists and technologists to turn their attention to the use of potential alternatives to the traditional fuels. Among the alternatives are solar energy, wind power, geothermal energy, trash combustion, methane gas, tidal and wave power. Although technological experiments in all these new sources have been tried, the current global energy situation will compel man to take more than a perfunctory interest in these various possibilities.

Certain general points should be established prior to a more specific analysis of the EEC energy situation (*see* Fig. 10). First, unlike the world's two other major industrial units (COMECON and the United States of America), the EEC relies heavily upon, indeed is almost entirely dependent upon, energy from external suppliers. In 1973 over 60 per cent of the Community's primary energy requirements, principally oil, had to be imported. Strategically, this was a vulnerable state of affairs in a world increasingly dominated

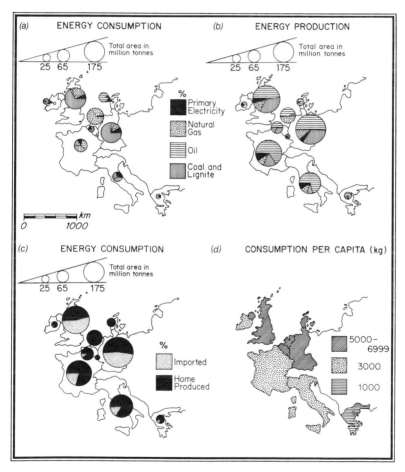

[Adapted from B. W. Ilbery,
Western Europe: A Systematic Human Geography, 1981, Fig. 4.1.
FIG. 10.—The energy situation in 1974: (*a*) energy production; (*b*) energy consumption; (*c*) dependence on imported energy; (*d*) consumption of energy per capita.

by resource politics, and economically it represented a significant financial drain upon the balance of payments of member states. Secondly, by way of an internal complication, the geographical distribution of energy resources between member states is disparate. The full extent is analysed below, but in an over-all picture it means that some member states are much more energy sufficient than others as Table 21 clearly indicates.

TABLE 21

Primary energy in the EEC, 1973
(million tonnes coal equivalent)

	Production	Gross consumption	Percentage dependence upon imports
West Germany	171.0	378.2	55.0
France	56.5	256.4	78.3
Italy	34.3	182.6	83.0
Netherlands	82.5	87.2	5.7
Belgium	8.2	66.4	86.4
Luxembourg	0.0	7.3	99.6
United Kingdom	166.1	318.1	48.3
Ireland	1.7	10.7	80.5
Denmark	0.1	28.0	99.6
EEC Total	520.4	1,334.9	61.4

NOTE
Primary energy refers to energy usable in its basic form including solid fuels, hydrocarbons, nuclear fuels, hydro-electricity and alternative sources such as solar energy, wind and tidal power.

Table 21 deliberately relates to 1973, the year of the first major energy crisis. The Community's external dependence upon imports had risen from around 30 per cent in 1960 to over double this level by the outbreak of the Yom Kippur War. For all member states the conflict precipitated a supply crisis, and for some it served to illustrate the vulnerable nature of their supply positions. The Netherlands was a significant exception as a result of its high natural gas production. West Germany and the UK, the major coal producers, had some degree of flexibility between primary energy sources, but for the remaining six member states the impact of the crisis was more sudden and severe. Since 1973 the expansion in the North Sea oil output has reduced the over-all import dependence of the EEC and of the UK in particular, but the oil dependence of the Ten is still at a dangerously high level.

Net imports of energy, constituted mainly of crude oil and petroleum products, have fallen since their 1973 peak. The U K, in particular, has experienced a dramatic decrease in its needs for imported
oil with North Sea crude oil production reaching 80m tons in 1979.
Energy imports are now only around one-tenth of over-all U K
energy consumption. In contrast, the remaining industrialised members of the E E C remain heavily dependent on imported oil. Overall,
oil consumption in the Community is falling steadily, partly as a
consequence of recession but also as a result of determined efforts to
make a more rational use of expensive imports. Energy imports still
remain at over half of total needs, making the Community still most
vulnerable to rising import prices and supply dislocations.

Coal

Coal energised the industrial revolution which began in the U K in
the late eighteenth century and which subsequently spread to the
continent of Europe during the nineteenth century. The U K and her
continental neighbours were fortunate in that they possessed supplies
of coal, though these varied in quantity and type. Moreover, coal
was a versatile commodity which was used as a domestic fuel, in the
form of coke for smelting iron ore, for firing bricks, pottery and
glass, as a fuel in most industrial processes, and as a source of gas.
Coal powered steam-driven machinery, the locomotive and the
steamship, without which the industrial revolution could never have
happened. Furthermore, since coal was the primary source of energy,
it led to the new, growing, industrial regions becoming largely co-
terminous with the coalfields, especially since coal was low in value
in relation to its bulk and costly to carry. By the beginning of the
present century electricity was becoming of growing importance but
it, like coal-gas, was a converted form of coal energy.

The coal-producing regions

The coal resources of the Community fall into two main areas: those
of the U K occurring principally in South Wales, the Midlands, the
Yorks–Derby–Notts field, Lancashire, Northumberland and Durham, and in the Central Lowlands of Scotland; and those located
within the "Heavy Industrial Triangle" of the Community, i.e. the
Nord–Pas-de-Calais and Lorraine fields of France, the Sambre–
Meuse and Kempenland fields of Belgium, the Limburg field of the
Netherlands, and the Aachen, Ruhr and Saar fields of West Germany
(see Fig. 11).

Apart from the above France has a few pockets of coal around the
northern and eastern edges of the Central Plateau but the total
output is small; Italy has a few minute deposits but the output is

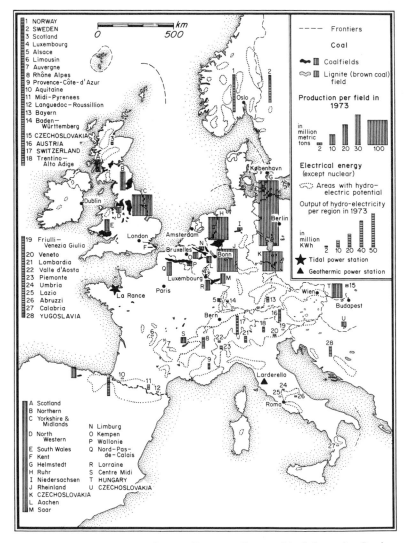

[*Source*: European Communities Information Service.

FIG. 11.—Coal and electrical energy production.

negligible and she has been compelled to import almost all her needs of coal; Luxembourg has no indigenous coal resources at all but can import her requirements from her neighbours; Denmark, too, lacks coal and must import her needs; while the Republic of Ireland, though almost devoid of coal, has ample supplies of peat which, in dried pulverised form, is used to generate electricity. Table 22 shows the coal production of the five Community producers and over-all trade in coal in 1979.

TABLE 22

Coal and lignite production, 1979 (m tons)

	Coal production	Net trade in coal[1]	Lignite production
West Germany	93.3	−7.2	130.6
France	18.6	+26.7	2.5
Italy	—	+13.1	2.1
Netherlands	—	+5.0	—
Belgium	6.1	+9.3	—
Luxembourg	—	+0.3	—
UK	120.6	+2.2	—
Ireland	0.1	+1.2	—
Denmark	—	+7.5	—
EEC Total	238.7	+58.1	135.2

NOTE

1. A positive value in this column denotes that the member state is a net importer of coal.

Source: Basic Statistics of the Community, 1982, Eurostat, Table 56.

The Declining Demand for Coal

The role of coal as a source of energy has fallen dramatically since the end of the Second World War. The falling demand has resulted from the increasing use of newer sources of energy and from technological changes. The growing exhaustion of the thickest and most accessible seams, the labour-intensive nature of winning coal, and the increasing transport costs in comparison with alternative sources of energy has meant that coal has declined rapidly in its importance. This decline has been assisted by the development of gas- and oil-fired central heating systems, by the switch from coal to oil and electricity by such former large users as the railways, ships, electricity producers and many industries. Other factors, too, have contributed to the decline as, for example, the campaign against air pollution and the fact that, until fairly recently, imported oil was cheaper than coal. "Paradoxically coal has also suffered from the increased efficiency with which it can now be used. In some of its largest markets, for example, the generation of thermal electricity, a far smaller amount of coal is now required to produce a given quantity of power than in the past."[3] Thus, notwithstanding the research which has gone into increasing coal's efficiency, it has become a high-cost as well as an inconvenient fuel for modern usage. In 1952, when the European Coal and Steel Community (ECSC) came into being, coal provided two-thirds of its primary energy but fourteen years later it had dropped to one-third. Coal output by the EEC Six was reduced from 234m tonnes in 1961 to 146m tonnes in 1972 and a similar decline is to be seen in the UK's production which in the same period dropped from 193.5m tonnes to 119.5m tonnes.[4]

The Future of Coal

Partly because of the competition from oil, gas and the other sources of energy, and partly because coal was dirty, cumbersome and expensive to transport, the demand for it has declined massively since the EEC came into being. Because of the dramatic shrinkage in demand, it has necessitated the contraction and modernisation of coal-mining in the countries of the Community.

The significance of coal to the economies of Western Europe was recognised by the establishment in 1952 of the ECSC (*see* Chapter II). Subsequently integrated into the EEC, the Six members came to possess the single resource of some 230m tonnes of coal a year which was marketed at a common price.[5] At the time of the setting up of the ECSC, coal dominated energy supplies, providing two-thirds of the total energy required by its members. In this initial period of post-war industrial growth and the need for more energy, the aim was to maximise coal output and, for example, coal production in France achieved its peak in 1958 with a figure of 59m tonnes. But during the 1960s this pattern began to change as a result of the growing competition from oil and natural gas and the availability of cheaper coal imported from outside the Community. Accordingly, the ECSC had to change its policy and it now had to effect the closure of the less economic pits, phase a reduction in output, and amalgamate collieries to achieve more efficient production. As a result of this rationalisation and the growing use of oil, coal production dropped from 245m tonnes in 1950 to 134m tonnes in 1974 in the original Six.

In the UK there has been a similar story of decline, although the degree of dependence upon coal is substantially greater than on the continent and it continues to account for around 37 per cent of the UK's total energy needs. The National Coal Board (NCB) has been compelled to rationalise and restructure the coal industry and is concentrating production in its more modern and more efficient pits. Since 1976 output has been more or less stabilised at around 120m tonnes.

Since 1973, the year of the oil crisis, the cost of oil has escalated dramatically as a result of the actions taken by O P E C, and the high cost of oil could well have important repercussions for the coal-mining industry. It may well lead to a reversal of the policy which has been followed over the past twenty years. As Minshull has commented: "Two new developments would seem likely: the urgent tapping of the newly discovered hydrocarbon resources in the North Sea and adjacent continental shelf, and the re-examination of energy policies in the light of the new more highly competitive position of coal."[6] For example, British production of oil from the North Sea reached 100m tonnes by 1980 while the N C B is going ahead with the exploitation of the newly-discovered Selby coalfield with its esti-mated reserves of 500m tonnes and an annual production of 10m tonnes. It should also be recalled that, although many British and continental coalfields are largely exhausted, there are some fields such as the Yorks–Derby–Notts and Northumberland and Durham fields in Britain and the Kempenland, Ruhr and Lorraine fields on the continent that possess very rich reserves and their output could be very substantially increased.

Oil

Since the 1950s oil consumption in Western Europe has shown a massive increase, averaging around 10 per cent annually. This very substantial growth has arisen for four principal reasons:

(*i*) the relatively low cost of refined petroleum compared with coal;
(*ii*) the big advantage of oil in servicing such large, growing and non-competitive markets as automobile and aviation fuels;
(*iii*) its competitiveness in electricity production in thermal power stations;
(*iv*) the expanding use of oil in the production of synthetic fibres and in the plastics industry.[7]

The enlarged E E C is dependent upon oil for some 60 per cent of its energy needs and its consumption of oil in 1974, at the time of the energy crisis, was running at some 580m tonnes, since almost all of its oil requirements had to be imported, mostly from the Middle East and North Africa (*see* Table 23). This vast import accounted for about one-third of the total international movement of oil. In the E E C Six's total fuel bill the proportion accounted for by oil in-creased from 25 per cent in 1958 to 60 per cent in 1972, and this

TABLE 23
EEC consumption of crude oil, 1974
(in '000 tonnes)

	Production	Imports
West Germany	6,191	103,319
United Kingdom	411	111,646
France	1,175	129,814
Italy	1,093	120,236
Netherlands	1,574	63,927
Belgium-Luxembourg	—	30,398
Denmark	86	9,363
Ireland	—	2,625
TOTAL	10,530	571,328

growing reliance upon imported oil was making the Community particularly vulnerable, not merely strategically but also from the point of view of growing pressure on the balance of payments.[8]

A quarter of a century ago the tendency was for petroleum to be refined on or near to the oilfields, but with the rapidly increasing consumption of oil by the West European countries and the introduction of super-tankers the oil-refining process began to be increasingly located in the consuming countries. Accordingly, crude oil was shipped to coastal and estuarine tanker terminals in Western Europe where it was refined and then distributed by pipeline, railway or road to the consuming areas. "As consumption increased so the refining capacity has enlarged dramatically. In the original Six, the refining capacity increased from 90m tonnes in 1958 to 360m tonnes in 1967, and in the enlarged EEC it reached 540m tonnes by 1973"[9] (see Fig. 12). At the time of the oil crisis (1973), Italy had the largest oil-refining capacity (174m tonnes), followed by West Germany (126m tonnes), France (125m tonnes), the UK (121m tonnes), and the Netherlands (78m tonnes).[10]

The Oil Crisis

The energy crisis which suddenly afflicted the world, and more particularly the developed world, in 1973 was due in general terms to man's extravagant use of energy and more especially oil, to unprecedented rates of increase in energy consumption, and to the gradual exhaustion of some of our energy resources. There were, however, other factors of an economic and political nature which aggravated, and, indeed, may be said to have precipitated the crisis. Certain fundamental changes in the power supply/demand situation were

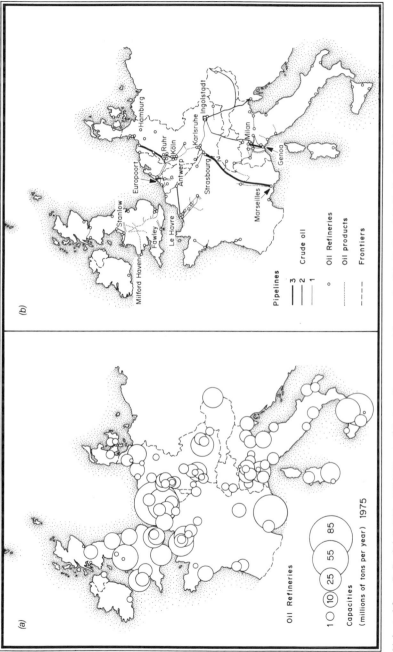

[Adapted from P. R. Odell, "The EEC Energy Market: Structure and Integration" in R. Lee & P. E. Ogden (eds.), *Economy and Society in the EEC*, 1976.

(a) Oil refining capacity; and (b) pipelines.
FIG. 12.—Oil refining capacity and pipelines.

recognised in the 1960s but they developed more rapidly than was generally expected with the result that the oil situation changed, over a relatively short period of time, from one of reasonable abundance to relative scarcity.

Certain long-term and certain short-term factors help to explain the recent and continuing crisis. First, there has been a very rapid and ever-growing consumption of oil, especially in the highly industrialised developed countries, notably in the EEC and Japan which have highly restricted indigenous oil supplies. Secondly, *per capita* consumption of oil has grown rapidly, especially in the developed countries which enjoy high living standards; the reason for this mounting *per capita* consumption lies very largely in technological changes—these refer not only to the introduction of the motor car and domestic central heating, which consume petrol and heating oil, but to the whole complex of production in manufacture, agriculture and transport. Thirdly, the world's population is growing rapidly and as some of the developing countries move out of the underdeveloped stage they add to the total of oil consumed. Cumulatively, therefore, there is an ever-growing demand for oil.

In addition to the above long-term factors, there have been several short-term factors and it is these which have been responsible for the sudden and alarming oil crisis. First, the worldwide demand for oil during the past decade grew more quickly than the long-range forecasts predicted; it had been generally believed that the tremendous expansion in the demand for oil during the 1960s would begin to level off in the early 1970s, but this did not happen and growth persisted. Secondly, the availability of energy supplies generally was less than was anticipated since coal production declined more rapidly than was believed, the nuclear power industry suffered setbacks in bringing new capacity into service, while the development of some of the newly-discovered oilfields, e.g. the Alaskan and North Sea deposits, was delayed. Thirdly, because of the shortfalls in other sources of energy oil had to be used as a substitute, hence creating great pressures upon the oil industry. Fourthly, domestic production of oil in the United States seemed to have reached its peak and the country was beginning to import increasing amounts of oil; thus oil which hitherto had been available to other countries was now being competed for by the United States. Finally, the Arab–Israeli War not only dislocated oil transportation, but the Arabs cut off oil supplies to the alleged pro-Israeli countries and at the same time imposed swingeing increases on the cost of oil.

As a result of all these various factors OPEC is in a very strong position and virtually able to control the international trade in oil. Most of the OPEC countries are developing countries with underdeveloped economies, substantial populations and finite oil reserves; hence it is natural that they should want to capitalise fully upon their precious natural resource and should be ever ready to increase the price of it. The Arab Middle Eastern countries are also prepared to use their oil for political ends. So, the developed countries, especially those of Western Europe which have little or no oil resources of their own, are in effect being held to ransom and the punitive costs they are having to pay for oil has not only led to an energy crisis but given rise to acute financial difficulties as the economic predicament of the UK, before it began to realise its North Sea oil resources, so vividly illustrated. The oil crisis has indicated quite clearly that, in the first place, energy should now be conserved and, secondly, that new sources of energy must be sought and quickly; otherwise the economies and the standards of living of the Community countries will be seriously at risk.

Oil Resources on Land

The raising of oil prices, more especially through the pressure exerted by the Arab countries of the Middle East, together with the nationalisation of the Western oil companies put an end to the low-cost advantage of oil. The early months of 1974 marked a watershed and the advantage which oil had had for more than a decade began to be reversed. One important result of the attempt by OPEC to blackmail the West was to cause the EEC to intensify the search for oil within its own boundaries. Land deposits of oil have been few and the yields disappointing but the search goes on.

The oil-producing fields of France are located in the Alsace, Aquitaine and Paris Basins. The first field to be discovered was at Pechelbronn in Alsace from which oil was pumped as early as 1881; although several wells were sunk the output was small, 20,000 tonnes in 1962.[11] Other fields in Alsace were one near Staffelfelden in the southern part which produced 24,000 tonnes in 1962 and the field at Scheibenhard discovered in 1956. But the Alsace accumulations are small and now virtually exhausted. The principal producing area is the Aquitaine Basin where between 1949 and 1964 six fields were discovered, but only the Parentis and Cazaux fields are of any significance: the former was producing 26,200 barrels per day (b.p.d.) in 1969 and between 1954 and 1962 had yielded some 9m tonnes while the Cazaux field, discovered in 1959 was yielding 10,780 b.p.d. in 1969.[12] The Lacq oilfield was discovered in 1949 but in 1962 produced only 85,000 tonnes of oil. In the Paris Basin, where four fields are known, only the Coulommiers and Chailly-en-Bière fields are of significance and their output is very small. Extensive and systematic exploration did not really begin in France until after the Second World War but there have been no major finds and total production is only just over 1m tonnes a year.

Germany's first oil discovery was made in 1876 in the Hannover area. Since that time over twenty-four fields have been found. The chief oil-producing areas are in the valley of the lower Ems and in the Hannover area but there are minor oilfields in Schleswig–Holstein, in the Rhine Rift Valley, and in Bavaria. Since the Second World War there has been intensive exploration in West Germany, and the Federal Republic, until the finds in the North Sea, was the most important oil-producing country in Western Europe. Her output is currently around 5.5m tonnes a year, although this is but a tiny fraction of her very large oil requirements.

Exploration for oil began in the Netherlands in 1932 and was intensified during the war period when the country was under German occupation. The Schoonebeek field in the north-east was discovered in 1943, but development was delayed until the post-war years. An important find was made at Rijswijk near the Hague in 1953 and a number of other fields were subsequently located in this area, the most important of which was Ijesselmonde in 1956. Total production is about 1.5m tonnes a year (*see* Fig. 12).

Although an oil find was made at Cortemaggiore in 1949, Italy's first major oil discovery was the Ragusa field in Sicily in 1954. In spite of fairly active exploration in the Plain of Lombardy and in the south-central part of peninsular Italy, oil output in Italy is small; the greater output comes from the two Sicilian fields, Ragusa and Gela. Total Italian production in 1976 was 1.1m tonnes.

In the UK small quantities of oil have been produced since the discovery, in 1919, of oil at Hardstoft in Derbyshire. A systematic and more concentrated effort to find oil was begun in the 1930s and the first successes from this exploratory effort were at Formby and Eakring in 1939, followed by further finds at Kelham Hills in 1941, Dukes Wood in 1941 and Caunton in 1943, all in east central Nottinghamshire.[13] Further exploration throughout the 1950s and early 1960s resulted in further small oil discoveries. The total production has never been large and is only about 400,000 tonnes a year.

Total oil production from the land in the whole of the EEC is only around 10m tonnes, a minute fraction of the 575m tonnes which is imported.

North Sea Oil

The research into, and exploration for, hydrocarbons in the North Sea commenced in the early 1960s; surveys indicated there were wide areas in which hydrocarbons were likely to be found. The Continental Shelf Act of 1964 led to the delimitation of the sea areas in respect of the seven countries bordering the North Sea and "the territorial agreements based upon the Geneva Convention have favoured the United Kingdom and Norway as 71 per cent of the North Sea comes under their jurisdiction and, within this area almost all of the "proven" oil reserves and around 81 per cent of known commercial gas reserves have been discovered."[14] Most of the oil deposits appear to lie along the median line which separates British from Norwegian waters.

By 1977 "the known discoveries of oil in the North Sea amounted to an estimated 22 billion barrels, of which the UK has 16–17 billion and Norway has 5–6 billion barrels. The small Dan field in the Danish sector is the only discovery of any significance outside the Norwegian and UK sectors."[15] From the initial British discovery of the Montrose field in 1969, some 28 oil fields have been found in the British sector along with 20 other oil finds. In the Norwegian sector 13 oilfields have been discovered. Many of the other oil finds which have been located in the British sector have yet to be appraised as to their commercial viability. Although estimates of North Sea oil reserves vary considerably, from about 1.5 to 2.0 billion tonnes, it seems very possible that Britain could become a producer similar in status to Nigeria or Kuwait long before the end of the century; and the same could well apply to Norway.

A high proportion of the North Sea reserves is found in several "giant" fields; for example, the Statfjord field accounts for about half of the Norwegian reserves, while the Brent, Forties, Brae, Ninian and Piper fields probably share more than two-fifths of UK reserves. The increasing cost of oil has made exploitation more economically feasible, but as exploration moves further polewards into deeper and stormier seas exploitation is bound to become increasingly more difficult and costly (see Fig. 13).

Whereas exploration drilling has been fruitful in the blocks near the median line, as also have been the Norwegian discoveries, the other countries have not been successful to any extent: Denmark has located four oil finds, the Netherlands two, while "West Germany, the greatest consumer of energy of the countries concerned, drilled more wells than Norway from 1964–73 but no commercial discoveries were found."[16]

In the late 1970s the UK consumption of crude oil was around 110m tonnes a year, with import dependency rapidly diminishing. Conservation policies are likely to deliberately restrict output and the North Sea output is most unlikely to be able to meet more than perhaps a substantial fraction of EEC needs. At least there will be some contribution and the Community "should benefit from having a politically stable source of oil."[17]

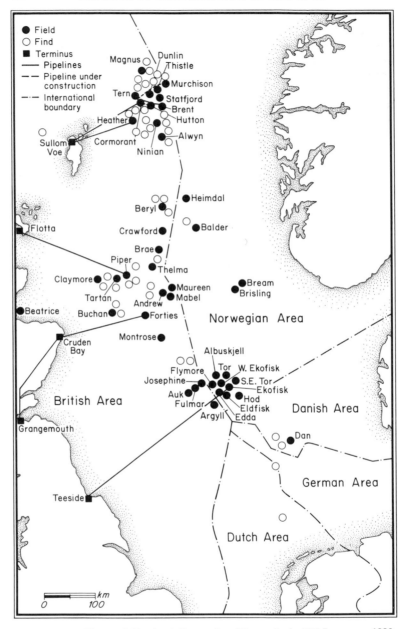

[*Source*: J. Fernie, *A Geography of Energy in the U K*, Longman, 1980.
FIG. 13.—Oil discoveries in the North Sea.

Natural Gas

Although the use of natural gas or methane in Italy goes back to 1946, it is only since about 1960 that natural gas has begun to play a substantial role in the energy pattern of the EEC. The gas which is commonly found in association with petroleum is termed "natural gas" to distinguish it from coal gas. Methane, popularly known as marsh-gas, and ethane are the principal constituents of natural gas. Frequently tapped in oil-drilling processes, it was, formerly, allowed to escape and burn to waste. The United States, which possesses large resources of natural gas, was the pioneer in the use of natural gas. But nowadays it is highly valued as a source of energy and its importance in Europe and in the USSR has grown by leaps and bounds during the past twenty years. Indeed, gas now provides about 15 per cent of the world's total industrial power (*see* Table 24).

TABLE 24
Natural gas production, 1979
(in '000 TJ (GCV))[1]

Belgium/Lux.	1.4
Netherlands	3,292.8
West Germany	740.9
Italy	482.3
United Kingdom	1,498.3
Denmark	—
Ireland	21.5
France	300.3
EEC Total	6,337.4

NOTE
1. TJ = Terajoule, gross calorific value.

Use of natural gas in the Old World tended to lag behind that in the Americas because:

(*i*) at first there were major difficulties of transporting it from the Middle East and North Africa;
(*ii*) the discoveries of natural gas in Europe are of recent date.

"In 1946 natural gas was discovered at Caviaga, twenty miles south-east of Milan. Since that date a whole series of natural gas fields have been discovered in the Plain of Lombardy, e.g. at Cortemaggiore, Ripalta, Cornegliano, Bordolano and Ravenna. The conversion of the gas into a marketable commodity demanded processing plants and a pipeline distribution network; by 1954 methane production amounted to 95,000m cu. ft. and there were some

3,700 km of pipeline."[18] By 1957 some 480m cu. ft. a day were being produced; by 1976 total production had reached 15.4 billion cu. metres.

Since the early days the search for natural gas has continued both into the peninsula where small fields were found in the Marches, Basilicata, Apulia and on Sicily, and offshore in the shallow waters of the northern Adriatic where several gasfields were located off the coast of Emilia–Romagna. Pacione says that "at present (1977) about 10,000 million or 70 per cent of annual domestic gas production comes from the Romagna offshore fields".[19] The total Italian production of natural gas, some 15.4 billion m³ as already noted, satisfies half of the national demand, the rest being met by imports from Libya, the Netherlands and the Soviet Union (*see* Fig. 14).

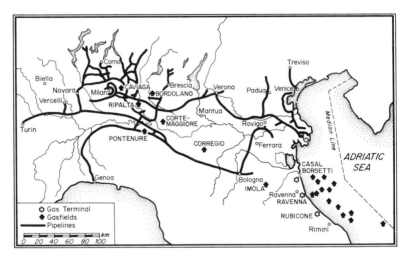

FIG. 14.—Natural gasfields and pipelines in Northern Italy.

In August 1959, while prospecting for oil in the province of Groningen in the northern Netherlands, a major gas-field was discovered at Slochteren. This has proved to be one of the largest gas-fields in the world, on a par with the Texas gas-field, and "the estimated reserves of gas in this field are 2,400 million tonnes of coal-equivalent."[20] The Slochteren field now yields abundant supplies (over 30,000 m m³ annually) and gas exports to Belgium and West Germany began in 1966.

In the Netherlands, 50 per cent of energy demand is met by natural gas; however, the discoveries in the offshore zone have been smaller than were predicted after the major onshore discovery at Slochteren. The Dutch will become importers of natural gas by 1980 as almost half of their reserves are on long-term export contracts to West Germany, Belgium, Italy and Switzerland. Production from the Groningen field will level off in 1977 and the Dutch Government is intensifying exploration in the North Sea in an attempt to add to the present thirteen small discoveries.[21]

Since Fernie wrote this, further reserves of natural gas have been discovered in Groningen, and the Netherlands remains an exporter of such energy to neighbouring E E C member states.

West Germany has a number of gas-fields, principally on the northern plain, and has a substantial output: 740,900 TJ (terajoules) in 1979. There is a well-developed gas pipeline network, especially in the north-west of the country and along the Rhine valley.

The gas pipelines in France carry gas from the fields at Lacq and St Marcet in the Aquitaine–Pyrenean to important consuming areas: to the towns of Bordeaux and Toulouse and a number of other smaller centres in the south-west, while a pipeline runs to Paris and another to Lyon. Indigenous production is not very large and has declined slightly in very recent years.

Largely as a result of the rich gas finds in the Netherlands, attention was drawn to the possibility of there being natural gas deposits under the bed of the North Sea. The first British strike occurred in 1965 by British Petroleum and since that time eleven large gas-fields have been located: West Sole, Ann, Viking, Rough, Amethyst, Indefatigable, Leman Bank, Sean, Dottie, Deborah, and Hewett. Three pipelines carry gas from the gas-fields in the North Sea to coastal locations, i.e. to Easington in Holderness, to Theddlethorpe in Lincolnshire and to Bacton in Norfolk. Inland, natural gas is now piped to all areas of Great Britain; the result of this is that whereas in 1960 95 per cent of the gas used in Britain was made from coal by 1970 95 per cent of the gas used was natural gas. Britain's southern group of fields have, for the most part, probably already reached their peak production and it is unlikely that production levels will be maintained after 1985; moreover, it is generally believed that after the end of the century yields from these southern fields will begin to decline, perhaps sharply. On the other hand, there have been ten finds in this southern group which have not yet been exploited and Britain's newest gas-field in Morecambe Bay is expected to come on stream by 1984. Fernie writes: "U K exploration continues to be successful. . . . The encouraging discovery by British Gas in the Irish Sea may promote further exploration activity in this area to augment contracted reserves from the Frigg, Brent and Heimdal fields."[22] (*See* Fig. 15).

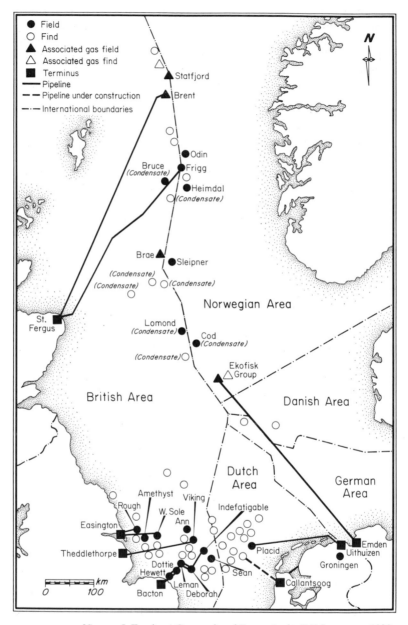

[Source: J. Fernie, *A Geography of Energy in the UK*, Longman, 1980.
FIG. 15.—Natural gas deposits in the North Sea.

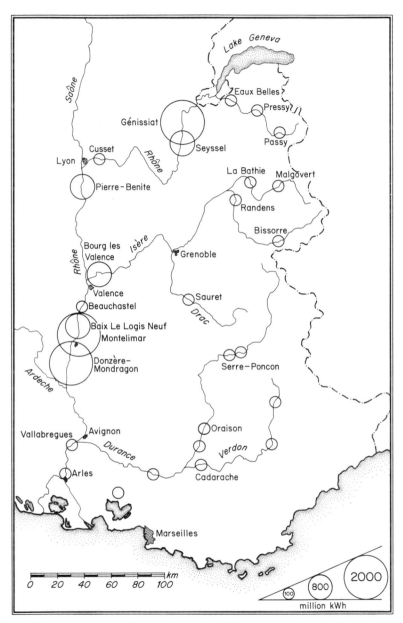

FIG. 16.—Hydro-electric power development in the Rhône valley.

Hydro-Electric Power

Hydro-electric energy is one of the least important sources of primary energy in the EEC and in 1975 contributed but 5.9 per cent of total energy production. It is most unlikely that its contribution to the total energy output will increase since most of the best water-power sites have already been harnessed. Out of total electricity production, i.e. thermal electricity, hydro-electricity and nuclear electricity, hydro-electric power is responsible for only 12 per cent (1976). The most significant producers are France and Italy, with respectively 34 and 26 per cent of the total electricity output being produced by HEP.

Current output of hydro-electric power in France is around 65 billion kWh. This very substantial production has been made possible by the construction of dams in the French Alps, the Central Plateau, the Pyreneés and by the harnessing of the great rivers the Rhône and the Rhine. The Rhône–Alps region is the single most important area for HEP supplying over 25 billion kWh. "Half is supplied by mountain power stations in the Alps and the other half by the stations belonging to the *Compagnie Nationale du Rhône* at Génissiat upstream from Lyon, Bourg-lès-Valence, Beauchastel, Baix-Logis-Neuf, Châteauneuf-du-Rhône and Bollène downstream, and recently at Pierre-Bénite on the edge of the Lyon agglomeration."[23] (*See* Fig. 16). The main function of the French section of the Rhine is the production of energy and "four billion kWh are delivered annually to the grid system by the five power stations of Kembs, Ottmarsheim, Fessenheim, Vogelgrün and Markolsheim, arranged in a chain and soon to be reinforced by a sixth power station at Rhinau."[24] The Central Plateau (with major stations on the Dordogne at L'Aigle, Bort, and Chastang) and the Pyrenees, together with the power station which uses tidal energy (the first in the world) in the estuary of the Rance, near St Malo in Brittany, and opened in 1966, share the rest of the HEP production. Two schemes are worth mentioning: the *Enytrac* scheme which links up all the hydro stations in the Central Plateau; and the *Emalp* scheme which links up the French, Swiss and Italian Alpine stations so that seasonal variations resulting from irregular river flow can be evened out.

One of the greatest assets of the Alps is their water-power resources and Italy has made very good use of the resources which occur within her boundaries; already 70 per cent of them are being used. The first hydro-electric power station in Italy was constructed in the Valtellina, in the central Alps and almost every suitable river in this sector has been harnessed with the result that more than half of the country's hydro-electricity comes from here. In the western Alps, too, the rivers have been harnessed to provide about 25 per cent of Italy's hydro-electricity. Thus, three-quarters of Italy's total hydro-electric power is to be found in the Alpine region as a whole. In peninsular Italy the upper Nera and Velino rivers have been harnessed and upstream from Terni is a large hydro station. There is a hydro-electric plant on the Sele river and the crystalline plateaus of Sila and Aspromonte in the "toe" provide good water catchment areas for the winter rainfall and a number of lakes have been transformed into reservoirs for hydro-electric power generation; indeed, Calabria's power stations generate about 3 per cent of Italy's hydro-electricity supply.[25] In 1976 hydro-electric power supplied 26 per cent of Italy's total electricity production of 160.6 billion kWh. This puts Italy, next after France, as a major hydro-electricity producer in the Community.

The Federal Republic of Germany is the largest producer of electricity with an output in 1976 of 333.6 billion kWh but the contribution made by hydro-electric power is small, a mere 6 per cent. Because of West Germany's great coal resources, together with lignite, and her huge import of oil for transforming into thermal electric power, she has not developed her water-power resources to any great extent. However, it should be borne in mind that the conditions for making hydro-electric power are less favourable than in either France or Italy. Most of the potential lies in the central hill country and in the mountainous south-east. Only about 20 billion kWh is produced by hydro plants. The greater part of West Germany's HEP is generated in the Alps in the extreme south. The largest single station here is the Walchensee–Köchelsee plant which makes use of two natural lakes, one lying some 200 metres above the other; it is the most important hydro-electric power station in the country and supplies current to the whole of Bavaria.[26]

Only a small fraction of the UK's energy supplies comes from hydro-electric power. With the exception of three small schemes on Dartmoor, five in Wales, chiefly in the Snowdon area including the pumped-storage at Ffestiniog, and two in southern Scotland, most of the hydro-electric power generated comes from the Highlands of Scotland where there are ten main schemes. While the UK receives enough rainfall the total catchment area is not big enough to allow much extension of HEP. The result is that out of a total electricity production of 276.9 billion kWh, a mere 2 per cent is hydro-electric power and this is fed into the national grid.

The Republic of Ireland, virtually destitute of indigenous resources of coal, oil and natural gas, has had to use its resources of peat to make thermal electricity and its rivers to produce hydro-electric power. Nine per cent of the electricity produced comes from hydro-electric power plants.

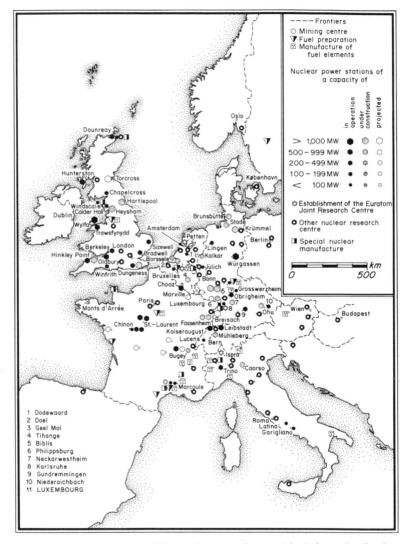

FIG. 17.—Nuclear industry.

[*Source*: European Communities Information Service.

Nuclear Power

Hydro-electric power, unlike coal, petroleum and natural gas, all three of which exist in finite quantities and will one day be used up, is an inexhaustible source of energy. But hydro-electric power, by itself, could never meet all the demands for power, hence the scientists' search for some additional source of energy. Since the hydro-carbons are a wasting asset and since the world demand for power continues to increase, the advent of nuclear power appears to have come at a propitious time.

What is known as nuclear fission (the "splitting of the atom") results in the release of tremendous amounts of energy and the idea behind nuclear energy as a source of power was the control of this released energy; in other words, the aim was to produce a steady flow of energy which could be harnessed for use. This has now been achieved through the medium of the nuclear reactor or "atomic pile". The first experimental commercial reactor was designed by British scientists and established at Calder Hall, Cumbria, in 1957. Energy produced by this reactor was fed into the National Electric Grid system. Britain now has some sixteen nuclear power stations in operation and by 1976 approximately 11 per cent of the UK's electricity output was produced by nuclear power stations (*see* Fig. 17).

The "fuel" used in nuclear reactors is provided by radio-active metals, the most important of which are uranium and thorium. Only very small quantities of these are required; 30 grams of uranium, for example, has the energy equivalent of more than 100 tonnes of coal. Although uranium ores are not especially common, the small amount of uranium used means there are ample supplies for a very long time to come. Most of the uranium is refined from two of its ores, pitch-blende and carnotite, and these are concentrated into uranium oxide from which uranium metal is finally produced. The development of the fast-breeder reactor ensures vastly increased energy from each tonne of uranium and its by-product, plutonium, which is produced in larger quantities than it is used. The importance of nuclear energy lies, first, in the fact that countries lacking sources of conventional fuels can now develop industry and, secondly, that its use will lead to a greater dispersion of industry.

Among the original six members of the EEC France was the first to produce nuclear power; this was from the plant near Chinon, in 1957, built by Electricité de France. "This was brought about by the lead which she built up in research after the war when both Germany and Italy were very weak, and which she succeeded in maintaining throughout the 1950s. It was made especially attractive by her home reserves of uranium coupled with her serious energy deficit."[27] Other nuclear stations were built at Chooz in the Ardennes (in collaboration with Belgium), Gravelines, Monts d'Arrée, St Laurent, Dampierre, Bugey, Marcoule, Tricastin and a high capacity station at Fessenheim in Alsace. France has also developed a uranium enrichment plant at Tricastin, and a reprocessing plant at Cap de la Hague. With planned and partially completed reactor plants, about 27 per cent of France's energy needs will by met by the nuclear sector by 1990.

Italy did not commence to produce nuclear energy until 1963 and when one considers that Italy only produces about one-third of her energy requirements, it is rather surprising that she has not involved herself more in a nuclear energy programme for she has the technological ability to construct successful nuclear installations. So far her total nuclear output comes from only three stations: Latina and Garigliano in the coastal lowlands south of Rome and at Trino–Vercellese midway between Milan and Turin. Nuclear electricity production, in 1976, accounted for a mere 3 per cent of the total electricity output (*see* Fig. 17).

Understandably the late development of nuclear power in West Germany issued from the war, but her tremendous demand for energy caused her to seek alternative sources of energy. However, by 1965 West Germany had only one large nuclear power station located at Gundremmingen, west of Munich.[28] During the past fifteen years, no doubt urged on by the vast cost of her oil imports bill, West Germany has applied herself more assiduously to a nuclear programme and now has nuclear plants at Kiel, Lingen, Brunswick, Biblis, etc. From eight major and two minor nuclear power stations, nuclear power contributes 7 per cent of the total electricity production of 333.6 billion kWh. The development of nuclear power in West Germany has been constrained by the strong anti-nuclear lobby in the country.

Belgium has two major nuclear power stations, Doel and Tihange, with a contribution from Chooz, and 16 per cent of its electricity is contributed by the nuclear plants. Since the Netherlands has been able to generate much of its electricity from its natural gas resources, it has not become involved in the nuclear business to any very great extent, although nuclear power contributes 6 per cent of the total electricity supply.

Denmark and the Republic of Ireland have no nuclear power stations. In the E E C Nine, notwithstanding considerable nuclear development, only 8 per cent of the total electricity output is contributed by nuclear power.

Euratom

Simultaneously to the setting up of the European Economic Community, the Treaty of Rome also provided for the establishment of a separate European Atomic Energy Community (E A E C or Euratom). Its objective was to promote an efficient civil nuclear industry in the Six, based on the assumption that nuclear power was to be essential for future industrial expansion. The logic for creating Euratom should be viewed in the light of the Six's energy supply situation at that time. Coal output was declining and the scale of its replacement by oil supplies was by no means anticipated. Its founders, therefore, saw nuclear power as a vitally important future energy source. The E A E C Treaty laid down various procedures for the Community financing of joint undertakings, particularly in nuclear research, and the fixing of prices for nuclear fuels. There have been, however, no Community powers to guide the generation of energy from nuclear fuels, this decision remaining with individual member states. In 1967 the executives of Euratom, the E C S C and the E E C, were merged into a single Commission so that the former's administrative functions are now handled by the Directorate-General (Energy).

Following the 1973 oil crisis, the Commission's view has been increasingly that the E E C's strategy should be to develop its own energy resources in order to fill the energy gap. A substantial nuclear power programme would seem to be a necessary part of such an approach. In 1977 the E E C's energy commissioner, Dr Guido Brunner, announced a Commission plan to make a sum of 300m u.a. available to finance nuclear power stations and requests for loans from this source were subsequently made by the four largest member states. The final decision on this plan rests, of course, with the Council of Ministers, who will undoubtedly have to take the various counter-arguments into account when making their decision. On safety and environmental grounds there are many objectors especially in West Germany, France and Italy, although in the U K there has also emerged a growing anti-nuclear lobby. Before a large scale programme goes ahead, there will be a considerable effort needed to convince the Community's population that nuclear energy is not only a necessary but also a controllable future source of energy.

Towards a Common Energy Policy

Previous sections of this chapter have analysed energy sources within member states. This was largely deliberate due to the fact that energy policy has been primarily regarded as a domestic rather than a Community issue. Since 1973, however, there have been repeated

TABLE 25

EEC energy demand and supply forecasts, 1975–85

Year	Annual demand growth from 1975	Total demand[1]	EEC production[1]	Net Imports[1]	Import dependence
1975		1,282	55[2]	730	57%
1985	2%	1,560	1,050[2]	510	33%
	3%	1,720	1,050[2]	670	39%
	4%	1,900	1,050[2]	850	45%

NOTES
1. Million tonnes coal equivalent.
2. Mid-point estimate based on marginal increase in coal production and substantial expansion of nuclear energy.

Source: "European Coal 2000", *Association of Coal Producers of the European Community*, June 1977.

soundings from the Commission for the need to move towards a common energy policy in order to provide a better basis for dealing with future supply problems. Although there had been discussions on energy before 1973, they were overtaken by the sudden supply crisis. The Copenhagen Summit of December 1973 failed to agree on a common stance to OPEC and instructed the Commission to draw up a programme for debate. Entitled "Towards a new energy policy strategy for the Community," its main objectives were to reduce the growth of energy demand through improved resource utilisation and to reduce energy import dependence to 40 per cent of total supply by 1985. Tables 25 and 26, although from another source, show how this position could be achieved.

TABLE 26

Composition of EEC energy production, 1975–85

Primary energy source	Production 1975[1]	Production 1985[1]
Coal	237	240–250
Lignite	37	40
Oil	17	300
Gas	192	250
Nuclear	27	140–180
Hydro	42	50
TOTAL	552	1020–1070

NOTE
1. Million tonnes coal equivalent.

Source: "European Coal 2000", *Association of Coal Producers of the European Community*, June 1977.

The Tables highlight the need for energy conservation and also the importance of promoting energy production from indigenous sources. To achieve the Commission's figure of 40 per cent import dependence by 1985, energy demand must grow at no more than 3 per cent per annum in the period 1975-85. Although longer-term forecasts are more hazardous, for this stated level of dependence to remain in the year 2000, energy demand growth must be kept to no more than 2 per cent per annum over the entire period.

The world-wide recession from 1973-5 reduced the EEC's total energy consumption and temporarily masked the longer-term energy outlook. In 1976 recovery in the EEC economy was accompanied by a corresponding increase in energy demand, and in July of the following year the Commission published a further report on energy objectives to 1985. This investigation concluded that the original targets could not be reached. It showed that, in particular, the estimates for nuclear energy's contribution (Table 26) were too optimistic and that coal and oil production would also be less than previously forecasted. Consequently, import dependence would still be around one half of total energy consumption.

In June 1979 France provided an initiative, prior to the Luxembourg summit of energy ministers, designed to try once again to develop a common energy policy. The call was for a ceiling on oil imports into the Nine and Community discussions on energy conservation measures. Such moves were accepted, but there was no agreement on the call to control the "spot" markets for oil such as Rotterdam and Genoa. The smaller countries of the Community, possessing no supplies of their own, were not willing to accept this aspect of the French plan.

In spite of recent attempts to forge a common energy policy, member states still tend to consider the fundamental aspects of energy policy as domestic issues. "The Nine have shown through their lack of agreement on the bulk of Commission proposals that the Communities can do no more than set objectives to guide independent national policies."[29] It is yet another example of where it would seem logical for there to be a Community policy, yet where the feelings of member states are in favour of separate domestic policies. But, as Roy Jenkins, former President of the European Commission, has warned, "The problem of energy, if neglected, could not merely damage our economies, but can bring them into a state of dislocation, if not collapse, within the next decade."

Further energy policy recommendations from the Community chiefs came in November 1979. The Eurocrats would like to see gas prices in Britain increased to bring them into line with those in other Common Market countries. The French, who pay twice as much for their gas as the British consumers, urge that the latter should pay VAT on their gas bills, as do the French. The over-all aim is, of course, to make people use less fuel. Jurgen Kuhn, the Energy Commission chief commented: "We do not think it is right for EEC countries to subsidise fuel prices. Gas prices are too low, and we are making recommendations accordingly."[30] The report says that fuel policy must encourage energy-saving, help stimulate investment, and bring in new sources of energy, especially nuclear power. The EEC Commission is also considering mounting a counter-campaign to the anti-nuclear lobby which is currently growing up throughout Europe. Already France has launched a big nuclear power station programme and the EEC is pressing Britain to follow suit. French and German ministers are also urging that North Sea oil should be sold to the Community at a lower price than it is sold to the rest of the world. Britain is determined to resist this, however, since it would give other member states the opportunity to sell it on the world market at a profit.

The dramatic oil and energy crises of the 1970s have made the Community acutely aware of the need to develop alternative sources of energy and to seek ways of helping member states overcome future oil shortages. Substantial financial resources have been allocated to Community research projects in the field of solar and geothermal energy and, as reported at the 1981 United Nations' Conference in Nairobi, the EEC are also willing to contribute to energy development projects in the Third World.[31] Even so, the impact of such alternative energy sources on total needs must remain limited for the next decade. Simultaneously, as part of its energy policy, Community ministers have asked the Commission to investigate schemes for mutual assistance should the oil supply situation deteriorate. Such aid could take the form of joint oil stocks or even a type of "oil bank" from which member states could draw once their own stocks fell below a certain level.[32] In short, the EEC sees the above developments forming part of its more general energy policy objectives of reducing dependence on imported oil, promoting conservation and developing indigenous energy resources such as solid fuel and nuclear energy.

NOTES

1. Gentry, J., "A New Look at the Energy Crisis," *Plain Truth*, Vol. XXXVIII, No. 7, July–August 1973, pp. 2–8, Ambassador College.
2. Minshull, G. N., *The New Europe*, Hodder & Stoughton, 1978, p. 17.
3. Parker, G., *The Logic of Unity*, 2nd edition, Longmans, 1975, p. 47.
4. Minshull, G. N., *op. cit.*, p. 20.
5. Minshull, G. N., *op. cit.*, p. 22.
6. Minshull, B. N., *op. cit.*, p. 23.

7. *Ibid.*
8. Minshull, G. N., *op. cit.*, p. 24.
9. *Ibid.*
10. Clout, H. D., "Energy and Regional Problems," in *Regional Development in Western Europe*, ed. Clout H. D., John Wiley & Sons, 1975, p. 49.
11. Monkhouse, F. J., *The Countries of north-western Europe*, Longmans, 1965, p. 439.
12. *Our Industry Petroleum*, The British Petroleum Company Ltd., 1970, p. 422.
13. *Ibid.*
14. Fernie, J., "The Development of North Sea Oil and Gas Resources," *Scottish Geographical Magazine*, Vol. 93, April 1977, pp. 21-31.
15. *Ibid.*, p. 24.
16. *Ibid.*, p. 21.
17. Minshull, G. N., *op. cit.*, p. 29.
18. Robinson, H., *The Mediterranean Lands*, 2nd edition, University Tutorial Press Ltd., 1964, pp. 226-7.
19. Pacione, M., "Natural Gas in Italy," *Geography*, Vol. 64, Part 3, July 1979, pp. 211-15.
20. Minshull, G. N., *op. cit.*, p. 27.
21. Fernie, J., *op. cit.*, pp. 21, 24.
22. Fernie, J., *op. cit.*, p. 24.
23. George, P., *France: A Geographical Study*, Martin Robertson, 1967, p. 165.
24. *Ibid.*, p. 162.
25. Branigan, J. J., *Europe*, Macdonald & Evans, 1965, p. 545.
26. *Ibid.*, p. 317.
27. Parker, G., *op. cit.*, p. 60.
28. *Ibid.*
29. Black, R. A., "Plus ça change, plus c'est la même chose: Nine Governments in search of a common energy policy," in Wallace, H., ed. *Policy Making in the European Communities*, p. 192.
30. *The Daily Telegraph*, 29th September 1979.
31. *Europe '81*, No. 11, November 1981, pp. 19-22.
32. *Europe '81*, No. 5, May 1981, p. 19.

Chapter VI

Industry

THE European Economic Community, with over 260 m domestic consumers, constitutes one of the great industrial agglomerations in the world. Its output bears comparison with both the United States and the USSR, the world's two industrial superpowers (*see* Table 27). Historically, Western Europe was the first part of the world to experience industrialisation, yet towards the end of the nineteenth century, the emergence of Japan, the USA and Russia challenged its

TABLE 27
Production of EEC, USA and USSR in 1979

	EEC	USA	USSR
Coal (million tonnes)	238.7	666.9	553.8
Crude Oil (million tonnes)	87.2	479.3	586.0
Natural Gas (thousand TJ (GCV))	6,396.1	20,961.7	14,209.1
Electricity (billion kWh)	1,178	2,319	1,119
Iron[1] (thousand tonnes)	12,358	48,427	131,885
Crude Steel (million tonnes)	140.2	126.1	151.4
Motor vehicles[1] (thousands)	11,917	12,892	2,201

NOTE
1. 1978.

Source: Basic Statistics of the Community, Eurostat, 1982.

position of superiority. Geographically, therefore, the die, both in terms of industrial production and location, was cast long before the integrated Community became a reality.

As indicated in Chapters I and II, Western European industry lay exhausted and in ruins after the Second World War. An unprecedented scale of co-operation was required if former power, influence and prosperity were to be regained. The mechanics of recovery have been previously analysed and assessed: their significance is, of course, that they have ensured that Western Europe persists as an industrial superpower. Since 1952 the forces of integration have come to bear upon the industrial geography of the EEC. The ECSC still exists and a competition policy has emerged in order to ensure that the benefits of the customs union are not distorted although surprisingly there has been little or no progress in other areas of industrial policy. Less noticeable, yet extremely significant, has been the impact of integration upon the spatial economic structure of the Community. Industry has grown and prospered in a series of core areas and at the same time, the decline of traditional industries in less favoured regions has been accelerated (*see* also Chapter XI).

The Traditional Industrial Pattern

The Industrial Revolution began in the UK which became the first industrial power, accruing to itself a power and an influence in the world which remained unchallenged for nearly one hundred years. Throughout the nineteenth century a characterising feature was the heavy reliance placed upon heavy and staple industries such as coal-mining, iron- and steel-making, heavy engineering, shipbuilding and textiles. The Industrial Revolution brought a radical change in the methods and organisation of manufacture: a change from hand-work to machine work, from the domestic system to the factory system, and from wide dispersion to the centralised location of industry in particular areas. The central and distinguishing feature of the Industrial Revolution was the new relationship which emerged between men, machines and resources. The traditional technology which had been based upon wood, water and wind, was supplanted by a new technology based upon coal, iron and steam.

The Industrial Revolution introduced a new pattern of manufacturing which was to last for 150 years until the Great Depression of 1929–34. Two main factors exerted an overwhelming influence throughout this long period: first, was the powerful attraction of the coalfields since coal became the primary source of energy and it led to the new, growing industrial regions becoming co-terminous with the coalfields: secondly, regional specialisation began to develop, e.g., iron and steel where coal and iron ore were found in conjunction, cotton manufacturing in Lancashire, woollen textiles in West York-shire, and pottery on the North Staffordshire coalfield. Major industrial concentrations accordingly developed on all the principal coalfields and the bonds remained firm until about fifty years ago.

As the Industrial Revolution spread to Germany, France, Belgium and the United States, this pattern persisted and the coalfields became the great magnets of industrial development, e.g., the Franco-Belgian Coalfield, the Ruhr, the Pennsylvania Coalfield.

Modern Industrial Change

The beginnings of industrial change began about fifty years ago when electrification and the development of motor transport helped to undermine and finally to break up this long-established pattern. Gradually a new pattern began to emerge: that of industrial dispersion and the growth of consumer goods of great variety aided by new sources of energy, new forms of transport, and politico-economic factors. The former basic industries have suffered a relative decline in their importance (though not in absolute terms, with one or two exceptions) since the First World War, but, to quote Minshull, "The growing complexity of industrial structure has meant that they have been supplemented by the assembly-line techniques of the car industry, the technical accuracy of the machine-tool industry, the consumer-based light industries, and science and technology-based, sophisticated and specialised industries."[1]

Industrial production, like many other forms of production, has gone through an evolutionary development. Let us, therefore, briefly review the changes and developments which have come to characterise modern industry:

(*i*) while industry in the past was strongly orientated to the coalfields, because coal was the chief source of energy and its weight and bulk militated against its long distance movement, the use of newer sources of energy such as electricity, oil and gas facilitated "foot-loose" locations. Heavy industries are still prone to be located on the coalfields but they owe their continuance and survival, in part at least, to new factors which have been conducive to the maintaining geographical inertia;

(*ii*) one of the most significant changes has been the tremendous growth in the size and complexity of industrial plants and their mass production methods. Large, integrated plants are more economical to run than smaller ones. for production can be streamlined, large-scale mechanisation can be applied, standardisation can be adopted, by-products can be used, and big firms can employ their own research and training staffs;

(*iii*) the logical development of such major-scale mass production is automation, the use of electronic devices to supersede man in the supervision and control of machines. In automation the bulk of the manufacture is done by automatic processes, and the need of human intervention and control is reduced to an absolute minimum. The future will see an increasing application of automative techniques associated in particular with micro-processors. The British Steel corporation already has one large plant that is practically fully automated while the Fiat company of Italy is

producing a motor car (the Strada) by robots. Precisely how
quickly and to what extent, as well as with what results, automative
processes will be introduced, it is difficult to forecast but automation in the future is bound to have far-reaching effects upon industrial production, organisation and employment;

(iv) another notable feature of modern industry is the trend
towards concentration: in Zimmerman's words "a powerful and
almost universal trend towards combinations, giantism, inter-
company understandings, and cartelisation."[2] This concentration
proceeds along three lines—horizontal, vertical and circular. Horizontal integration is the joining together of two or more firms
engaged in manufacturing the same products; industrial expansion
in Britain in the past was often effected in this way and one of the
best recent examples is British Leyland which now incorporates
six former car companies—Austin, Morris, Standard-Triumph,
Jaguar, Daimler and Rover. Vertical integration, formerly more
typical of German industry, brings successive stages of manufacture under single ownership and management. The German firm
of Krupps, for example, owned coalmines, iron ore fields, steel-
making plants, shipyards and engineering works which were all
linked together into a single vast concern. Circular combination
applies to the absorption of cognate or allied types of production.
Concentration along these lines ensures more effective control over
sources of raw material supplies, over the markets, and it tends to
reduce or spread the risks;

(v) industry, as indicated above, was becoming more foot-loose,
largely because of the growth and extension of the electric grid and
the rapid growth in the motor transport, both of which made for
greater flexibility and mobility. The growth of large or specialised
consumer markets, resulting from increasing standards of living,
also became a decisive factor in the location of many new-type
manufacturing industries. The vast growth in the production of
consumer goods is more especially a post-Second World War
phenomenon. One can recognise two types of consumer goods:
goods for immediate consumption and consumer durables. In the
former group are: bakery products, pre-packed convenience foods
of which there has been a tremendous growth, cigarettes, drinks—
both soft and alcoholic, toilet requisites, cosmetics, and pharmaceuticals, clothing and footwear. Consumer durable goods
include such things as electric heaters and gadgets, electric- and
gas-cookers, refrigerators, washing machines, vacuum cleaners,
radio and television sets, along with typewriters, calculators and
data processing equipment. This newer type of manufacturing
has often sprung up along major roads and in out-of-town

locations and, although it is widespread, it is especially concentrated in the south-eastern and Midlands areas of the United Kingdom;

(*vi*) one of the most striking changes that has taken place in the post-war period is the transfer from goods-producing economies to service economies, i.e. economies providing services as distinct from those manufacturing goods. Every EEC country has more people engaged in the provision of services than in manufacturing industry. The service industries include, for example, transportation and the distributive trades, recreation and tourism, communications, professional and scientific services, and insurance, banking and financial services.

The Iron and Steel Industry

The remainder of this chapter will be devoted to a consideration of the chief industries in the EEC and to the changes which have occurred in their locations and structure. Let us begin with the iron and steel industry for two reasons: first, because the EEC has become one of the world's most important producers of steel (*see* Table 28) and, secondly, the size and buoyancy of the industry is a fair reflection of the economy as a whole (*see* Figs. 18 and 19).

The iron and steel industry fulfils a special role in the economy of any country since iron and steel is the basis of a very wide range of manufactures ranging from armaments, ships and oil-rigs, to motor cars and cutlery. The significance of coal and steel was clearly apparent in the fact that the ECSC was set up as early as 1952. As Parker commented: "Not only were they together of such vital importance, but they were very closely related both economically and geographically, since practically all smelting was done with coal and was carried out at the coal and iron-ore fields."[3] This traditional association has gradually loosened, however, over the past quarter of a century as the importance of coal as a source of energy has been substantially reduced and as supplies of iron ore have also declined and increasing reliance has been placed upon foreign ore supplies from outside the Community. In Britain, for example, home-produced iron ore is now only about 1m tonnes annually.

Traditionally the coalfields were unrivalled as sites for the iron and steel industry, partly because the Carboniferous strata contained iron ore and limestone as well as providing coal and partly because the transport of coal over any appreciable distance was strongly discouraged by the fact that it was of low value in relation to its bulk. Within the Community, at least until quite recently, the iron and steel industry was concentrated on the coal belt which stretched in a great arc from the Pas-de-Calais (in Artois) to the Ruhr. The Ruhr

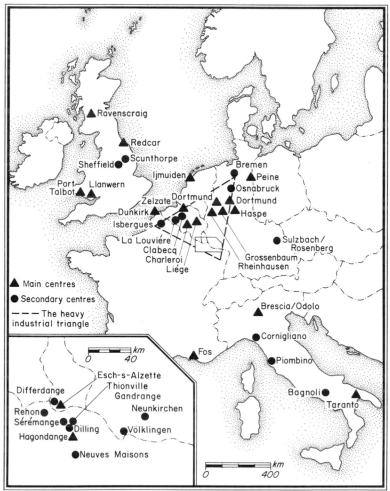

Main centres

Secondary centres

The heavy industrial triangle

[*Source*: I. M. Evans, "Europe's steel industry fights for survival in the 1980s",
Geographical Magazine, July 1982.

FIG. 18.—Principal iron and steel centres, 1981.

provided almost ideal conditions since not only did it provide very
large quantities of high-grade, easily-mined coking coal together with
supplies of blackband iron ore but supplies of iron ore and limestone
were available in the adjacent Siegerland. Furthermore, when the
Coal Measure iron ores ran out, the Rhine was available for the
import of the high-quality iron ores from Sweden. The cheap water
transport provided by the Rhine was augmented by the completion
of the Dortmund-Ems canal (1898) and the Herne canal (1906). Not

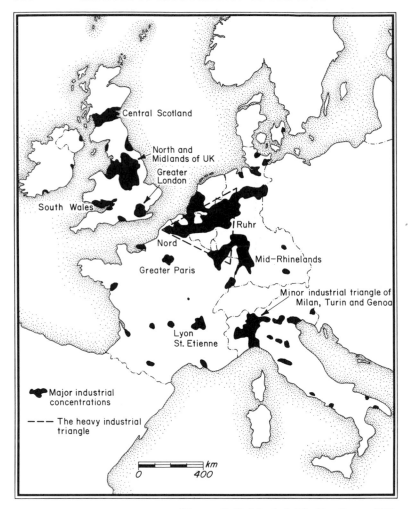

Major industrial
concentrations

The heavy industrial
triangle

[*Source*: G. N. Minshull, *The New Europe*, 1980.
FIG. 19.—The heavy industrial triangle.

surprisingly, therefore, the Ruhr became the seat of the greatest
steel-producing area in Western Europe and in 1938, immediately
prior to the Second World War, the Ruhr was producing 15.4m
tonnes out of Germany's total steel output of 22m tonnes. Notwithstanding the pastoralisation policy immediately after the Second
World War, the Ruhr was once again producing 27m tonnes of steel
by 1964 and a decade later output was over 34m tonnes. This vast
output came mainly from large integrated plants at Duisburg, Dort-

TABLE 28
EEC steel production (in million tonnes)

	1952	1964	1973	1975	1977	1979
West Germany	18.6	37.3	49.5	40.4	38.9	46.0
France	10.9	19.8	25.3	21.5	22.1	23.4
Belgium	5.1	8.7	15.5	11.5	11.3	13.4
Luxembourg	3.0	4.6	5.9	4.6	4.3	4.9
Netherlands	0.7	2.6	5.6	4.8	4.9	5.8
Italy	3.6	9.8	20.9	21.8	23.3	24.3
EEC-6	41.9	82.8	122.7	104.6	104.8	117.8
United Kingdom	16.4	24.7	26.6	19.7	20.5	21.5
Denmark	0.0	0.0	0.5	0.5	0.7	0.8
Ireland	0.0	0.0	0.1	0.1	0.1	0.1
EEC-9 TOTAL	58.3	107.5	149.9	124.9	126.1	140.2

mund, Oberhausen and Rheinhausen. The other principal steel-producing area is located on the Saar coalfield at Saarbrucken, Neukirchen and Volklingen, which have been producing something of the order of 10 per cent of West German output. Other foci of substantial production occur at Bremen and Salzgitter. As a result of the expansion in steel producing capacity and the repercussions following the fuel crisis of 1973, West Germany, like many other members of the EEC, has been obliged to undertake re-structuring programmes in respect of its steel industry.

In contrast to the West German steel industry, the French steel industry traditionally has been much more dispersed and certainly much less concentrated. The chief major concentration in the early days of steel-making was on the Nord Pas-de-Calais coalfield and even as recently as 1967 the region produced 5.2m tonnes of steel out of a total French production of some 20m tonnes, i.e. about one-quarter of the total output. Traditionally the industry was located in three areas:

(*a*) around Denain, Valenciennes, Henin and Lietard, the focus of the heavy industry;

(*b*) at Boulogne and Isbergues near the coast; and

(*c*) at Maubeuge and Hautmont in the Sambre valley, which were centres of minor production.

All these small-scale steel producing centres have been overshadowed by the highly automated USINOR steelworks at Dunkerque with a capacity of 4m tonnes a year and which is planned to have a capacity of 6 to 8m tonnes. Already Dunkerque enjoys three-quarters of the region's steel-making capacity. Lorraine is the leading steel-making area and accounts for over 60 per cent of French production. The abundant, but lean Jurassic ores with their high phosphorus content had to await the invention of the Gilchrist-Thomas process before they could be used. The ore deposits stretch along the Côtes de Moselle from Nancy in the south to Longwy in the North and extend across the frontier into southern Luxembourg. The extensive iron ore deposits in Lorraine led, as in eastern England, to the growth of steel-making and by 1973-4 had seventeen integrated plants five of which have over 1m tonnes capacity, e.g., those at Gandrange, Hagondange, Longwy, Rombas and Seremange. Many of the smaller steelworks have been subjected to rationalisation and modernisation, but Lorraine will continue to be a major steel-making area as the major development of the Sacilor steel works at Gandrange suggests.

A number of nineteenth century iron and steel centres grew up near the coal basins of the Massif Central, notably at St. Étienne and Le Creusot, while more recently a steelworks was developed at Caen using local iron ore and at Quevilly, near Rouen, using imported ore. Finally, an ultra-modern plant at Fos-sur-Mer, near Marseille, has been set up which employs 6,000 workers and whose output in 1977 was 4m tonnes (see Fig. 18).[4]

In recent years the French steel industry has been in difficulties and the Government, in 1978, took steps to implement a rescue plan for the ailing industry which was losing about £480m a year. The companies most affected are the giants of the steel industry: Usinor, Sacilor with their joint subsidiary Sollac, and Chatillon-Neuve-Maison, which together account for 71 per cent of all steel production in the country and 60 per cent of the turn-over. All three groups are to be reorganised with the loss of some 20,000 jobs. The riots in Longwy in the summer of 1979 were a reaction to this cutback in the steel industry. "Sixty-two point five per cent of the steel France produces is in the form of sheets or plates, which are most in demand on the market today, especially for automobile manufacture. On the other hand, 27.5 per cent of the production is in the form of girders, pipes, rods, etc, manufactured in older factories which are not competitive with those in some other countries. Priority is therefore being given to expanding and modernising sheet and plate-steel plants, while the number of factories producing girders, pipes, rods and the like will be substantially reduced."[5]

The Benelux countries are responsible for about 23m tonnes of steel. Substantial iron and steel industries early developed along the line of the Sambre-Meuse coal trough using the haematite iron-ores which outcropped along the valley. La Louvière, Charleroi and Namur, located on the Centre coalfield, developed blast furnaces and iron foundries while Liège and Seraing on the Liège coalfield came to specialise in steel manufactures of all kinds. These towns continue to retain a very substantial proportion of Belgium's steel industry, although it is concentrated in fewer, larger, integrated plants. A new steelworks at Marcinelle, near Charleroi, came into production in 1977. The local supplies of iron ore are now totally exhausted and supplies are now imported from Lorraine, Luxembourg and Sweden, while Kempen and Ruhr coal is used. At Zelzate, north of Ghent and near the border with the Netherlands, a major steel-producing centre has been set up and it is likely to grow into a prime development site. The Sidmar Zelzate plant has an output of some 2m tonnes a year but is capable of trebling this figure; the chief limiting factor is its location on the Ghent-Terneuzen canal which can only accommodate 60,000-tonne ore-carriers.

The iron and steel industry in the Netherlands is of relatively recent origin but has grown rapidly. Most of the Dutch production comes from the huge integrated plant at Velsen, near the port of Ijmuiden, which has a capacity of 4m tonnes. Because Velsen lies on the North Sea canal, its harbour can take 80,000-tonne ore carriers. A large new steel complex was planned at Maasvlakte, downstream from Rotterdam, in the delta region, but this failed to be implemented due to recession in the EEC steel market.

In southern Luxembourg a very substantial steel industry is based upon the northern extension of the Lorraine ore-field. Coal supplies in very substantial quantities have to be imported from Belgium and France to support the iron and steel industry. There are five integrated steelworks at Petange, Differdange, Esch-sur-Alzette and Dudelange. Since 1964 crude steel production has varied between 4 and 6m tonnes, a truly remarkable output for such a small country.

The last of the original six Community members is Italy and its post-war history of steel production is one of dramatic growth and marked locational change. Almost completely deficient in the necessary raw materials for iron and steel production, such steel as was produced, around 2m tonnes, was confined to northern Italy using mainly scrap metal and hydro-electric power. A number of small specialised steelworks, turning out quality steel, in electric furnaces, were located in Turin, Milan, Bergamo and Brescia. At Piombino on the mainland opposite the Isle of Elba, Italy's only source of iron ore, a small steelworks existed. In 1952, the year of the establishment of the Coal and Steel Community, Italy's steel output was only 3.6m tonnes. This pattern of steel-making, with its limited output, remained substantially the same until the early 1960s when changes in the economic and technical background to steel-making were reflected in the gradual emergence of new centres.[6] Since the early 1960s Italian steel output has increased very rapidly, expanding from 9.8m tonnes in 1964 to 17m tonnes in 1968 and reaching its peak output in 1975 with 21.8m tonnes. This phenomenal increase together with changes in the location of the steel industry have resulted from Government participation and control. "The state has taken a controlling interest through the holding company of Finsider, which now controls some 60 per cent of total production."[7] The developmental programme was geared to the establishment of coastal plants which are able to import iron ore, scrap and coal cheaply and four large integrated plants sited at Cornigliano, Piombino, Bagnoli and Taranto, each having up to 8m tonnes capacity, together account for 60 per cent of the country's steel. The steel plants at Bagnoli and Taranto were part of the Government's *Cassa per il Mezzogiorno* programme to stimulate industrial development in the backward south. The Taranto steelworks, opened in 1964, may be viewed as a growth pole in the extreme south of the peninsula.

Of the three countries joining the Community in 1973, the UK alone is of any consequence as a steel producer. The UK's iron and steel works grew up on the coalfields where there were supplies of coal and iron ores and usually nearby limestone. By the early twentieth century the lean Jurassic ores began to be used and new steel-making centres arose, notably at Scunthorpe and Corby. After the First World War, the traditional coalfield-based steel-making centres, which in the first place had had unrivalled sites for steel-making, began to experience difficulties, not least of which was the growing exhaustion of home-based iron ores, but the decline of the major areas was aggravated by the effects of the Great Depression 1929–34. In the mid-1930s an attempt was made to rationalise the iron and steel industry and many of the numerous small, uneconomic plants were closed down. The demands of the Second World War gave the iron and steel industry a shot in the arm but Minshull has well summarised the situation in the mid-1940s: "There was an unintegrated structure and much duplication of products. Control was in the hands of many private companies, often in small factories, under-capitalised, and with obsolescent equipment. The processes of change begun in the 1930s were continued and intensified: the movement to the coast; technological change and the increasing advantages of size gained by amalgamation and concentration in large factories; and the residual areas of steelworking maintained by inertia and increasing state intervention."[8]

During the 1950s and 1960s the iron and steel industry developed strongly and reached a peak of production in 1973 with an output of 26.6m tonnes. Up to this date the world steel-making industry had been expanding and the UK had shared in this expansion. The nationalisation of the steel industry by the Iron and Steel Act 1967 led to the British Steel Corporation's plans to rationalise and build up the industry so that it could compete in the world market. Unfortunately the energy crisis in 1973 and the subsequent economic recession which set in led to a drop in consumer spending and in the demand for steel. Since 1974 there has been large-scale over-capacity and the BSC in the year 1975-6 suffered a loss of £255m, in 1976-7 £520m, and in 1977-8 £450m. The BSC has already closed down many plants and the unions co-operated in the reduction of 17,000 steel jobs in 1978. The further deterioration in the UK iron and steel markets has posed grave financial problems for the BSC and resulted in extensive plant closures in Wales (especially at Ebbw Vale and Shotton), the North-East (Consett), Bilston and Corby. Some redundant workers have benefited from the EEC's Iron and Steel Employees Readaptation Benefits Scheme and ERDF aid for infrastructure development has helped to improve the attraction of former steel towns for new industrial development.

Until about 1968 the iron and steel industry was heavily concentrated in an area known as the "Heavy Industrial Triangle" which embraced the Nord Pas-de-Calais region, the Belgian Sambre-Meuse coalfield, the Ruhr, the Saar, and the Lorraine and Luxembourg areas. In 1952 when the ECSC was established the Triangle accounted for about 86 per cent of the steel produced in the Community and in 1968 it still accounted for 60 per cent of production. After 1968, however, there was a rapid growth in the output from the newer coastal steelworks: between 1953 and 1963 it had increased from 1.3m tonnes to 7.1m tonnes, thereby increasing from 3 to 10 per cent of the Community's total; by 1966 the capacity of the eight coastal works was 15.1m tonnes or 14 per cent of that of the Community and by 1973 36 per cent. The output from the coastal steelworks is bound to increase very substantially in the future for the capacity of most of the coastal plants is growing to around 8m tonnes (*see* Fig. 19).

In 1979 the Community of the Nine had a crude steel production capacity of around 200m tonnes, although crude steel production in that year was 140m tonnes as against 155m tonnes in 1974. The future trends would seem to indicate that first, with the increasing size of the steel-making plants there will be fewer, if larger, units and, secondly, that something of the order of two-thirds of the total production will be controlled by eight large companies. Mergers and rationalisation would seem to be the pattern in the future.

General Manufacturing

Although heavy industry—iron and steel, heavy engineering, non-ferrous metal smelting and refining, chemicals and oil-refining—is substantially concentrated in the Triangle, manufacturing of a highly varied nature is very widely spread throughout the Community and without the Triangle there are particular areas exhibiting a high degree of industrial concentration, e.g. the Paris region, the Lyon conurbation, the Marseille area, Randstad Holland, the Turin–Milan region, Lower Saxony, the Middle Rhinelands and Mid-Bavaria, together with, in Britain, the London region, the West Midlands, Merseyside, Teeside and the Central Lowlands of Scotland.

Paris is a great industrial city, the greatest in France, and its manufactures are very diverse: steel castings, machine tools, engines, rolling stock, motor vehicles, aircraft, chemicals, and a large range of consumer goods and luxury industries. In the Paris agglomeration the chief factories tend to be located on the outer fringes of the city while many new industrial developments, closely associated with the port, for Paris is an important river port, are spreading downstream along the banks of the Seine. At Billancourt is the main Renault plant, though at Nanterre and Clichy to the north-west there are other Renault works. There are a number of satellite towns, e.g. Suresnes, St. Ouen, St. Denis, and Aubervilliers, the latter three to the north-west, which are industrial areas.

Lyon (1.152m) is the second city of France and, in addition to its own industries, dominates the local manufacturing activities. Around it are a number of small towns closely associated with the silk and synthetic fibre industries. Lyon's principal industrial district is the commune of Villeurbanne (80,000), now a suburb of the city. Once the most important silk manufacturing centre in the world, in more recent times it has begun to produce synthetic fibres and the Lyon area is now responsible for about half of the total nylon and rayon output of France. Lyon has numerous other industries including metallurgical, electrical manufactures, chemicals, glassworks, potteries, and tanneries, as well as a wide range of food-processing industries, breweries and distilleries. A town of great manufacturing and commercial importance, it ranks after Paris as France's greatest industrial centre. About 50 km to the south-west of Lyon lies the St. Étienne coalfield upon which are located the towns of St. Étienne (330,000), Rive de Gier, St. Chamond and Firminy, all mining towns. St. Étienne is an important producer of iron and steel and there are small steelworks at the other centres. The coalfield towns produce a wide range of metal goods including textile machinery, motor-car parts, tools, implements, and nuts and bolts. The area is also important for specialised textile manufactures and St. Étienne shares with Lyon the silk and synthetic fibre industries.

Marseille (1.004m) is France's premier port and third city. Founded as long ago as c. 600 BC by the ancient Greeks, it grew up around a creek which formed the old harbour. Although flourishing

in medieval times on the Levantine trade, with the discovery of the
ocean routes to the East it suffered a relative decline. The opening of
the Suez Canal and the development of French colonies in North
Africa and Indo-China led to the resuscitation of Marseille and its
trade, and within the last hundred years its population has trebled.
Although it has functioned as an outlet for the Rhône Valley, the
port's chief activity was to collect and distribute imported "colonial"
commodities. The latter provided the basis for many of its industries
such as flour-milling, sugar-refining, leather-processing and the
manufacture of chemicals, soap, margarine and paper. Marseille has
grown into a major industrial centre, with all the multiform activities
normally associated with ports. Just as the old Lacydon harbour,
based on the creek, became inadequate for its growing trade after
the opening of the Suez Canal and led to the development of the
"New Port" northwards along the coast, so, in turn, the "annexe
ports" of the Étang de Berre, e.g. Lavera, Berre, together with Port de
Bouc and Fos-sur-Mer in the Gulf of Fos are beginning to supersede
the New Port. The spacious Étang de Berre offers ideal accommodation for oil-refining and storage, and has been developed as an
ancillary harbour to Marseille. At Fos-sur-Mer, as already indicated,
a major integrated steelworks of up to 8m tonnes capacity has been
developed (see Fig. 20).

Randstad Holland in the western part of the Netherlands covers,
for all intents and purposes, the provinces of North and South

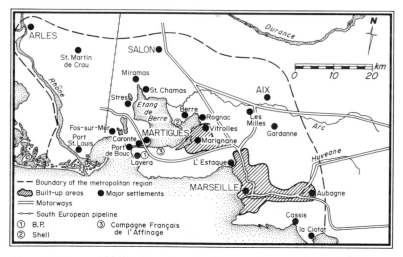

[*Source*: R. N. Gwynne & B. D. Giles, "The Concept of Fos: An Interim Assessment",
IBG Annual Conference, 1979.
FIG. 20.—Marseille metropolitan region.

Holland and Utrecht. The polderlands, or agricultural heart of these provinces are girdled by urban settlements: Ijmuiden, Haarlem, Zaandam, Amsterdam, Hilversum and Utrecht form the northern arc of towns, Leiden, The Hague, Rotterdam and Dordrecht the southern arc. This ring of towns, make up what has come to be termed "Randstad Holland", i.e. ring city Holland. It is one of the wealthiest, most urbanised, and fastest growing regions in the Community, concentrating some 6.5m of the Netherlands 13.7m population. The various towns comprising the Randstad all lie within a circle of 35 km radius. Since they are in fairly close proximity, they constitute, in effect, a ring-like conurbation. This concentrated urban growth has given rise to many serious problems of regional planning including escalating land prices, urban sprawl into the countryside, traffic congestion, pollution and social stresses which have developed from shortages in housing and the necessity for residents to commute over long distances (*see* Fig. 21).

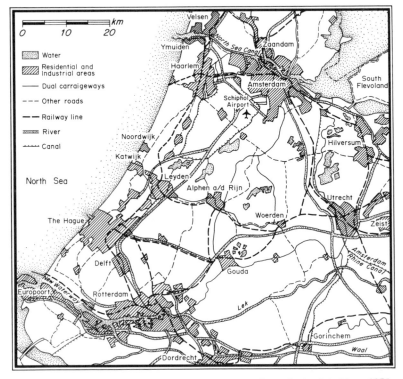

[*Source*: *The Netherlands in Maps*, 1975.

FIG. 21.—Randstad Holland.

Amsterdam, with a population of around 1m, is *the* main port importing for the home market, and traditionally has had a large tropical trade upon which many of the city's industries have grown up, e.g. sugar-refining, chocolate-making, the making of margarine and pharmaceuticals. Amsterdam also became the chief diamond market of the world and continues to be renowned for its highly specialised diamond cutting and polishing industry. It is also one of the world's greatest tobacco markets. In addition to the industries which grew out of its former colonial trade, Amsterdam has varied metallurgical and engineering industries and is a shipbuilding and ship-repairing centre. In 1968 a giant oil refinery was opened. From Amsterdam to Ijmuiden, along the banks of the North Sea Canal, is a continuous belt of heavy industry with highly-developed industrial complexes at Zaandam and at Ijmuiden-Velsen, where, as already noted, there is a great integrated iron and steelworks.

From the Hook of Holland to Rotterdam, along the New Waterway, is a continuous string of port and industrial development at Pernis, Botlek and Europoort. Here are numerous processing industries including oil refineries, petrochemical plants, chemical works and plastic factories together with ship-building and ship-repair yards, a giant fertiliser complex at Europoort completed in 1968, container handling docks at Pernis-Eemhaven and in the newly-developed Rijnport basin, together with the new iron and steel complex at Maasvlakte. In addition to its function as the biggest port in Europe, Rotterdam is a major industrial centre:

> "Its manufactures are manifold but, broadly, they fall into five groups: (*i*) shipbuilding and ship-repairing, which are carried on in some fifty shipyards; (*ii*) marine and general engineering concerned with the production of lock-gates, caissons, bridges and pumping equipment; (*iii*) vegetable-oil refining which has led to the large-scale production of margarine and soap (Unilever have two large factories here); (*iv*) mineral-oil refining, there being three petroleum refineries owned by Shell, Caltex and Esso, which have a total capacity of some 20 million tonnes a year; and (*v*) consumer goods covering a wide range of commodities and articles."[9] (*See* Fig. 22.)

Seawards of Rotterdam and on the north bank of the New Waterway are Schiedam (82,000), noted for its gin and strawboard manufactures, and Vlaardingen (73,000) concerned with shipbuilding. A few kilometres south-east of Rotterdam is Dordrecht (182,000) which has important and varied industrial activities including shipbuilding, engineering, chemicals, glass and vegetable oil extraction.

German industry has several distinguishing features: among them

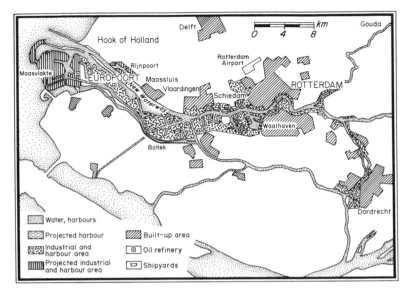

FIG. 22.—Rotterdam–Europoort.

are a highly concentrated heavy industry, a very large chemical industry, a large-scale production of substitute, synthetic and derivative materials, a very wide range of manufactures, and a widely dispersed pattern of industry. The Ruhr industrial region became the seat of the most concentrated heavy industry not only in pre-war Germany but in Europe as a whole. As we have already seen the coal-mining and iron and steel industries were primarily concentrated here but it also became a major engineering, chemical and textile area. Outside the Ruhr, however, industry tended to be located in loosely grouped clusters of towns as in Saxony and Württemberg or scattered in a large number of relatively isolated centres, e.g. Hamburg, Ludwigshaven-Mannheim, Nürnberg (Nuremburg) and Munich.

Since the Second World War the area of Lower Saxony has grown greatly in importance. The Salzgitter iron and steel works near Brunswick, founded on the Salzgitter iron-ore field, the Ilsede works near Hannover, and Klockner plant at Bremen, an early example of a coastal works, serve two other large-scale industries, the shipbuilding industry at Hamburg and Bremen-Bremerhaven and the motor car industry at Wolfsburg, Hannover and Brunswick. The Volkswagen factory at Wolfsburg employs some 70,000 workers. The efficiency of the company, and the high reputation of the Volkswagen product, have enabled expansion to occur in nearby Hannover and Brunswick, thereby making Lower Saxony the second motor-vehicle-producing region in West Germany.

In the south Rhinelands region there are two principal industrial areas, the first focusing on Frankfurt, Mainz, Darmstadt, Ludwigshaven and Mannheim which are concerned with engineering, motor vehicles (Daimler-Benz at Mannheim and Gaggenau and Opel at Russelsheim, near Frankfurt), electrical goods, and chemicals around Frankfurt and Darmstadt and Ludwigshaven-Mannheim; and the second in the mid-Neckar valley at Heilbronn, Pforzheim, Stuttgart, Ludwigsburg and Esslingen where there is general engineering, electrical engineering, motor vehicles (Porsche at Stuttgart), and textiles, especially cotton goods, and knitwear at Geislingen.

In Bavaria, the two great manufacturing centres are Nürnberg and Munich. Nürnberg, with a population of half a million, developed important handicraft manufactures in medieval times and became one of the greatest towns in Europe. The city now specialises in the manufacture of goods which have a high value but require only relatively small amounts of raw material, e.g. electrical apparatus, typewriters, precision instruments, toys, and pencils. Fürth, immediately to the west, is now continuous with Nürnberg and so forms a conurbation. Munich, the second largest city in West Germany, has a population of 1.337m and has become a great regional centre; its manifold industries include mechanical and electrical engineering, motor vehicles (B M W), chemicals, textiles and brewing (see Fig. 23).

Not only is the north Italian Plain the most outstanding agricultural region of Italy, but it is also the dominant industrial area. Its industrial importance is very much a post-war growth, but even in pre-war days it was the most significant manufacturing area in the country. A number of factors combined to foster industrial development: a variety of industrial raw materials, e.g. small iron-ore supplies, silk, hemp, straw, hides; abundant supplies of cheap hydro-electric power; large supplies of cheap, efficient and skilled labour; a large and gradually growing internal market as well as an expanding foreign trade; and the accessibility of the region to both the sea and central Europe. Many of the towns also had a long tradition of craft manufactures. Manufacturing towns are scattered throughout the plain, although most of the important industrial establishments are concentrated in Lombardy and Piedmont, and especially in and around the two great industrial cities of Milan and Turin. Manufactures include iron and steel goods, motor vehicles, engineering and electrical products, chemicals, rubber goods, pottery, a wide range of textiles, clothing and footwear (see Fig. 24). Milan, with a population of 1.743m is a great banking and commercial and transport centre as well as a major manufacturing town. Its principal industries

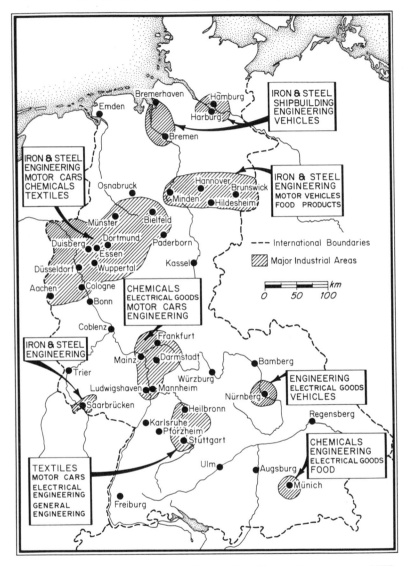

[*Source*: H. Robinson, *Western Europe*, UTP.

FIG. 23.—West Germany: industrial areas.

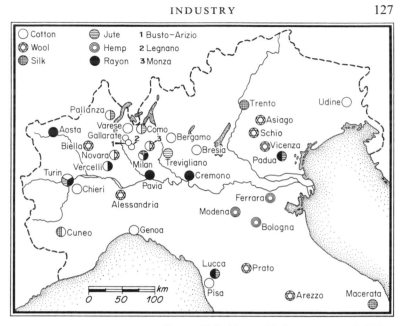

Cotton ○	Jute ⊜	1 Busto–Arizio
Wool ◎	Hemp ◎	2 Legnano
Silk ⊕	Rayon ●	3 Monza

[Source: H. Robinson, *Mediterranean Lands*, UTP.

FIG. 24.—Textiles in Northern Italy.

are engineering, including the production of motor cars, agricultural machinery, chemicals, textiles, clothing and footwear. Crowding closely around Milan are a number of satellite towns—Gallarate, Busto Arsizio, Legano, Monza and Saronno—which have metallurgical, engineering, chemical and textile industries. Turin, population 1.199m, is the great centre for the manufacture of Fiat motor cars with the firm employing 186,000 workers. Other industries, mostly ancillary to the car industry, are the manufacture of sheet steel, machine tools, electrical goods, tyres; also engines of various kinds are turned out along with tractors, railway rolling stock and domestic electrical appliances. Other important towns are Bologna, a communications and marketing centre, with machinery, textile, leather, glass and macaroni manufactures; Verona an important textile centre; and Porto Marghera (Venice) a major centre of the chemical industry.

In the United Kingdom the traditional industrial areas were mainly located on the coalfields since coal was the major source of power, and the growth of centres of heavy industry (iron and steel, engineering, shipbuilding, the smelting of non-ferrous ores) and textile manufacturing congregated on the coalfields. Since the First

World War the pull of the coalfields for the establishment and expansion of manufacturing activity has steadily weakened and factors other than coal have become increasingly more important for economic activity, e.g. the spread of the electricity grid and the development of motor transport enabled manufacturing to become much more foot-loose, while nearness to large consumer markets drew the newer, rapidly developing light industries to new locations. The newer industries which began to grow up during the inter-war period, but which have expanded especially vigorously after 1945, showed different locational preferences from many of the older industries which were the foundation of the country's economy in the nineteenth century. Those new industries, which use raw materials of the lighter kind and are less bulky and more valuable, manufacturing consumer goods such as cookers, refrigerators, electronic goods and a host of modern gadgets, as well as clothing, cosmetics and pharmaceuticals, are not tied to the traditional industrial areas; they are much more mobile and readily attracted to large towns which at once afford a ready supply of labour and a big consumer market.

Some of the UK's formerly important industries are contracting in importance, notably textiles, which for half a century has been running down as a result of acute foreign competition; shipbuilding largely through foreign competition, especially Japanese, and overproduction; the iron and steel industry partly as a result of overcapacity and reduced demand; and the motor-vehicle industry because of foreign competition and internal structural, management and union problems. On the other hand some industries, more especially the engineering, chemical and food and drink industries, are expanding.

It was the presence of coal and iron in the early days which gave rise to some of the leading engineering areas in the UK but since electricity is the main form of power now used the industry has become more widely dispersed. The Midlands is the chief area for the production of machines and tools but south Lancashire and West Yorkshire have grown into major engineering areas. In Scotland the Central Lowlands has long formed a leading engineering area. The motor-vehicle industry is largely dependent upon sheet steel and engineering products and the presence of an already well-established engineering industry contributed to the rise (initially at Coventry) and progress of motor manufacture in that region. Most of the industry is to be found in the Midlands and the South-East but since the early 1960s the government has been the most powerful locating factor and developments at Halewood (1963), Ellesmere Port (1966) and at Linwood and Bathgate in Scotland were built in areas designated by the government. Rationalisation, a consequence of a falling domestic share and recession, has concentrated production in distinct regions.

The chemical industry is currently experiencing rapid development and in the UK, as well as in Europe, is a major growth industry; it is a key industry since chemicals are required in a host of activities. The UK industry, which is capital intensive (it accounted for 17 per cent of manufacturing capital expenditure in 1975), is dominated by several large companies, largest of which is Imperial Chemical Industries (ICI) with some 150 factories. Three areas are of special significance: Teesside, Merseyside and London, while Severnside is rapidly growing to become the fourth. Among other important centres are Bristol, Birmingham, Huddersfield, Leeds, Newcastle, Hull, Immingham, and Nottingham with Glasgow and Grangemouth in Scotland.

The UK processes all the important textile fibres—cotton, wool, flax, jute and silk, as well as rayon and the truly synthetic fibres. The once important Lancashire cotton industry, which at one time provided the country's leading export, is a mere shadow of its former self. The woollen industry of West Yorkshire is also less important than formerly, although it has not suffered to the extent that the Lancashire cotton industry has. Smaller woollen industries continue to exist in the Tweed valley and in the West Country. Nottingham, Leicester and nearby towns are centres of the lace and knitwear industries. Belfast and its hinterland area is still concerned with linen production, along with Dundee. Dundee is also the focus of the jute-processing industry but Barnsley is a minor centre. Silk manufacture, never very important in the UK, has declined but is still carried out, on a small scale, at Macclesfield, Congleton and Leek. The rayon industry has grown rapidly during the past fifty years and to it has now been added the even more important petroleum-based synthetic fibre industry. Among the more important, but widely dispersed, centres are Bradford, Manchester, Derby, Spondon, Lancaster, Flint, Wolverhampton, Coventry, Braintree and Pontypool. "Mixtures of fabrics such as polyester-cotton and wool-Terylene are increasingly rendering the traditional divisions within the textile industry obsolete. The influence of markets has become more important as half of the textile industry's output of cloth goes directly into consumer clothing. Rapid fashion changes have thus dictated a much closer identity of interests between the branches of the industry. The old processing distinctions are breaking down, and spinning, weaving, knitwear and clothing manufacture are increasingly part of one organism, the vertically integrated company. This has involved new capitalisation, rationalisation, amalgamation and the introduction of new production techniques."[10]

Denmark and Ireland traditionally have been farming countries but each has 30.5 per cent of its workforce engaged in industry. They are alike, too, in that their capital cities overwhelmingly concentrate industrial activity. In Denmark over 45 per cent of the industrial workers are employed in Copenhagen which has a very wide range of industrial activities including shipbuilding and repairing, marine engineering, the production of artificial fertilisers, textiles, footwear, furniture, pottery and glassware, tobacco processing, brewing and food processing and packing. Towns in Jutland, such as Ålborg, Randers and Vejle make agricultural machinery and equipment. Ålborg is the major centre of cement-making, and Vejle has textiles. In 1978 Denmark produced 0.8m tonnes of steel but this, of course, does not meet her needs and she must import substantial quantities. Three hundred and sixty merchant vessels were produced in 1978, but this was a reduction by almost a half on the previous year.

In the Republic of Ireland Dublin concentrates the country's manufacturing activity and employs over two-fifths of the industrial workforce. The capital is responsible for half of the total industrial output. The chief activities are engineering, fertiliser production, clothing, footwear, brewing and distilling, meat canning, bacon processing, and biscuit-making. Wexford, Waterford, Cork and Limerick have a small industrial base. Shannon industrial estate adjoins Shannon airport: here some thirty companies employ over 4,000 workers and the industrial estate produces about 30 per cent of Ireland's manufactured export goods. Two textile factories have been opened in Sligo and Courtaulds have a factory in Donegal.

Greece, the newest member of the Community, is not a highly industrialised country and only 28.9 per cent of the working population is employed in industrial manufacture. Greece has a small steel industry producing about 700,000 tonnes of crude steel and produces about 1m tonnes of rolled products. Until quite recently Greece confined itself to ship-repairing but in 1976 75,000 gross registered tonnes of merchant shipping was built. Some 18,000 GWh of electricity is produced. The port of Piraeus is the chief industrial centre with many large modern factories concerned with the making of textiles, chemicals, soap and engineer-products. Piraeus also has steelworks and shipyards. Athens is not, as yet, a major industrial centre, although it has some manufactures, notably textiles, carpets, and leather goods. Thessaloniki, the second largest city in Greece, has a considerable range of industries, including textiles, leather goods, brewing, flour-milling and tobacco processing. The processing of agricultural produce is widely spread and embraces flour-milling, distilling, sugar-refining, the production of currants, the extraction of olive oil, the making of wine and tobacco-curing.

Industrial Policy in the EEC

Despite the unquestioned fundamental importance of secondary activities in the EEC economy, very little progress has been made towards an integrated industrial policy. Forty per cent of the Community workforce is employed in this sector, yet unlike agriculture which employs around 8 per cent, a Common Industrial Policy (CIP) is more pipedream than reality. The policies of the ECSC, covering iron and steel products, are an exception to this general state of affairs, for in all other sectors industrial policies remain the function of individual member states. "In a Community context, industrial policy is a strategy to develop industrial activity in such a way that the single market presaged by the achievement of the customs union in 1968 will become a reality"—by establishing, in the words of the 1972 Paris Summit Communiqué, "a single industrial base for the Community as a whole."[11]

Generally speaking, industrial policy operates in two main areas. First, it seeks to influence industrial structure, i.e. the size and geographical distribution of firms in a particular activity. In the UK, for example, the industrial strategy of the 1974-9 Labour administration, through the operation of the National Enterprise Board, is one aspect of this type of industrial policy. Similar policies have operated in the other member states, notably France and Italy, with in all cases, the emphasis being upon increased government intervention in the operation and affairs of manufacturing industry. Secondly, industrial policy seeks to regulate the behaviour of firms. A good example of this is the UK legislation on monopolies and restrictive practices, which exerts control on the general business environment. Similar legislation is to be found in other member states, and at EEC level, in the responsibilities of the Competition Directorate-General. Unlike industrial structure, this second aspect of industrial policy is explicitly spelled out in the Treaty of Rome. For this reason, let us briefly discuss this aspect of industrial policy.

The relevant articles are 85 to 102 inclusive, covering rules of competition, taxation policy and the harmonisation of national laws.[12] Taken collectively, they are concerned with the achievement of a truly common market in which goods can move freely between member states. For example, it is the responsibility of the Competition Directorate-General to eliminate restrictive business practices such as market-sharing arrangements and the operation of cartels (a manufacturer's union designed to control the production and prices of a particular good). If unchecked, such agreements could hold back the full process of integration of trade in industrial goods. Swann clearly illustrates instances where Community action has been taken to break down these barriers.[13] The Commission has also used its powers to investigate various industries such as textiles, shipbuilding and aerospace where state aids have been given to firms. The reason for this intervention has been on the grounds that subsidisation by member states can distort the relative competitive position between them, although in some cases, it has been permitted. To be allowed, the Commission has stipulated that aid must be selective and of a regressive nature, designed to make the recipient industry competitive in the long run. More specifically, progress has been made towards the harmonisation of regional aid schemes—as noted in Chapter XII. This has come through an agreement to make ceilings to the level of investment aid available in problem regions. Finally, there have been measures aimed at achieving fiscal and company law harmonisation, but as Blake and Nevill-Rolfe point out, these above aspects of industrial policy are "classic examples of negative integration."[14] They also note that "it is striking that neither of them is the responsibility of the Commission member in charge of industrial policy."[15]

To return to the structural aspects of industrial policy, and in view of Blake and Neville-Rolfe's comment, it is significant to note that there is no explicit reference to a CIP in the Treaty of Rome. The development of a CIP, therefore, relies heavily upon its need being recognised by member states in order to "steer industry in a direction that the Community regards as desirable."[16] There must, therefore, be an even greater will to integrate than in the case of Transport Policy, which was laid down in 1958, or Regional Policy, which was implied by the Treaty of Rome. Like the two aforementioned policy areas, a considerable convergence of national industrial policies would facilitate the creation of a CIP.

The objectives of a common industrial structure policy have been laid down by the European Parliament.[17] Primarily, these involve the creation of optimum conditions for existing measures to redevelop and adapt industry to the realities of a common market. Also included as objectives are the co-ordination of national structure measures and the promotion of research and development to increase the productivity of Community industries. In March 1970, the Commission produced a memorandum entitled "Industrial Policy for the Community", which has popularly become known as the Colonna Report.[18] This lengthy report contained many proposals, which have been summarised by Hodges into five broad themes.[19]. These are:

(*i*) creation of a single market—the removal of the remaining technical barriers to trade;
(*ii*) harmonisation and standardisation of the legal, fiscal and

financial framework within which firms operate in order to encourage firms to expand throughout the Community;

(*iii*) merger promotion—the active encouragement of industrial mergers between firms in different member states, particularly in high technology industries, in order to enable E E C industry to withstand increasing competition from outside;

(*iv*) industrial adaptation—measure to ensure a smooth and speedy adaptation to changing industrial conditions, this policy being closely linked with regional and social policies;

(*v*) external economic relations—greater solidarity required, especially in the control of multinational companies and technological collaboration.

Hodges outlines in detail some of the fundamental disagreements which emerged in the preliminary discussions of the Colonna Report.[20] From a geographical point of view, the Commission's stand on industrial adaptation is particularly pertinent. On the one hand, it is suggested that industry should be persuaded to move to predominantly agricultural regions like the *Mezzogiorno* and to regions such as North-East England which face the decline of traditional industries. The means of achieving this, however, is not contained within its industrial policy—instead, it is the work of Community social and regional policies. On the other hand, the regulation of state aids to industry comes under the Competition Directorate-General, as mentioned earlier. So, there is a strong possibility that the economic and social well-being of problem regions could actually worsen due to problems of member states reaching agreement on the size and distribution of the European Regional Development Fund (*see* Chapter XII).

As noted earlier, the final communiqué of the 1972 Paris Summit was the first major breakthrough. As with regional policy, January 1974 was set as the deadline for the adoption of a programme and timetable for an industrial policy. The Commission has produced material, but the progress made to date has been disappointingly slow. The only progress made to date has been in the "negative" area of competition policy referred to above and in harmonising the technical framework within which industry operates. Not all-embracing structural industrial policies have been agreed and this aspect of a C I P has remained a low priority throughout a period of low industrial growth. "The major cause of this lack of progress has been an absence of a consensus among member governments that an industrial policy is needed."[21] A C I P may yet have its day; but in order to become reality, it must overcome the basic problem facing all common policies—the early idealism will have to be rejuvenated to replace the current fear that each member state must get out at least as much as it puts in.

Industrial change, Integration and Spatial Structure

Finally, it is appropriate to make some comment on the impact of industrial change and economic integration on the spatial structure of the EEC economy since 1958. The relationship is indeed a complex one and only a broad outline will be attempted.[22] The changes in industrial production as outlined earlier have had a significant impact on the spatial structure of the EEC economy. Manufacturing industry is such that most industries are foot-loose and no longer tied down to a traditional power or market-based location. Moreover, as economic integration has proceeded, the physical barriers to the free flow of industrial goods have been progressively removed and industrial capital is free to migrate between member states of the EEC. Between them, industrial change and economic integration have served to promote the economic growth of the geographical centre of the Community, repeating the gravitational process previously at work within individual member states. It is, therefore, no coincidence that in five countries of the Six, the major concentration of industrial growth during the 1960s was close to the continental centre of western Europe, while in Italy the northern industrial belt reached towards this core.

Various empirical and theoretical studies have categorically shown that a centre-peripheral model of economic structure can be applied to Western Europe as a whole. The growth of economic integration has been achieved through the progressive establishment of an internal free trade area for industrial products (*see* Chapter III). Geographically, a central location can confer significant advantages in the form of both internal and external economies of scale. Transport accessibility for the wider market is good and distribution costs can be reduced in comparison to a more peripheral location. The result is that a central location can lead to lower unit costs of production and so, promote the concentration of productive resources.

Within Western Europe, core regions such as the Paris basin, south-eastern England and the Randstad were established industrial regions before integration became a reality and as noted earlier, a Heavy Industrial Triangle was also recognisable. During the 1960s, with the growth of economic integration, there was a noticeable concentration of industrial resources around the Rhine Valley, as Parker clearly and enthusiastically notes:

The centripetal changes have led to concentration into the most favoured regions and ... it is around the Rhinelands that this has been most in evidence. The economic unification of this great area is certainly one of the most significant results of the Community, since up to then it had been the archetype of artificial fragmentation of a natural unit.[23]

Clark also observed this trend in his desk study of economic potential in an enlarged Community[24] (*see* Fig. 25). Using accessibility coefficients based upon income data for 1962, Clark suggested that the maximum market potential of a Community including the U K would be in the Antwerp-Cologne area. The U K's most favourable market potential area, concentrated in the South-East, recorded a value on a par with northern Italy and southern France. Since his study, the income gap between the U K and the rest of the E E C has widened, so presumably, the market potential of the central European core *vis-à-vis* the U K will be even greater. (*See* also Chapter XI).

In general, therefore, the continental centre of Western Europe, stretching from Lombardy to Paris and Hamburg would seem to be the most favoured industrial location in the Community. Figure 26, showing the industrial headquarters of the 100 largest E E C firms, would largely support this claim, in spite of the large concentration in south-east England. Conversely, a peripheral location would seem to be relatively detrimental, as Brown notes with respect to the U K peripheral regions.[25] Not all commentators, however, would support this view. Keeble outlines some of their arguments.[26] In particular, he notes that in peripheral regions, there is a good supply of labour and wages costs are lower than in core regions due to lower living standards. Regions such as Wales and the northern region of England could offer an attractive location for expanding domestic firms and for E E C-directed investment from outside, e.g. from the U S A and Japan. An effective regional policy, backed up by the European Regional Development Fund, could well channel manufacturing firms into such regions (*see* Chapter XII). Theoretically, at least, there would seem to be scope for the fruits of the E E C membership to fall on less prosperous regions; but in a period of slow economic growth, uncertain energy supplies and political uncertainty over Community regional policy, an industrial location in the central European core would seem to have more positive advantages than one on the periphery. Moreover, as integration advances (*see* Chapter X), these benefits seem likely to be sustained.

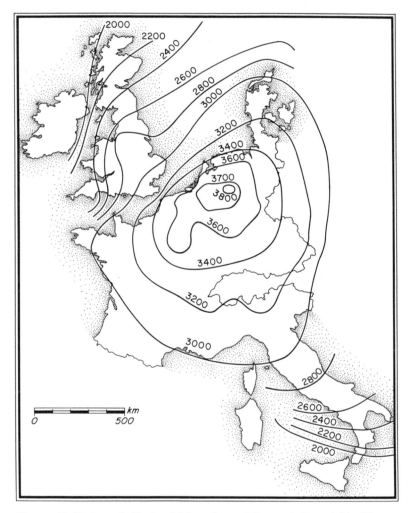

[*Source*: C. Clark *et al.*, "Industrial Location and Economic Potential in Western Europe", *Regional Studies*, 3, 1969, p. 205.

FIG. 25.—Economic potential in the enlarged Community. The contours on the map represent locations of equal economic potential measured by regional income and transport costs to all other European regions. They are spaced at 200 unit intervals. The higher the potential of a region, the more attractive it would be to manufacturing industry.

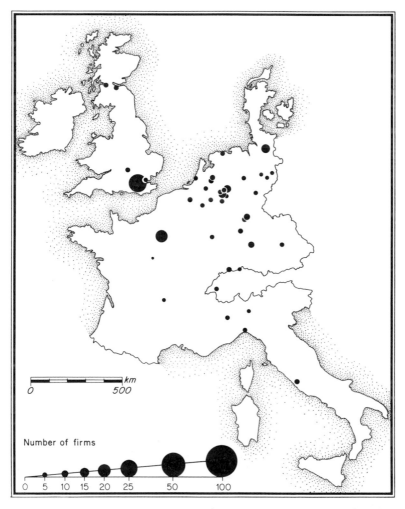

[*Source*: R. Lee & p. E. Ogden, *Economy and Society in the EEC*,
Saxon House, 1976, p. 27.

FIG. 26.—Industrial headquarters in the EEC c. 1974 (100 largest firms).

NOTES
1. Minshull, G. N., *The New Europe*, Hodder & Stoughton, 1978, p. 35.
2. Zimmerman, E. W., *World Resources and Industries*, Harper, revised edition 1951, p. 790.
3. Parker, G., *The Logic of Unity*, Longmans, 2nd edition, 1975, p. 57.
4. *News from France*, Vol. 5, No. 3, December 1978, p. 8.
5. *Ibid.*, p. 9.
6. Parker, G. *op. cit.*, p. 61.
7. Minshull, G. N., *op. cit.*, p. 73.
8. Minshull, G. N., *op. cit.*, p. 60.
9. Robinson, H., *Western Europe*, 5th edition, University Tutorial Press, London, 1977, p. 297.
10. Minshull, G. N., *op. cit.*, p. 88.
11. Hodges, M., "Industrial Policy: A Directorate in Search of a Role", Wallace, H., ed. *et al.*, *Policy-Making in the European Communities*, John Wiley & Sons, 1977, p. 113.
12. See *Treaty of Rome*, Cmnd. 5179-II, HMSO, 1973 pp. 32-8.
13. Swann, D., *Economics of the Common Market*, Penguin, 1975, pp. 79-89.
14. Blake, D. and Neville-Rolfe, M., *Little in Common for the Common Industrial Policy*, in The Open University, *The European Economic Community: Work and Home*, 1974, pp. 16-18.
15. *Ibid.*, p. 16.
16. *Ibid.*, p. 15.
17. The European Parliament, *Europe Today*, 1975, section 4.210.
18. COM (70)100. For full details, see The Open University, *The European Economic Community: Work and Home*, 1974, section 3, pp. 29-37.
19. Hodges, M. *op. cit.*, p. 113.
20. Hodges, M., *op. cit.*, pp. 122-4.
21. Hodges, M., *op. cit.*, p. 130.
22. For details, see Lee, R. "Integration, Spatial Structure and the capitalist mode of production in the EEC", in Ogden, P. E. and Lee, R. eds, *Economy and Society in the EEC*, Saxon House, 1976, Chapter 2.
23. Parker, G., *The Logic of Unity*, Longmans, 1975, p. 155.
24. Clark, C. *et. al.*, "Industrial Location and Economic Potential in Western Europe", *Regional Studies*, 3, 1969.
25. Brown, A. J., *The Framework of Regional Economies in the UK*, Cambridge University Press, 1972, p. 337.
26. Keeble, D., *Industrial Location and Planning in the UK*, Methuen & Co., 1976, pp. 279-83.

Chapter VII

Aspects of Tertiary Industries

HAVING described and discussed the primary activity of agriculture and the secondary industrial activities in the EEC, it is necessary, if only briefly, to look at some of the tertiary activities which now are of such great and growing importance. The following table gives the percentage distribution of employment by sector in each member state in 1980. Like all modern economies, the service sector is the majority employer in all cases.

TABLE 29
Civilian employment, 1980 (in percentages)

	Agriculture	Industry	Services
Belgium[1]	3.0	34.8	62.2
Netherlands	4.6	32.0	63.4
France	8.8	35.9	55.3
West Germany	6.0	44.8	49.2
Italy	14.2	37.8	48.0
Luxembourg	6.3	38.4	55.3
Denmark	8.3	30.2	61.5
Ireland	19.2	32.4	48.4
United Kingdom	2.6	38.0	59.4
EEC Total[2]	7.4	38.6	54.0

NOTES
1. 1979.
2. Estimate.

Source: Basic Statistics of the Community, Eurostat, 1982.

It is impossible here to look at all the varied types of services that occur and we shall limit our field to three very significant aspects: to office location and regional development, to the distributive trades, and to tourism and its importance in regional development.

Office Location and Regional Development

The location of offices and research into office location policies have been relatively neglected fields of study by both academics and governments until the late 1960s. Over the past twenty years there has been a rapid growth in office development within cities which has given rise to problems at the urban and regional planning levels. British geographers, notably Cowan, Daniels, Goddard and Fernie, have made very useful contributions to the analysis of the varied aspects of office geography. In other E E C countries there has perhaps not been so much interest and, for example, Burtenshaw has commented that "In West Germany, geographers, economists and regional planners are only just awakening to the need to understand the patterns and processes of office location."[1] In many studies on office location, frequent reference is made to the dearth of official data and no doubt this is a major reason why the study of office location in geography has been neglected.

Office occupations in the U K

The past twenty years has seen a substantial change in the occupational structure within the country and office-based professional, technical and clerical workers have come to occupy an ever-increasing proportion of the workforce. Daniels has commented:

> "Centrality exerts a strong pull on the location of office occupations and although the pull exerted by this factor may diminish in the longer term as the full impact of post-industrial technology begins to emerge, it seems reasonable to assume that it will continue to focus demand on major urban areas."[2]

Notwithstanding the growing number of government incentives, government decentralisation, and the efforts of the Location of Offices Bureau (L O B) since 1963, the regional imbalance in the distribution of office activities appears to be persisting.

Using data from the 1971 Census returns, it has been possible to identify, in broad terms, the growth and structural change taking place between 1961 and 1971. In 1961 office occupations accounted for some 20 per cent of the national workforce, but a decade later it had increased to 25 per cent. The rate of increase between 1961–6 had been about 13 per cent, but this had decelerated to 9 per cent during 1967–71. According to Daniels this slowing down concealed some interesting trends, notably the restructuring of the workforce away from clerical jobs towards administrative and professional occupations.[3] It seems likely the reduced growth rate in clerical occupations will continue and will not be entirely compensated by the increased demand for administrative and professional workers. Just as automation has done much to change manufacturing industry and led to cutbacks in the workforce, so it is now having a growing impact on office work. Technological innovations, such as electric typewriters, photocopying machines and mini-computers in office work, is making it possible to dispense with some office staff; on the other hand, these innovations are creating a need for new, highly specialised workers such as computer programmers and systems analysts.

Table 30 shows the regional inequalities in the growth of office occupations in the various Economic Planning Regions in England and Wales. Careful study of the table makes it clear that national trends in office occupation change are by no means consistent. The South-East Region had the same share of office jobs in 1971 as it had in 1966, notwithstanding the attempt to control the location of office activities. Outside Greater London, growth in the Outer Metropolitan Area and in the Outer South-East proceeded at twice the national rate. East Anglia alone of the economic planning regions, with its low base total, achieved the rapid expansion of office employment attained in the Outer South-East. Elsewhere in the country the regional growth rates were much nearer the average, notably in the North-West, Yorkshire and Humberside, and the West Midlands which had a declining share of all office occupations. Says Daniels:

Although almost all parts of the country have shared in the expansion of office occupations, significant inequalities remain at the

TABLE 30

Growth of office occupations in Economic Planning Regions, England and Wales, 1966–71

Region	Regional share (per cent)		Percentage change of employment between 1966 and 1971
	1966	1971	
Northern	4.8	4.8	9.4
Yorkshire & Humberside	7.9	7.7	6.7
North-West	13.0	12.7	6.3
East Midlands	5.5	5.6	12.9
West Midlands	9.8	9.6	6.3
East Anglia	2.3	2.7	23.5
South-East	46.9	46.9	9.1
Greater London	30.6	28.8	2.4
Outer Metropolitan Area	9.6	10.5	19.4
Outer South-East	6.7	7.6	24.5
South-West	6.2	6.3	12.5
Wales	3.6	3.7	10.9
Total	100.0	100.0	9.1
	(4,986,310)	(5,440,000)	

Sources: *Census of Population 1966*, 1969; *Census of Population 1971*, 1975.

regional level. Decentralisation has caused some downward transfer of office employment through the urban hierarchy but some areas such as those parts of the South-East Region outside London continue to attract a larger share of office jobs than they really require.[4]

Office Concentration and Control in the EEC

As might be expected, the spatial distribution of office activities is heavily concentrated in the "growth" areas of countries. In 1971, 24.4 per cent of the working population of the UK were employed in offices, but the proportion of office workers to total employment in the South-East Region amounted to 31.2 per cent, compared to only 18.5 per cent in the Northern Region. Such regional imbalances in job opportunities are also evident in other EEC countries and there is a concentration of office work in the national capitals and their regions in the cases of France, the Netherlands and the Republic of Ireland.

Various national governments have attempted to control the growth of office developments in the zones of concentration and systems of control were introduced in Britain and France in the 1960s and in the Netherlands in the late 1970s. In West Germany there is no official policy in respect of office development largely because of the nature of the governmental system, that of a federal state. Thus, although there is no federal government policy, "in the early 'seventies the Federal Government became aware of the problems posed by office development, particularly in Bonn."[5]

Since Bonn, the capital, is only a small city of 283,000, it has not the concentration of offices which, for example, characterise the great capital cities of London, Paris or Brussels. Office location in West Germany tends, therefore, to be dispersed and found more particularly in such major commercial and industrial cities as Cologne, Frankfurt, Dusseldorf, Mainz, Stuttgart, Munich and Hamburg.

In the smaller of the EEC member states such as Ireland and Denmark the respective capitals, Dublin and Copenhagen, concentrate the administrative, industrial and commercial functions and hence office location is emphatically centralised in the two capital cities.

Because of the high degree of office development in the South-East economic planning region of the UK, firms can be prevented from locating offices in specific sites, and before office developments—conversions, extensions or new buildings—in excess of 30,000 square feet are allowed, an Office Development Permit (ODP) is required; and even if permission is granted, development is subject to local planning regulations. In the western provinces of the Netherlands, a

20 per cent selective investment levy used to be imposed on new office building; this "congestion" tax increased the location costs for firms wishing to develop within the Randstad, although, if a firm was prepared to pay such increased costs, there was no ban on office construction. This has now been replaced by a system of licensing and control more akin to the French system. In France a system of control has existed since 1960. Firms desirous of constructing or occupying offices in the Paris region have needed an *agrément* from the *Comité de Décentralisation*. An *agrément* is similar to an ODP but this planning control is also linked to a policy of *redevance* (a development tax similar to the Dutch selective investment levy) which varies from 100 to 400 francs per square metre according to the attraction of a location for office development.[6] However, the French Government, in 1971, concerned about the differential rate of economic growth within the Paris region, excluded redevelopment zones in Paris and the new towns in the Paris Basin from this tax.

Office Dispersal

The UK and Netherlands governments as part of their regional development policies have decentralised considerable amounts of government work from traditional centres. Between 1945 and 1970 in the UK, something of the order of 70,000 headquarter jobs were dispersed from central London, with about a third of the jobs being decanted to the development areas. With the publication of the Hardman Report in 1973, a further 31,400 jobs were recommended for dispersal.[7] Finally it was decided that these should be phased over a ten-year period with Glasgow, Cardiff and Newport being the chief recipients, although this government decision was decidedly unpopular with the staff who were likely to be affected by such moves.

Similar civil servant resistance to re-location has also been strongly voiced in the Netherlands, where the staff do not want to be moved from the Randstad. The Dutch Government plan to move 22,500 jobs from The Hague to five other centres: to Groningen, Emmen, Leeuwarden, Heerlen and Zwolle. Some moves have already taken place, e.g. the Government Pension Fund has moved to Heerlen, but there has been criticism of such moves because of the additional communication costs incurred as a result of the decentralisation. The approach of the Dutch Government to office dispersal differs from that adopted in Britain: while in the Netherlands government jobs are being dispersed to a limited number of centres, in Britain a much larger number of jobs have been re-located but they have been more widely distributed to a larger number of cities.

In France, unlike the UK,

there are few centres sufficiently well-developed to take some of
the office demand away from the capital despite government decentralisation policies such as the designation of the *métropoles
d'équilibre*. Indeed, only Lyon of the provincial centres can be said
to take any significant share of the demand for office space away
from Paris.[8]

Government office dispersal in France has been difficult to effect
because of trade union opposition and the unwillingness of union
members to move from Paris. Again, the *métropoles d'équilibre* attracted office development at the expense of nearby rural areas and
this led to political pressures to arrest the decline and depopulation
of the countryside. The lack of success in promoting office dispersal
has, accordingly, resulted in the government having to modify its
policies. The *métropoles* have been abandoned in favour of the smaller
scale *"contrats de pays"* and *"villes moyennes"* policy.[9]

Conclusion

Locational forces shaping patterns of office development are broadly
similar in all the EEC countries with the national capitals—London,
Dublin, Paris, Brussels, The Hague and Bonn—together with the
large conurbations of Amsterdam, Rotterdam, Frankfurt, Hamburg,
Lyon, Milan, etc. concentrating office activities. The attraction of
large conurbations for office agglomeration is undermined where, as
in the cases of Britain and the Netherlands more particularly, there
are government policies of control and dispersal. Though governments are the primary agents effecting decentralisation, where trade
union movements are strong there is strong hostility by employees
who view movement to the provinces with misgivings. Private firms,
too, in times of economic recession, such as the mid-1970s, are loath
to relocate their central offices notwithstanding lucrative financial
incentives. It can also be appreciated that firms prefer central locations because of their links with the business community, the greater
ease of attracting appropriate staff, and the availability of retail and
social facilities. The principal pressures urging movement are shortage of office space, unsuitable premises, cost considerations and
inadequate car-parking facilities. Re-location decisions, however,
have to conform to the planning framework operating in each city
and Fernie's comparative study of the historic city of Edinburgh and
the redesigned post-war centre of Leeds well illustrates how the
pattern of office development differs according to city planning
policies.

To conclude, let us use two quotations. The first is by Bateman
who writes:

In looking at any planning policy in Paris, one must not forget the power which central government is able to exert. It was de Gaulle who set up the first major effective plan for Paris since Haussman and in the last ten years, government and the president have had some influence. Currently, Giscard d'Estaing appears to have adopted a policy of "toning down" many of the projects envisaged in the late 1960s and early 1970s. Some of these affect office development in the city. For instance, the redevelopment of the Italie sector, originally planned to have 59 tower blocks with the highest rising to 528 feet, has been curtailed with only 28 blocks completed or under way. The debate over the future of les Halles similarly illustrates the manner in which central government in the form of the president can intervene in the planning of Paris. One very direct act by central government has been to place an embargo on its own departments to prevent more government offices being built in the city centre.[10]

The second quote is by Burtenshaw who states:

West Germany needs an office location policy but the reasons for it arise much more from the nature and evolution of the West German urban system since 1945. While the experience of London and Paris might have some validity, the absence of a world city and the already dispersed nature of office employment do present the cities with more intractable problems particularly as office employment is the growth sector.[11]

The Distributive Trades

The distributive trades within the EEC account for some 15 per cent of the workforce and contribute approximately 12 per cent of the GDP of the member countries.[12] Variations, of course, exist between country and country and, indeed, within each country but, in the Community at large, distribution forms a major sector of all national and regional economies. At the beginning of 1977 the Chartered Institute of Transport in the UK estimated that employment in the movement of passengers and goods was over 2.3m with 42 per cent of jobs being in the field of physical distribution. Materials handling costs in the UK runs at about £6 billion or 15 per cent of the GNP. As yet there is no all-embracing Community policy in existence to provide guidance in the distributive system; moreover, in most member countries no integrated national development policies exist in relation to either wholesaling or retailing, the two principal aspects of the distribution process. Dawson says, "French national and regional economic planning provides the nearest approximation to overall distribution planning but even in this case the state plays an indirect and not a direct role."[13] Policies within the countries of the EEC tend to be piecemeal and variable, and this diversity of public policies in the matter of distribution provides a serious handicap strongly militating against full economic integration within the EEC.

The distributive trades are usually defined as "those intermediary activities involved in the transfer of goods from producers to consumers, namely wholesaling and retailing."[14] These two activities, though characteristically small in their scale of operations, collectively form one of the largest industries and, for example, in the UK they account for about 11 per cent of the GDP and a comparable proportion of the national workforce.

Physical Distribution

First we must begin by thinking about the distribution and transport functions as one. Transport is the movement by some form of vehicle of goods (and people) from one place to another; implicit in this statement, transport involves a carriage function and a change of location. Most commodities are moved from their areas of production to the places where they are processed and then consumed and such transference, in the economist's language, is a change in *place utility*; in other words, a commodity becomes enhanced in value after it has been transported. Such increase in value accrues through moving the commodity to places where it is in demand. To effect changes in location some form of carriage is necessitated: this may be in a wooden box on a lorry, in a container in a ship's hold, or in a bulk carrier such as an oil-tanker. The carriage function may involve handling, packaging, storage and warehousing, just as the physical movement is likely to involve related activities such as the routeing of vehicles and the assembly of vehicles at depots. It will be apparent that a wide range of activities may be involved before commodities which have been produced from field, forest, mine or factory finally reach the consumer, and to these activities it has become customary in more recent years to apply the term *physical distribution*. The purposes of these manifold activities is to bridge the geographical distances, impediments and hazards between the producer and consumer. Enormous quantities of foodstuffs, raw materials and manufactured goods are moved from place to place and may be subjected to attack and spoilation by climatic vagaries such as frost, desiccation, humidity, by animal and insect pests, and even by human theft. In order to protect goods in transit or in store from deterioration or loss, precautions must be taken to protect and safeguard them to ensure that they reach the consumer in perfect condition at the place and time they are wanted; in other words, the movement and carriage of goods (or, for that matter, people) involves *organised* transport. Another pre-requisite for successful transport operations is that of *economic viability*; that is, the final cost to the consumer must fall within what he can afford. To ensure economic operations becomes a major concern of physical distribution.

Physical Distribution Strategy and Costs

Any firm involved in distribution should evolve a strategy based upon a careful consideration of its own operational activities and its customers' requirements. The aim of such a strategy is basically and simply to minimise as far as possible the operating costs. The strategic plan must consider the total distribution operation and devise a working system which will effect the most efficient distribution at the least possible cost. Table 31 shows the total distribution costs as they manifest themselves in Britain.

TABLE 31
Total distribution costs

	Percentage of total costs for average firm
Transport	$5\frac{1}{2}$
Inventory	3
Packaging	2
Warehousing	$2\frac{1}{2}$
Administration	3
Total	16

Source: Murphy, G., *Transport and Distribution*, Business Books, 1972.

The cost of transporting goods and their storage are closely inter-related and, indeed, can be seen as complementary costs since clearly the more efficient movement is, the less need will there be for storage while, conversely, greater warehousing efficiency allows goods to be safely and economically stored until transport is arranged for their distribution. Indeed, all of the distribution cost factors listed in Table 31 influence each other and the over-all performance of the firm. Let us illustrate this further. If, for instance, the market is dispersed and demand fluctuates then certain functions are brought into existence. Inventory management must be held to act as a buffer between fluctuations in demand and production so that the predetermined service level can be met. As most markets are geographically dispersed, service stock will be held in warehouses to facilitate distribution to individual markets. The level of inventory will be affected by a time factor which depends upon efficiency of the transport operation. If markets are widely dispersed, then the number of warehouses within the distribution network will increase and therefore the amount of inventory in the pipeline will increase, thereby adding to the over-all total distribution costs. The transport decision also has a very important bearing on inventory levels: the basis decision to be made is often one between low cheap inventory levels and more expensive fast and reliable transport, or expensive inventory and slow cheap transport. The shorter the time goods are in transit, the more inventory levels should be cut down. It is also important that stocks should be turned over, since stocks which are not being turned over represent capital investment which is tied up without giving any return.

The Distribution Process

Following on from the above remarks, we can now turn our attention to the distribution process. As will be realised from what has just been said, distribution is not merely a matter of moving goods from the place of origin to the consumer market. There are, in fact, a considerable number of functions in the total distribution process, though not all of them will necessarily occur in every distribution system; nevertheless, most of them are present in any system. The factors in physical distribution may be enumerated as follows:

> (i) a purchasing function;
> (ii) a collection or assembly function;
> (iii) packaging, unitisation and containerisation;
> (iv) storage and warehousing;
> (v) inventory management;
> (vi) transportation;
> (vii) depot activity;
> ($viii$) a marketing function.

Attention may be drawn to three matters relating to physical distribution or logistics: first, much will depend upon the nature and operating conditions of the firm as to how many of the functions listed above will be essential to its successful operation, but it may be accepted that most of them will be necessary; secondly, the distribution process is becoming increasingly sophisticated as management involves itself and hence it now includes some activities which once were thought of as being quite separate functions; and, thirdly, the use of the computer to simulate proposed distribution systems under a variety of operating conditions makes the decision-making process for management's future activities not only more accurate but cost saving.

Public Policy in Relation to Distribution

Some allusion to the role of public policies in relation to distribution is required. The distributive system in any country or region is a reflection, first, of the socio-economic environment and, secondly of the degree of governmental involvement influencing distributive development.[15] Whereas in some countries, as in the UK in pre-war days, the growth of departmental stores and chain stores was almost completely uninhibited, in others such as Belgium, France and Germany, multiple-store development was restricted, often because of the political strength and influence of small traders.[16] As a result, multiple-store development in these countries did not manifest itself in any substantial sort of way until the retail revolution during the late 1950s and the 1960s.

Dawson has written:

> While the presence of vernacular distributive institutions in the EEC—the Danish country co-operative, the Italian street trader, the French épicerie, the Irish country general store—is a response to socio-economic factors in the respective nations, the spatial imbalance in the development of megacultural distributive institutions—the supermarket, the chain store, the shopping centre, the voluntary chain—is largely a response to the attitudes of public policy.[17]

Table 32 lists some of the variables in the distributive trades within the EEC member countries.

The purpose of EEC trade policies is the manipulation and harmonisation of international trade rather than domestic trade, although, Dawson avers, it would seem that the effects of such policies are bound to influence domestic marketing, for the outcome of EEC policy on freedom of entry of new firms will, in the long run, probably lead to a reduction in the variety of wholesale and retail institutions.[18] Thus far, however, EEC policy in regard to this situation is generally ignored by the member countries who continue to insist that domestic marketing is the concern of the individual Community members.[19]

In most countries in the Community there exist already regulations which govern and restrict the entry of new firms into distribution and, more especially, into retailing. Some countries have long had such controls; in others they date from the time of the Great Depression when protection was invoked against competition from growing large-scale retail organisations. However, as a consequence of fuller economic integration within the EEC and as firms engaged in distribution develop wider operations, inevitably there will be strong

TABLE 32

Distribution within EEC member countries

	Belgium	Denmark	France	W. Germany	Ireland	Italy	Luxembourg	Netherlands	UK
Contribution to GDP (%)	11.2	13.8	14.1	14.0	13.4	9.7	11.0	13.6	12.0
Contribution to employment (%)	16.1	16.8	15.8	14.6	15.3	14.8	14.2	17.6	17.0
Population per shop	65	95	97	115	118	57	69	87	106
Population per wholesaler	300	500	650	550	1300	680	350	450	1300
Population ('000) per supermarket	21.6	22.1	30.5	21.6	59.0	121.0	22.5	23.4	28.0
Percentage share of retail sales accounted for by:									
multiples	9.9	6.0	15.2	14.6	10.2	3.0	A	20.3	29.1
department stores	3.9	3.6	4.2	8.8	6.6	0.5	A	4.8	4.5
consumer co-operatives	2.4	10.3	2.6	3.1	A	1.3	A	1.7	10.2
voluntary chains	7.0	16.7	15.6	39.6	13.2	5.6	10.0	24.7	10.0
10 largest firms	16.2	9.7	12.0	15.0	18.4	4.7	n.a.	15.2	18.6
Percentage of food sales through self-service shops	34	51	42	60	20	6	12	47	42
Number of superstores	55	2	147	410	1	2	n.a.	18	22
Grocery shops per cash and carry warehouse	590	n.a.	470	230	210	5000	n.a.	140	185

NOTES
Data refer to 1971 or thereabouts. Because of differences in definition the detailed comparison of figures is not valid.
A = negligible.
n.a. = not available.

Main source: National Economic Development Office (NEDO), 1973.

pressures to harmonise policies relating to restraints on domestic trade.

Within the Community the means of restricting entry to firms and of protecting small retailers vary widely and range from the tight restrictions imposed by Italy and Luxembourg to the almost complete absence of restraint in West Germany. So far, there have been few changes in policy resulting from membership of the Community and entry into distribution has been affected only slightly by EEC policies; nevertheless, the policies on free entry will eventually lead to some curtailment of the more restrictive policies adopted by some of the member states.[20] Complete harmonisation of policy will, almost surely, create a big problem before full integration can be achieved.

Components of the Distributive Trades

Wholesaling

The term wholesaling is variously used and it is not easy to define it precisely; briefly, it is the intermediary process between production and retailing, but Davies defines it as "the business of bulk commodity transactions, ranging from the warehouse storage of industrial goods to the traditional market exchanges of livestock and horticultural products."[21] In Britain the Standard Industrial Classification gives three principal groups of commodities: the wholesale distribution of food and drink; the wholesale distribution of petroleum products; and other wholesale distribution, although this third grouping is not all-embracing for as Davies points out, dealers in coal, builders' materials, industrial machinery and agricultural supplies are excluded.

Tietz has suggested an alternative classification which cuts across the above systematic groupings and introduces some further dimensions into the function of wholesaling.[22] Tietz distinguishes between:

(i) Wholesaling which is geared to the storage of goods
    (a) with customers calling, e.g. general merchants serving mainly small shopkeepers;
    (b) without customers calling, e.g. dealers delivering coal, builders' materials, and other heavy items.
(ii) Wholesaling which is geared to the disposition of goods
    (a) with customers calling, e.g. wholesalers selling through samples, mainly in trade fairs and marts;
    (b) without customers calling, e.g. agents and brokers (including importers and exporters) who oversee the transfer of goods.

Davies writes:

The main geographical significance of these distinctions lies in the different location patterns that may be observed. While there are clearly many exceptions, storage wholesaling which depends on customer visits remains much more strongly constrained to inner city locations whereas that which operates through deliveries is much more widely dispersed. In Britain, a marked contrast is emerging between those activities agglomerated on the fringe of the main centre or central area and those linked with manufacturing firms on outlying trading estates and new industrial sites. Dispositional wholesaling is altogether less common in Britain compared to the USA and is mainly found only in the largest cities. Trade fairs and marts, dealing with such items as books, furniture and domestic appliances, often occupy permanent exhibition halls; while agents and brokers commonly associate with other general office activities in the central area or are concentrated around the terminals of major transport lines.[23]

Hanson has categorised the main functions of the wholesaler as follows:

(i) "breaking of bulk", that is, buying in large quantities from the producer and selling in smaller quantities to retailers;

(ii) warehousing, that is, holding stocks to meet fluctuations of demand;

(iii) helping to finance distribution by allowing credit to retailers although paying his own suppliers promptly;

(iv) sometimes preparing a commodity for sale by grading, packing and branding the goods.[24]

In more recent years, the traditional function of wholesaling has been quite radically affected by the frequent elimination of the wholesaler. When this happens, the job of wholesaling must be taken over by someone else, normally the manufacturers or the retailers. Large-scale retailers, such as multiple or chain organisations, frequently purchase directly from the manufacturers and in consequence the former must take on the task of warehousing and of distributing the stock to their branches. Moreover, these days there is an increasing tendency for manufacturers of branded products to undertake the distribution of their goods to retailers in order to make certain they attain the maximum number of retail outlets. Perhaps the single most important innovation has been the growth of the cash and carry method of wholesaling, especially in relation to the food trade. The number and size of these depots, characteristically located near main roads on the outskirts of cities rather than in, or near to, the central areas, has greatly expanded as has their turnover which, in total, increased from £344m in 1969 to £707m in 1972.[25]

Retailing

In the case of retailing, statistical information is fairly readily available; there is also a measure of agreement concerning the structure of retailing. A number of categories may be discerned which are mainly related to their method of organisation or ownership:

(*i*) The independent stores embrace a wide range of shops from itinerant stall-owners to family businesses and small chain groups of a few branches. They are the most common type of store in the EEC but their numbers vary from country to country. They are very common in the UK and Belgium while in Italy small-scale operators largely dominate the distributive trades for there are some 750,000 small shops and 170,000 itinerant traders. The independent retailers have suffered severely through the development of the supermarket, although specialist traders have suffered less than those engaged in the convenience trades. The decline in the competitive position of the independent stores has been partially arrested by the recent formation of voluntary trading groups such as, for example, the Spar grocery organisation. Groups such as this "are effectively federations of retail stores operating through a common wholesaling firm and selling standardised, branded products while preserving the rights of individual ownership".[26]

(*ii*) Multiple stores, in the UK, refer to retail firms with ten or more establishments. Although multiples are nowadays commonly linked with supermarkets, they have, in fact, a long history and the Home and Colonial Tea Company, the Maypole Dairy Company and Lipton Ltd had widespread stores in the early years of the present century. More localised food chains, especially in the North of England, were Drivers and Gallons stores. During the inter-war period multiples in menswear, e.g. Burtons, and Dunn and Co., and in household goods, steadily increased but were more particularly concentrated in the north of the country. First of the variety stores were the F. W. Woolworth stores which now exceed 1,000 in number in the UK, followed later by Marks and Spencer Ltd, and Associated British Foods; these variety stores, along with other multiple organisations concerned in specialist trades, e.g. Boots, W. H. Smith, C. & A. (a Dutch concern) etc., occupy prime sites in the main streets of major shopping centres. In the UK multiples account for around 30 per cent of total retail sales. Multiples are also common in continental Europe, especially in

France, West Germany and the Netherlands; they are least common in Italy and Denmark (*see* Fig. 27).

(*iii*) The retail co-operative stores had their origin in 1844 when the first store was opened in Rochdale. Their popularity spread rapidly in northern England and Scotland, especially in working class districts. According to J. B. Jeffreys, who made an estimate for the year 1919, 45 per cent of the 2,160,000 residents in North-

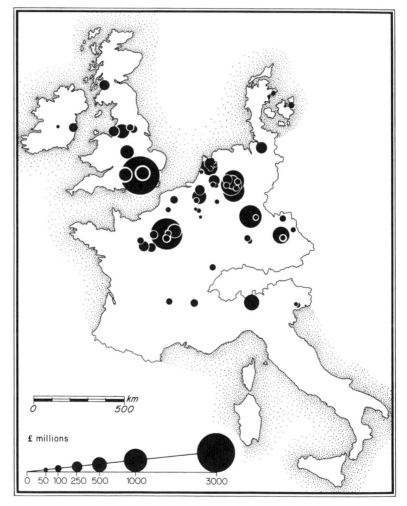

[*Source*: R. Lee & P. E. Ogden, *Economy and Society in the EEC*, Saxon House, 1976, p. 32.

FIG. 27.—Headquarters of leading retail firms in the EEC c. 1972.

umberland and Durham were members of local co-operative societies compared with only 5 per cent of 4,466,000 residents in London.[27] Although there was a very considerable increase in the co-operative stores both in the Midlands and the South in the inter-war period, they continued to be primarily patronised by working-class groups in industrial areas. Since 1950 the co-operative stores, like the independent stores, have suffered acutely from the competition of the multiple organisations. Writes Davies: "Despite the experience of self-service techniques and the advantages of having their own wholesaling system, the societies were slow to adapt to the modern methods of the supermarket and too much of their profits were dispersed as dividends rather than channelled as investments."[28] In an attempt to save the co-operatives modern management has introduced many major improvements including amalgamations of groups, the replacement of dividends by trading stamps, the adoption of a single brand name and more positive advertising.[29] There are still some 14,000 shops operated by 243 separate societies. While in the UK consumer co-operatives account for 10.2 per cent of retail sales and are almost exclusively an urban trading group, in Denmark where the co-operatives have a comparable proportion of sales they are found principally in the rural areas.

(*iv*) Department stores first appeared in London and Paris rather more than a century ago and were directed more especially to the middle-class market. During the inter-war years these department stores in the UK grew in both their numbers and size. Although London had numerous first-class stores, including Harrods, and Fortnum and Masons, many first-rate department stores also emerged in the provinces, e.g. Kendall Milne in Manchester, and Rackhams (formerly Brown Muff) in Bradford. In the larger cities on the continent there was much less development "primarily because of governmental restrictions designed to prevent any monopolies emerging in the retail field and also in some countries because of a fear of health hazards in serving several lines of trade together."[30] While the introduction of the Selective Employment Tax and planning restrictions militated against further departmental store growth in the post-war period in the UK, on the continent they expanded vigorously, notably so in West Germany but also in the Netherlands and the Republic of Ireland. In the UK, department stores are principally located in the central areas of large cities where they act as a strong shopping magnet. The family stores have declined drastically in numbers having been bought out by large organisations; Debenhams, the House of Fraser, the John Lewis Partnership and Sears Holdings between them control about half of all the department stores in the country.[31] Within the EEC member countries, department stores on the average account for from 4 to 5 per cent of total retail sales

(v) The Mail Order Firms originated in the United States about one hundred years ago where they have had conspicuous success. Mail order retailing was on a much smaller scale in Europe and in the UK mainly oriented towards working-class families in the industrial towns of the north of England and the Midlands. During the past fifteen or so years the mail order business has enjoyed an unexpected and vigorous impetus especially in the UK and West Germany where it has become geared to a much wider cross-section of the population. Most sales are in clothing and household textiles. Most of the mail order firms in Britain are concentrated in Lancashire and West Yorkshire where agents often form clubs. Great Universal Stores, Grattan Warehouses Ltd, Bradford, and Littlewoods, probably account for half of the total trade generated by the mail order business

(vi) Retail markets historically functioned as the principal form of selling and they continue to remain a significant feature in many British towns, either opening on one day a week (the traditional practice) or every working day in permanent, covered market halls. Originally selling mainly fresh foods, they have greatly widened their scope of retailing and the commodities they sell range from foodstuffs, to fancy goods and household requisites, as well as clothes, electrical goods and books. Until the middle of the last century, in the UK, retail markets were the most important outlets for foodstuffs. With the growth of other forms of retailing, markets have greatly declined in their importance and Davies says they "now account for less than one per cent of the total volume of retail trade"[32]

(vii) Many service activities are included in the retail classification of the British Census of Distribution as they function in the same way as shops and show similar locational characteristics. Among the service activities are such domestic services as opticians, osteopaths, hairdressers, dry cleaners and launderettes; leisure services such as cafés, restaurants, public houses, travel agencies and places of entertainment; business services, including post offices, banks, building societies, insurance agencies; and transport services embracing car showrooms, auto- and cycle-accessory shops, taxi agencies and garages. Clearly, similar services will be found in all member countries of the EEC.

Recent Trends in Retailing

Since the mid-1950s there have been momentous changes in the methods of retail trading, epitomised in the revolution in self-service techniques and in the vast growth of supermarkets. These developments have resulted in large numbers of small independent retailers in almost every line of trade having to close down since they found it impossible to compete with self-servicing and the explosion of price-cutting supermarkets. Davies has commented:

> The root causes for the overall decline in numbers of establishments since the 1960s are primarily explained by the expansion of chain stores which offered a greater range of products at generally lower prices because of the economies of scale that could be achieved in operating through large outlets. At the same time there were a series of credit squeezes imposed by successive governments which, together with the introduction of the Selective Employment Tax, tended to mitigate against the marginal businessman. The 1960s also saw the beginnings of some massive central area redevelopment schemes and other programmes aimed at the removal or renovation of commercial slums, and small businesses displaced in these ways found it difficult to re-establish in new shopping areas because of the high rents incurred.[33]

The repercussions felt in the retailing trade have varied widely between the different lines of trade—grocers and food shops, for instance, have been badly hit whereas electrical and television have flourished—and in different parts of the country. Moreover, the developments experienced in the UK have frequently occurred at a different pace and scale of change in comparison with those in other countries of the Community.

The war and its associated rationing of food and goods such as clothes, footwear, furniture, carpets, curtains, etc., marked a watershed in retail trading in Britain. When the war, and its aftermath, was finally over, new ideas in retailing, many of them American imports, were introduced and quickly found popularity. Self-service shopping, as we have already seen, was the first innovation; examples of self-service stores were to be found in the early 1950s but the great development of the self-service system came in the 1960s when supermarkets emerged owned by new and aggressive multiple groups. "By 1956 Britain had 3,000 self-service food shops and supermarkets, by 1962 11,850, and by 1967 almost 23,000."[34] Today there are probably around 50,000 of them. The public, by and large, liked the self-service store but was even more excited by the arrival of the supermarket which was bigger and better. As a result, "retailing organisations formed, grew and merged, and as they gained experience of the new kind of shopping, store planning evolved into a precise science, with purpose-built stores growing larger and more sophisticated every year."[35] According to Davies, in the decade 1961-71 the number of independently-owned shops decreased by 9.7 per cent with a total loss of some 43,000 establishments involved in some kind of food trade and that on average one new supermarket replaces from 10 to 15 of the traditional independent food shops.[36]

At this point we should recognise that, besides the independently-owned local shop and the town centre department store, there are four main kinds of retail store having the self-service principle:

(*i*) the self-service store—many of these are corner shops which have switched to self-service and linked up with one of the wholesale groupings thus enabling them to take advantage of bulk purchasing;

(*ii*) The supermarket—now a common sight in every shopping area, founded originally on the sale of food and using the self-service principle thus economising on staff, often, as part of a large chain of stores, they are able to indulge in bulk buying and sell their own "branded" products;

(*iii*) The superstore—a large out-of-town store, with a selling area of 2,000 to 4,000 square metres on one level, selling a wide range of household goods and with good car-parking facilities;

(*iv*) The hypermarket—with selling areas of over 5,000 square metres and sometimes up to 25,000 square metres and often placing its emphasis on non-food sales, these massive out-of-town shopping units are common in parts of the Community, especially in France and West Germany, but as yet are few in Britain.

In almost all of the EEC countries, during the past twenty-five years, new mass-merchandising techniques have emerged associated with a trend towards fewer but larger types of outlets. For long retailing in France remained largely unaffected by the new methods of selling and "the independent retailers still accounted for about ninety per cent of the shops and eighty per cent of the total turnover in the mid-sixties."[37] By 1970, there were still only 1,500 supermarkets proper. In view of the traditional conservatism in France, the dramatic development of the hypermarkets—from four in 1967 to 212 in 1973—has been nothing short of astounding. In West Germany there have been important recent developments in large discount and variety stores mostly in out-of-town locations. By 1973 about 406 such hypermarkets were in existence, accounting for approximately 6.8 per cent of the total retail turnover. Belgium is the only other country in the Community with a substantial number— 46 in 1973—of hypermarkets. The UK had only one hypermarket in 1973 but by 1980 there were five, all owned by Carrefours.

Tourism and its Importance in Regional Development

The Growth and Importance of Tourism

Tourism is merely an aspect of leisure activity, though probably its most important aspect. Travel, from very early times, has had a fascination for man: the urge to discover the unknown, to explore new and strange places, to seek new environments and experiences. Travel to achieve these ends is not new, but tourism, as we understand the term today, is of relatively modern origin. Tourism is distinguishable by its mass character from the travel undertaken in the past. The mass movement of people annually from their home location to some other temporary location for a few days or weeks is a product very largely of the period following the Second World War. The annual migration of large numbers of people began rather more than a hundred years ago but the present-day exodus, especially in relation to international tourism, is essentially a post-1945 phenomenon.

Over the past thirty years—since the world began to settle down after the years of readjustment immediately following 1945—there has been an astonishing growth in both domestic and international tourism. The United Nations reported that in the ten-year period between 1955 and 1965 the number of tourist arrivals (in some 67 countries) trebled from around 51m to over 157m.[38] By 1975 it was around 200m. Although since 1974, as a result of world economic difficulties, there has been a slackening off in the rate of expansion, prior to that date international tourism had been growing at a rate of about 12 per cent per annum.

What were the reasons for this growth in tourism? Four principal reasons underlie it:

(*i*) Increases in income and higher standards of living, including longer holidays with pay, have resulted in people in the developed industrial countries having more time and money to spend on holidays;

(*ii*) As incomes increase, the amount of surplus income at the disposal of the individual—i.e. that not spent on the essentials of life such as rent, rates, food, clothing, heating—increases, and there is more disposable income available for holidays;

(*iii*) Improvements in transport and in communications technology, such as the growth in private car ownership in particular, but also in air transport and the relatively decreased cost of air transport (especially through "package tours") have created a boom in holidaying;

(*iv*) There has also developed a new philosophy of leisure activity and holiday-making (partly stemming from changing social conditions, better education, and the influence of the mass media) which has stimulated active participation in leisure pursuits and promoted a desire to engage in sightseeing and adventurous activities. There are many factors at work, but these four have been fundamental and largely explain the "explosion" in tourism.

A number of changes have taken place in tourism which have fundamentally changed its nature.

(*i*) The whole concept of pleasure travel has changed since pre-war days. Foreign travel prior to 1939 was largely for the affluent, leisured and well-educated who enjoyed travel primarily for its own sake and who were content to enjoy scenery, works of art, and the flavour of foreign places. This concept, however, has been replaced by "tourism"—something altogether different. The present-day traveller has a different kind of background, and his ideas about travel are, mostly, very different. He comes from a wider social background and his tastes and desires are much more varied; his leisure time is much more restricted and, accordingly, he wishes to pack into it as much as possible.

(*ii*) There has developed what has been aptly termed the "democratisation" of leisure pursuits. For example, winter sports, which not so long ago were an activity almost exclusively confined to the wealthy, are now enjoyed by many. The "commercialisation" of many hobbies or leisure-time activities such as riding, yachting, water-skiing, hitherto rather exclusive pursuits, has made them available to the ordinary man who is interested. Large numbers of people are now going abroad to participate in the more exciting and exotic activities of mountaineering, under-water swimming, trail-riding, and safari holidaying.

(*iii*) There has also been the development of what is generally termed "social tourism". This kind of tourism, epitomised in the British holiday camp, not only bypasses the usual facilities provided by the traditional tourist resorts, but is responsible for the opening up and development of new areas. Organisations such as the Club Méditerranée cater for large groups of people and offer specially designed low-price accommodation, catering facilities and entertainment. There has also been a big growth in camping and caravanning and many camp and caravan sites provide varied amenities.

The Character and Organisation of Tourism

Although there is a variety of factors predisposing towards the development of tourist areas or centres, such as scenic attractions, good weather and cultural features, there are three elements or components which are essential: transport, accommodation and amenities. Transport is a very necessary condition since tourism involves going somewhere and making use of trains, coaches, ships, aircraft and the private car in particular. New increased speeds of movement are reducing travelling time, which is especially important to the tourist. All, in the process of travel or at the destination, require accommodation which provides food, drink and sleeping facilities. The nature of accommodation is very variable, e.g. hotels, motels, inns, boarding houses, hostels, camps, etc. The provision of facilities for bathing, boating, sporting activities, recreation, dancing and amusement is an important item in any resort holiday centre. The demands of the holidaymaker for a wide range of amenities has led to what has come to be known as "development", a matter which has preoccupied resort managements.

Strictly speaking, tourism, like recreation, is not an industry: it is an activity; but, in economic terms, it creates a demand or provides a market for a number of quite separate and varied industries. In some areas tourism represents the major part of the market, in others a complementary, but frequently highly profitable, demand for accommodation, catering, transport, entertainment and other services designed largely, perhaps even primarily, for a residential or industrial community.

If, according to Janata,[39] we consider tourism in economic terms, i.e. demand (or production) and supply, we can divide tourism into two sectors, the dynamic and the static. Within the dynamic sector fall the economic activities of

(i) The formation of the commodity,
(ii) The motivation of demand, and
(iii) The provision of transport.

Translated into practical terms, the dynamic aspects embrace the activities of travel agents, tour operators, transport undertakers and ancillary agencies. The static sector looks after the "sojourn" part of tourism, the demand for accommodation, food and refreshment in the main, the chief provider of which is the hotel and catering industry, although there are also other ancillary services involved.

For convenience we may talk about a tourist industry although, as noted above, tourism is an activity associated with a variety of industries; many activities each make their own individual contribution to a comprehensive service to tourists. The industry is primarily a service industry and a large proportion of those actively engaged in it find employment in tertiary occupations, e.g. catering, transport and entertainment. The industry is also usually marked by a fairly distinct seasonal rhythm; there are relatively few places enjoying an all-year-round trade. The seasonal character implies that casual work and seasonal employment are usually distinguishing features of the industry. In season, however, the industry is labour-intensive. Out of season, much of the tourism plant lies idle and this, of course, is uneconomic. Hence the attempts which are made through the staggering of holidays, out-of-season holidays at reduced rates, special celebrations, conference organising, etc., to extend the season. Anything which will help to lengthen the tourist season will help the industry generally.

The organisation and administration of tourism varies widely. In some countries it is closely regulated by the state; in others, it is more loosely controlled and the private sector is important. Nearly all countries, however, whether inside or outside the EEC, have some sort of National Tourist Office (NTO).

The Location of Tourism

Most of the Community member countries have urbanised populations which are becoming increasingly concentrated in fairly restricted areas of high population density. If a holiday is to bring a sense of escape from the thraldom of the city and industry, the tourist is obliged to move well away from the areas of economic attraction. Precisely how far the tourist is prepared to travel to achieve his escape is conditioned, theoretically, by the size of the place he is leaving and by the time and cost of travel.[40] The German geographer, Walthur Christaller has said that tourism by its very nature favours peripheral regions and is "a branch of the economy which avoids central places and the agglomerations of industry."[41] Thus areas which "are peripheral within the spatial arrangement of modern economic and industrial power can benefit from this very peripherality through the operation of tourist movements which take the form of centre-periphery migrations."[42] The development of tourism led, for instance, to large numbers of people being attracted to mountain areas, e.g. the Alps, which provided a new source of livelihood for the indigenes. This development came at a time when these regions were beginning to lose their populations because they were unable to compete with agricultural production in more favoured regions and farming provided a very precarious livelihood. Many other marginal areas have been likewise rescued from economic disaster and depopulation through the development of tourism. However, it should be emphasised that not all tourist demand is focused on peripheral areas; for example, London is the greatest centre of tourism in Britain, while George says: "Paris is France's greatest tourist centre."[43] Clearly, central places in themselves may become centres of tourist attraction, "since, as a result of centralising tendencies, they may build up a wealth of legal, social and cultural functions, the physical manifestations of which can themselves become important tourist attractions."[44] On the whole, however, tourism, by its nature, tends to encourage development in those parts of countries which suffer underdevelopment and which are the very ones needing an injection of economic capital; moreover, tourism can, and does, make use of resources which otherwise have no economic usefulness, e.g. snow, empty places, mountain tops.

Within the EEC countries tourism traditionally has flourished on south-facing coasts such as the coast of southern England, the Côte d'Azur in southern France, the Ligurian coasts—the Riviera di Ponente and the Riviera di Levante—of Italy; areas of scenic grandeur, often with watering places, such as the Auvergne and the Rhine gorge; mountain areas with winter sporting facilities, as in the Alpine regions; regions rich in archaeological, historical, artistic and cultural attractions such as Flanders and Tuscany; and the great capital cities of London, Paris, Brussels and Rome.

Tourism and Regional Development

For the more remote and essentially rural regions within the Community tourism development often has considerable economic potential and many governments have used tourism as a means of stimulating regional development. Perhaps the classic case is that of Languedoc-Roussillon, in France, which was the most ambitious single tourism development operation in Europe. Traditionally the region was economically backward with the population ekeing out a poor livelihood by producing *vin ordinaire*, raising sheep and goats on a transhumant basis or doing a little fishing and making salt by the solar evaporation of sea water. In Languedoc-Roussillon, a narrow coastal strip 193 km (120 miles) long, extending from Aigues-Mortes to the Spanish frontier, straight and flat, frequently fringed with sand-dunes and backed by mosquito-infested lagoons, marshes and water channels, sparsely populated and little known, has been transformed into a vast new tourist complex. This project, officially approved in March 1964, envisaged the creation of six new holiday resorts at La Grande Motte, Cap d'Agde, Embouchure de l'Aude, Gruissan, Leucate-Barcares and Saint Cyprien, taking advantage of the extensive beaches of fine sand and making use of the expansive areas of lagoons for the development of water-sports. The project demanded heavy capital investment but has already become of singular importance not only to the French economy but to French regional development. This vast and far-sighted tourism enterprise received 1.6m tourists in 1978 and, when fully developed, may well come to rival the Côte d'Azur[45] (*see* Fig. 28).

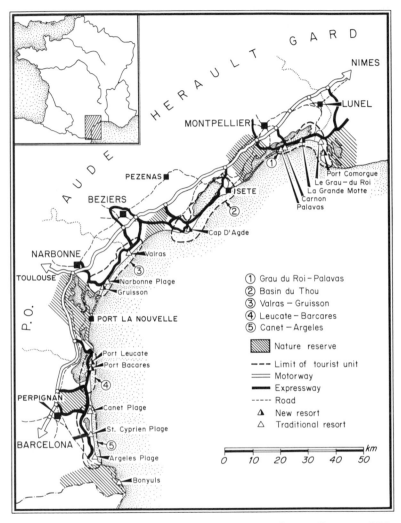

[*Source*: D. Pearce, *Tourist Development*, Longman, 1981.
FIG. 28.—Languedoc-Roussillon tourist development.

Governments have begun to promote tourism development in rural and problem areas by making available grants, loans and subsidies for improvements in accommodation and in infrastructure. Many rural areas of great tourist potential lack adequate roads, water supplies, sewerage, etc., which are prerequisites if foreign tourists are to be attracted to the areas. The range of government interest in tourism development as part of their regional policy may be illustrated by giving a few examples.

In the U K, for instance, the Highlands and Islands Development Board (H I D B) was set up in 1965 with what on paper appeared to be very wide powers to purchase land, direct investment and encourage initiatives across the whole range of economic activity. House has commented:

> Redevelopment and growth in the Highlands and Islands is almost an "act of faith" for many Scots and it is impossible to ignore the substantial achievements of the Development Board. ... These have been equally impressive whether one considers the many disseminated improvements in fisheries, tourism, manufacturing and land development or the larger-scale proposals to create growth areas.[46]

Tourism has been an inevitable area of the Board's interest and there has been much development in the Aviemore area (winter sports), around Inverness, Inverary, Arrochar, the Kyle of Lochalsh and on the Islands of Mull and Skye (*see* Chapter XIII).

In France guidelines for policies of rural tourism development "are carried out through D A T A R, which contributes technical assistance to the whole range of rural renovation policies."[47] Brittany and parts of the Central Massif have benefited by these schemes for development, especially through the construction and modernisation of rural hotels. Brittany's relative physical isolation and its remoteness from the more densely populated regions of France have tended to militate against tourist development, although the growth in motor transport has helped to make it more accessible. Nevertheless, there is considerable potential for further expansion and the C O D E R (Commission de Développement Economique Régional) plan aims at a substantial development of the tourist industry. Notwithstanding the efforts of C O D E R to develop tourism in Brittany, "the expansion of tourism is unlikely," says Thompson, "to make a far-reaching impact on the fundamental disequilibrium of the Breton economy. The employment created is highly seasonal and the chief benefits are felt indirectly, through the stimulus to the construction industry and the revenue derived from general tourist spending."[48] A plan to develop the Aquitaine coast for tourism was approved in 1970. This coast scheme consisted originally of a number of separate developments such as the open-air centre at Bombannes, the resort at Seignosse, the harbour works at Peyrehorade and the regional park at La Leyre but these have now been included in a comprehensive tourism development plan which included the creation of a 150 km Trans-Aquitaine Canal, running parallel with the coast. In time, this could become one of the finest holiday canals, providing sailing and water-sports, in Europe [49] (see, also, Chapter XIII for tourism developments in the Central Massif).

White writes:

> In West Germany there has been a concerted programme of tourist financing for the regional development areas (Bundesforderungs-gebiete) since 1969. In 1973 subsidies to privately owned tourist interests in these areas totalled DM 24.8 million while DM 77.2 million of federal or *Land* government money went into subsidies for the improvement of public tourist facilities. Federal grants are also available for improving quality and service in farm tourist establishments throughout the Republic: in 1973 such grants amounted to DM 30 million.[50]

In Italy the *Cassa per il Mezzogiorno* has launched a number of projects in which tourism investment and development is part and parcel of integrated economic development schemes. Robinson has written:

> Accordingly there have been efforts to create new centres of tourism in southern Italy and in the islands of Sicily and Sardinia as an integral part of the Government's programme of socio-economic development. Plans to build new tourist centres and applications to build new hotels in the South have received special favour and the results of these new investments are now beginning to manifest themselves: new resorts on the coast of Abruzzi, in Sicily and Sardinia have emerged and the Mezzogiorno "disposes of some 170,000 beds, an increase of 50,000 since 1965, and four times the total of twenty years earlier".[51]

The building and extension southwards of the *Autostrada del Sole* has also made it much easier for the tourist to visit the South.

Socio-Economic Aspects

Let us conclude this brief review of tourism development in the EEC by referring to some of the economic and social effects of tourism. Tourism can help a country's or a region's economy in a variety of ways.

(*i*) In countries where the industry is well developed, tourism provides employment on a large scale for it is a labour-intensive activity; in some areas or towns it is the main employer of labour. In many rural and marginal regions tourism is valuable since it offers almost the only alternative employment to such primary activities as farming and fishing.

(*ii*) International tourism can also assist the balance of payments; indeed, in some countries, where tourist receipts represent a substantial proportion of exports, tourism is vital. In 1978 the UK for the first time earned more than £3,000m in foreign exchange from tourism. It is estimated that 6p in every pound earned by the UK in 1978 came through tourism and that 18p in every pound earned by invisible exports was accounted for by tourism. Deducting what British people spent overseas gave a surplus of £954m in favour of Britain's balance of payments in that year.

(*iii*) Equally significant, although less immediately obvious, are the multiplier effects. For example, it has been estimated that £100m of expenditure by tourists in the UK creates £300m of total expenditure throughout the economy. Expressed in another way expenditure on tourism supports activity in other industries, e.g. transport, construction, agriculture, furniture, etc. The importance of "secondary" expenditure, which is inherent in tourism, cannot be overestimated.

(*iv*) Tourism, as indicated earlier, also aids a national economy in that it can help to develop and revitalise regional economies more quickly than many other industries and it tends to favour peripheral and rural regions which are the ones most needing an economic boost.

Along with economic benefits, tourism also brings some social benefits. On the other hand, tourism development may bring some social disadvantages. The social benefits stem mainly from the money brought into areas, especially underdeveloped areas, by the industry. The chief advantages are:

(*i*) employment which is probably the biggest single social advantage that the development of tourism can bring to a region;

(*ii*) the provision of infrastructure—communications, power supplies, piped water, shops, hospitals, schools, etc.—all become necessary when an area is developed for tourism; hence the local population also benefit from these developments;

(*iii*) the provision of "service industries", e.g., transport, laundries, etc., is also an advantage as the local communities would most probably not be able to support such facilities were it not for the demands of the tourist industry;

(*iv*) the provision of recreational facilities, ostensibly for the benefit of the tourist, also benefit the health and welfare of the people living within the region;

(*v*) tourism may bring cultural contacts which are beneficial. The attitudes and horizons of the indigenous peoples may be changed and widened as a result of rubbing shoulders with "foreigners".

Against the advantages must be set certain disadvantages; amongst these are:

(*i*) if tourism development, whether at national, regional or local level, has to depend largely upon imported factors of production, particularly of capital, then there will be leakages which will reduce the benefits to the host areas; such leakages will be siphoned-off to the centres of capital ownership and any such flow-back of tourist receipts is likely to weaken the effect which tourism may bring to regional development;[52]

(*ii*) there may well be conflict with local interests; for instance, where the land is devoted to agriculture, tourism development may make unacceptable demands upon the countryside, in terms of space and public access;

(*iii*) the development of tourism may adversely affect other economic activities; for example, the relatively high wages paid in the tourist sectors may lead to many workers leaving agriculture. Again, the employment of migrant labour, which is common in tourist areas, may deny jobs to the indigenous population;

(*iv*) there may be social problems—the greater the influx of tourists, the greater the risk of inconvenience and loss of amenity and facilities for those resident in the tourist areas;

(*v*) cultural contacts may not always be advantageous. Undesirable attitudes and modes of behaviour may be introduced which undermine and upset the traditional local life and customs. As White has said: "The very presence in a tourist area of a large body of migrant workers appears to be more important in inducing local social change than the presence of the tourists and the break-up of the old social communities may add to trends of local or regional depopulation."[53]

International Tourism in the EEC

Although international tourism had begun to grow from around 1950, large-scale tourist development occurred after the establishment of the Community. Table 33 following gives the gross receipts and total number of arrivals in 1976 and the percentage change in receipts over the period 1970-76.

In Table 33 the large number of arrivals in Denmark reflects the large number of tourists passing through Denmark en route to other destinations on the continent rather than to *bona fide* tourists holidaying in Denmark. It will be seen that the countries within the

TABLE 33

International tourism in the EEC

	Gross receipts 1976 ($m)	Percentage change per annum 1970-76	Total number of arrivals, 1976 (in '000s)
Belgium	959	18.4	8,040[3]
Denmark	803	n.a.	16,232
France	3,613	18.3	17,385[2]
West Germany	3,211	15.9	7,890[2]
Ireland	253	4.8	1,690
Italy	2,526	9.8	11,501[1]
Luxembourg	n.a.	n.a.	497
Netherlands	1,061	12.5	2,910[1]
United Kingdom	2,839	8.2	10,089

NOTES
n.a. = not available.
1. Arrivals at Hotels.
2. Arrivals at all accommodation establishments.
3. Accommodation nights.

Source: "The World in Figures", *The Economist*, 1978.

EEC 9 which are the major holiday destinations are France, Italy and the UK.

West Germany is remarkable because it vies with the United States as the world's greatest generator of tourism: in excess of 20 million Germans, out of a total of nearly 60 million nationals, travel abroad. This, in terms of proportion, makes the Germans the world's greatest travellers. The very large number engaging in foreign travel is a reflection, primarily, of the economic prosperity of West Germany but, also, to some extent, of the country's geographical location—an almost land-locked position in Central Europe having frontiers with nine other countries. West Germany accounts for about one-sixth of world tourist arrivals but, unlike the United States, nearly half of whose citizens travel to another region—mainly Europe—West Germans holiday preponderantly within the European region."[54]

NOTES
1. Burtenshaw, D., "Office Location Policy in West Germany", Dept. of Geography, Portsmouth Polytechnic, Paper prepared for I BG Urban Study Group, *Symposium on Office Location Policies in Europe*, University of Keele, September 1976.
2. Daniels, P. W., "Post-Industrial Britain", *Geography*, Vol. 63, July 1978, pp. 205-9.

3. *Ibid.*
4. *Ibid.*
5. Burtenshaw, D., *op cit.*
6. Bremond, M., "Les Bureaux: un march qui souffre de sa jeunesse", *Travaux Communaux*, No. 193, 1975.
7. Cmnd. 5322, The Dispersal of Government Work from London, London (The Hardman Report), HMSO, 1973.
8. Bateman, M., "Office Location Policy in the Paris Basin", Department of Geography, Portsmouth Polytechnic, Paper prepared for IBG Urban Study Group, *Symposium on Office Location Policies in Europe*, University of Keele, September 1976.
9. Bailly, A. S. and Fernie, J., "Office Location and Urban Development: Is the Western European Experience Relevant to Canada?" *Conference pour le Colloque de l'Association Canadienne des Sciences Regionales*, Victoria, May 1979.
10. *Ibid.*
11. Burtenshaw, D., *op. cit.*
12. Dawson, J. A., "Public Policy and Distribution in the EEC," pp. 256–71, in *Economy and Society in the EEC*, ed. Lee, R. and Ogden, P. E., Saxon House, 1976.
13. *Ibid.*
14. Davies, R., *Marketing Geography*, Methuen & Co., London, 1976, p. 47.
15. Dawson, *op. cit.*, p. 256.
16. *Ibid.*
17. *Ibid.*, p. 257.
18. *Ibid.*
19. *Ibid.*
20. *Ibid.*, p. 259.
21. Davies, R., *op. cit.*, p. 48.
22. Tietz, B., "Future Development of Retail and Wholesale Distribution in Western Europe", *British Journal of Marketing*, Vol. 5, 1971, pp. 42–55.
23. Davies, R., *op. cit.*, pp. 48–9.
24. Hanson, J. L., *A Dictionary of Economics and Commerce*, Macdonald & Evans Ltd., Plymouth, 1965, p. 398.
25. Davies, R., *op. cit.*, p. 49.
26. Davies, R., *op. cit.*, p. 51.
27. Jeffreys, J. B., *Retail Trading in Britain 1850–1950: A Study of Trends in Retailing with Special Reference to the Development of Co-operative, Multiple and Department Store Methods of Trading*, Cambridge University Press, 1954.
28. Davies, R., *op. cit.*, p. 53.
29. *Ibid.*
30. Jeffreys, J. B. and Knee, D., *Retailing in Europe: Present Structure and Future Trends*, Macmillan, 1962.
31. Davies, R., *op. cit.*, p. 54.
32. *Ibid.*
33. *Ibid.*

34. Irving, V., "The Great Shopping Race", *Sunday Times Magazine*, 23 Nov. 1975, p. 23.

35. *Ibid.*

36. Davies, R., *op. cit.*, p. 59.

37. *Ibid.*

38. Robinson, H., *A Geography of Tourism*, Macdonald & Evans Ltd, 1976, p. xxi.

39. Janata, G., "Tourism in HND Hotel and Catering Administration Courses", Paper presented at Ealing Technical College, 18th May 1971.

40. White, P. E., "Tourism and economic development in the rural environment", p. 151, in *Economy and Society in the EEC*, ed. Lee, R. and Ogden, P. E., Saxon House, 1976.

41. Christaller, W., "Some Considerations of Tourist Location in Europe", *Papers Regional Science Association* XII, 1964, pp. 95–105.

42. White, P. E., *op. cit.*, p. 151.

43. George, P., *France: A Geographical Study*, Martin Robertson, 1967, p. 196.

44. White, P. E., *op. cit.*, p. 151.

45. See Robinson, H., *A Geography of Tourism*, for an account of the Languedoc-Roussillon project, pp. 276–9.

46. House, J. W., *The UK Space*, 2nd edition, 1977, Weidenfeld & Nicolson, pp. 53–4.

47. White, P. E., *op. cit.*, p. 153.

48. Thompson, I. B., *Modern France: A Social and Economic Geography*, Butterworths, 1970, p, 272.

49. *French Regional Development*, Ambassade de France, Service de Presse et d'Information, p. 11.

50. White, P. E., *op. cit.*, p. 154.

51. Robinson, H., *op. cit.*, pp. 321–2.

52. White, P. E., *op. cit.*, p. 154.

53. White, P. E., "The Social Impact of Tourism as host countries: a study of language change in Switzerland", Research Papers, 9, School of Geography, University of Oxford, 1974.

54. Robinson, H., *op. cit.*, p. 281–2.

Chapter VIII

Transport

The Function of Transport and General Considerations

TRANSPORT provides a service which is essential for the well-being of all except the most primitive of economies. In the developed economies of the EEC, its function is to promote the efficient movement of goods and persons within and between member states. Historically, the evolution of a European transport network was one of the first stages of integration as discussed in Chapter II; as the pace of integration has advanced, especially since the Treaty of Rome, the transport network of the EEC has assumed even greater importance. National barriers to movement have gradually been broken down in order to meet the free trade requirements of the customs union (Chapter III) and the extensive migration of workers (Chapter IX). Without the elaborate network of motorways, railways, inland waterways, air routes and pipelines, the processes of integration would be unnecessarily hindered.

It will be useful to begin with some general considerations. Traditionally, trade movements in Europe have been aligned in two directions, a north-south movement between the countries of northern and southern Europe and an east-west movement by both land and water. These flows still persist—there are great volumes of goods moving along the Rhine navigation system and the transport network is best developed in this great industrial and commercial core of the Community. In addition, important lateral rail, canal and road networks spread out across the North European Plain linking France, the Benelux countries and West Germany. Secondly, given that the economies of Western Europe have been firmly based upon international trade, it has been necessary to accommodate the vast imports of raw materials, energy products and foodstuffs into the EEC countries and their subsequent export in the form of manufactured goods. In order to achieve this a well-developed carrying industry has been built up and its transport network makes use of every major mode of transport. Tables 34 and 35 give the basic characteristics of this network. A third general consideration is that the political fragmentation of Western Europe (at least until 1958) has resulted in each country developing its own transport network with varying degrees of government interference and control. There has

TABLE 34
Land transport in the EEC, 1979

| | Railways | | | Road[1] | |
	Length of line operated (km)	Passenger km (m)	Net tonne km (m)	Motor-ways (km)	Private cars per 1,000 popn
West Germany	28,546	37,466	65,092	7,029	346
France	34,076	53,564	70,010	4,603	326
Italy	16,072	39,678	17,525	5,760	300
Netherlands	2,880	8,514	3,376	1,714	293
Belgium	3,998	6,955	8,535	1,110	302
Luxembourg	270	242	714	44	427
UK	18,156	32,030	19,893	2,523	262
Ireland	1,988	1,113	629	—	194
Denmark	2,461	1,989	1,701	450	276
EEC total	108,447	181,551	187,475	23,233	306

NOTE
1. 1978.

Source: Revue, 1970–79, Eurostat, 1980, section 4, and Basic Statistics of the Community, Eurostat, 1982, Table 85.

TABLE 35
Water transport in the EEC, 1979

| | Inland waterways | | Maritime fleets | |
	Length in use (km)	Ton km hauled (m)	Number	Capacity ('000 tons gross)
West Germany	4,454	50,987	1,926	8,563
France	6,712	11,898	1,247	11,946
Italy[1]	2,237	n.a.	1,711	11,695
Netherlands	4,846	33,472	1,233	5,403
Belgium	1,510	5,908	276	1,789
Luxembourg	37	344	—	—
UK	538	84[2]	3,211	27,951
Ireland	—	—	118	201
Denmark	—	—	1,315	5,524
EEC total	20,334	n.a.	11,037	73,072

NOTES
1. 1978.
2. Navigable waterways of British Waterways Board.
n.a. Not available.

Source: Revue 1970–79, Eurostat, 1980, section 4, and Basic Statistics of the Community, Eurostat, 1980, table 87.

been a limited amount of international co-operation, but network integration, on the whole, has been haphazard rather than deliberately planned. Finally, with the exception of North America, the EEC member states contain a greater degree of personal mobility than any other area of the world. Over the last thirty years or so, car ownership levels have risen with better living standards and vehicle availability and the increase in transport use has been in excess of GDP growth.

The transport network of the EEC should be viewed as a single system, comprised of individual modes each of which has its own characteristics.[1] Between them these modes are seeking to meet the needs referred to earlier. The present-day importance of each mode within the system has been influenced by a variety of factors including geographical considerations, the degree of modal competition and government policy.

Geographical considerations, more especially topographical conditions, frequently affect transport networks; for instance, there is a distinct tendency for overland transport routes to follow the lines of least resistance, with roads, railways and canals often being channelled along valleys and through natural gaps. Canal transport in the EEC tends to be confined mostly to the North European Plain for both topographical and geological reasons. Other geographical factors can influence the over-all level of transport demand—these include climatic conditions, the location of mineral wealth and the distribution of population. As Bayliss has commented:

> In Germany and France the location of industry and natural products has meant that average hauls have been longer than in other countries, and this has favoured, therefore, the railway as a means of transport. In Italy, on the other hand, industry and population are principally concentrated in the north of the country, and coal and ores are produced in relatively small quantities, thereby depriving the railway of the types of consignment which it can carry most favourably.[2]

Modal choice in transport is determined by a complex set of considerations, the most important of which is the cost of carriage. Water transport is extremely competitive for certain types of haul and this helps to explain the continued use of inland waterways for goods transport in the Benelux countries, West Germany and France. Table 36 shows the modal split for internal and external goods transport between these member states in 1975 (Luxembourg excluded). The largest flow of goods carried is between the Netherlands and West Germany, with almost three-quarters of total tonnage being carried by inland waterways. There are substantial water-based

TABLE 36

Goods transport within and between selected Community members,
1975

('000 tons)

to from		West Germany	France	Netherlands	Belgium
West	C	238,804	8,466	2,084	3,260
Germany	F	78,804	3,191	30,636	8,780
	R	n.a.	5,532	12,733	5,151
	M	3,626	192	975	448
	T		17,381	46,428	17,639
France	C	7,290	161,779	370	5,917
	F	11,558	52,869	3,057	4,262
	R	9,386	n.a.	1,755	7,917
	M	731	16,459	1,066	581
	T	28,965		6,248	18,677
Netherlands	C	3,262	794	5,819	720
	F	62,062	4,904	77,063	20,779
	R	11,044	2,520	n.a.	8,219
	M	10,308	2,134	—	451
	T	86,676	10,352	—	30,169
Belgium	C	2,417	3,739	1,764	36,413
	F	6,896	3,289	9,844	21,461
	R	5,657	12,212	288	n.a.
	M	706	586	489	—
	T	15,676	19,826	12,385	—

NOTES
C = Railways, F = Inland waterways, R = Road, M = Sea transport,
T = C + F + R + M.
n.a. Not available

Source: Statistical Yearbook, Transport, Communications, Tourism, 1975,
Eurostat, 1977, Tables 1–2.

flows between these member states and also internally in West Germany and the Netherlands. Given the EEC's need to import fuel supplies for road transport, it is extremely fortunate that inland waterways carry substantial volumes of goods. Italy, the Republic of Ireland and the UK lack natural waterways suitable for inland shipping, except in a very limited way, so land modes are dominant.

The flow of goods between the member states of the EEC expanded rapidly during the 1960s as trade barriers between them were progressively broken down (*see* Chapter III). Since then, this flow has been more directly related to the general state of the EEC economy as measured by changes in the GNP of member states.

Some flows, e.g. between Belgium and the Netherlands have increased since 1975 while others, e.g. between France and West Germany, have fallen.

There are, finally, differences in government policy towards transport in the member states. All have state-owned railways and are generally striving to achieve "co-ordination through competition", but there are differences in emphasis. This is especially the case with regard to rail transport. In West Germany, the rail network operates at a great loss (£1,783m in 1975) and the networks are also heavily supported in France, Italy and the UK. In the Netherlands, by way of contrast, railways are not very significant and have traditionally been operated at a profit. In road transport, rail's main competitor in the passenger market, there are differences between member states in their approach to payment for the use of roadspace. In France and Italy, charges are made for using motorways, while in the UK, West Germany and the Netherlands, use is not restricted by toll payments. In total, the above differences constitute a major stumbling block towards the development of a common transport policy for the Community as a whole.

The Pattern of Transport in the EEC

The rivers of western Europe, especially those of the North European Plain, constitute an important transport asset of the EEC nations and neighbours; moreover, their significance has been enhanced by transverse links provided by man-made canal connections (*see* Fig. 29). The greatest and most effective use of inland waterways has been made in north-eastern France, the Benelux countries and West Germany: here, indeed, is to be found the densest network of navigable rivers and canals in the world, carrying vast volumes of goods traffic. Table 37 shows the extent of this traffic in 1975 for the main canals and river systems of the aforementioned Community members. At the very heart of this complex system is the axial river of the Rhine carrying more traffic than any other river in the world, with the possible exception of the Ohio in the USA. In European terms, it carries over three times the volume of traffic on the Waal and almost seven times the volume of traffic on France's great river, the Seine.

The northward-flowing rivers of the North European Plain became avenues of movement during the early Middle Ages, when vessels were small and of limited draught and could ply far inland. They were transformed into major avenues of movement in the eighteenth century when the construction of lateral canals provided the integrated network necessary for trade to prosper. The Rhine is both the key to this continental inland waterway system and the vital artery for a significant part of EEC manufacturing industry (*see*

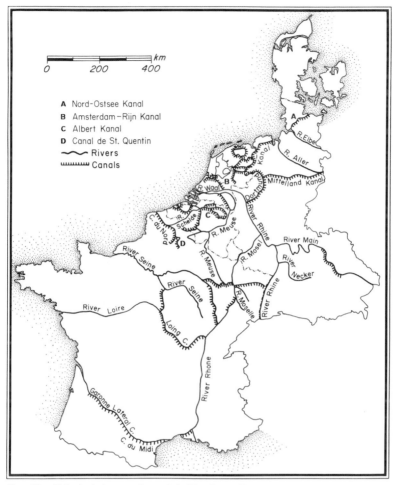

FIG. 29.—Principal rivers and canals in Northwest Europe.

Chapter VI). Canal construction reached its peak in the early part of the nineteenth century, but it required the progressive eradication of tariff barriers for trade to flourish. The Mittelland Canal, a great central east–west artificial waterway, was not finished until 1938 although its first section, the Rhein–Herne Canal was completed in 1914. Between them they make up the most notable of continental canals in terms of traffic volume as Table 37 shows. This modern canal, which has a minimum depth of over two metres, can take barges of around 1,000 tonnes. Its main purpose, however, has

TABLE 37

Inland waterway transport on selected canals and rivers, 1975

	Length in use (km)	Goods traffic ('000 ton km)	Density (tons per km)
Canals			
Dortmund–Ems Kanal (W G)	269	2,437	9,062
Mittelland Kanal (W G)	259	2,016	7,785
Nord–Ostsee Kanal (W G)	109	179	1,641
Wesel–Datten Kanal (W G)	60	983	16,394
Rhein–Herne Kanal (W G)	49	486	9,914
Canal Dunkerque à Valenciennes (F)	173	593	3,425
Canal du Midi (F)	240	17	73
Canal du Nord (F)	95	383	4,031
Canal de St. Quentin (F)	92	190	2,063
Amsterdam–Rijn Kanaal (N)	72	1,747	24,262
Gent–Terneuzen Kanaal (N)	16	368	23,008
Maas–Waalkanaal (N)	13	276	21,255
Albert Kanaal (B)	130	1,573	12,103
Brussel–Rupel Kanaal (B)	32	254	7,947
Rivers			
Rhein (W G)	653	32,691	50,064
Main (W G)	388	1,928	4,971
Mosel (W G)	242	2,331	9,631
Neckar (W G)	203	1,423	7,008
Seine (F)	536	4,724	8,813
Rhin (F)	129	1,903	14,759
Moselle (F)	106	308	2,903
Rijn en Lek (N)	123	3,011	24,484
Waal (N)	85	10,116	119,010
Merwede en Noord (N)	32	3,197	99,911
Schelde (B)	195	1,123	5,759
Meuse (B)	138	484	3,507

NOTES
W G = West Germany, F = France, N = Netherlands, B = Belgium.

Source: Statistical Yearbook, Transport, Communications, Tourism, 1975, Eurostat, 1977, Table 4–1.

proved to be incapable of fulfilment—the political division of Germany having reduced its potential importance as a great force in west–east integration. From the Rhine, itself regularised and canalised to take 2,000-tonne barges, waterways branch off laterally; noteworthy are the Dortmund–Ems Canal, the Neckar which is canalised to Stuttgart and the Lower Mosel which was canalised (completed 1960) to enable larger craft to reach the iron ore fields of Lorraine and to link the latter area with the Ruhr.

The Netherlands possesses a unique system of inland waterways. Altogether she has almost 500 km of navigable rivers and canals, about a quarter navigable by craft of 1,000–3,000 tonnes. The main network, intended to accommodate the largest vessels, is based upon the east–west flowing rivers of the interfluvial zone, the Merwede (Maas), Waal and Lek. Across these, and beyond them, are a series of inter-connecting canals. Two are of special importance, the first is the 25 km Noordzeekanaal, the second the new Amsterdam–Rijn Kanaal, opened in 1952, giving a direct connection from Amsterdam to the Rhine. This latter link is an extremely important goods carrier between the Netherlands and West Germany as Table 37 indicates. Internally, also, the inland waterways of the Netherlands carry a significant proportion (around 40 per cent) of total freight ton kilometres.

Belgium, in addition to the canalised Meuse, Schelde and Sambre rivers, has an extensive canal system. Of the twenty-six different canals, the major ones are the Albert Canal between Antwerp and Liège (opened 1940) and the Rupel Canal between Brussels, Bruges and Zeebrugge. The former is a significant continental waterway (*see* Table 37). In France, the inland waterway network is a long one but by no means as dense as that of the three other continental countries selected. Navigable waterways tend to be concentrated in the northeast. Table 36 shows that in 1975 goods transport by inland waterways in France was less than one-third that by rail, approximately ten per cent of the total. For external trade, inland waterways were more important than either road or rail for trade with West Germany and the Netherlands.

The traditional function of rail transport has been as a carrier over medium to long distances. Rail's advantages (and disadvantages) revolve around its fixed track, which enables very heavy loads of goods to be carried at speed. In this situation, the basic unit tends to be the whole train load rather than individual pieces of rolling stock. For passenger transport, rail's major function is as a provider of speedy inter-urban services and for urban commuter travel. Road transport is usually rail's main competitor, with rail's advantage being that it can achieve higher speeds and provide easier access into the heart of cities. Railways, however, are tied to a fixed track and (for passenger transport), a published service, so that for some trips road's greater flexibility may be the overriding factor determining modal choice.

Table 34 shows some basic features of the rail network in the EEC. The highest network densities are in north-west and central Europe. From the beginning the construction of railways was relatively easy and these were the most important parts of the continent agriculturally, industrially and commercially. In spite of political fragmentation, the adoption of a standard gauge has facilitated interchange across national frontiers for rolling stock can pass unimpeded between member states. Sea gaps, especially the English Channel, have been bridged by ferry services. The presence of a standard gauge prompted through routes in the nineteenth century— these were remarkably similar to the major through routes currently in operation (*see* Fig. 30). In the U K the industrial areas in the main

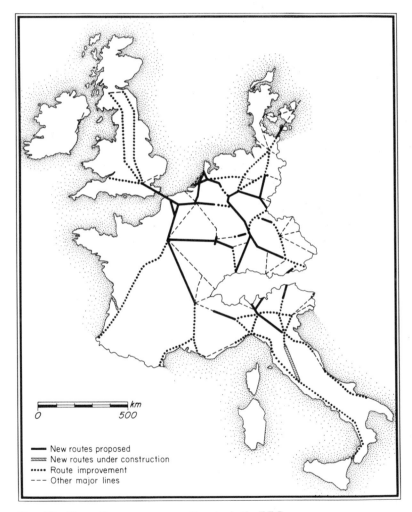

New routes proposed
New routes under construction
Route improvement
Other major lines

FIG. 30.—Trans-European express rail routes in the EEC.

already emerged before railway construction, but in other EEC countries the reverse was true. Industrial development as a consequence tends to be rather more widely dispersed. The economic impact of railways has been forcefully debated, but it is true to say that both in the past and at the present time, railways have played their part in the economic integration of the Community.

In the post-1945 period road transport has spectacularly emerged as the major carrier of persons for a variety of reasons. The private car is the "natural" state of transport and is the only transport mode which permits exclusive flexibility. Ownership levels have progressively increased in all EEC countries (*see* Table 34) and as Fig. 31 indicates, there is a comprehensive motorway network throughout most of the Community. The use of the private car for tourism purposes is especially significant, with many Europeans making the north–south journey in summer. In the UK road carries around 70 per cent of all goods (measured in terms of ton kilometres), although for the four countries shown in Table 36, it is by no means as dominant. Intra-EEC goods movement is now subject to the minimum of documentation and customs delays and this has promoted the trend towards increased goods movement by road.

The emergence of a European motorway network, especially during the 1960s, has been a forceful agent in promoting the flow of goods and persons. The Germans pioneered the way during the 1930s with the construction of *autobahnen*. Initially designed and laid down for military purposes, they have subsequently been adopted as the standard pattern for commercial highways. The post-war economic reconstruction and subsequent advance demanded an efficient road transport network and increasingly road transport has been developed. In France, as Fig. 31 indicates, Paris is the focal point in the *autoroute* system. When completed, the French motorway system will link the capital with all major regional centres. Progress towards an integrated international road system (E Roads) started in 1950 and covers a rather wider grouping of countries than the present Community. Eighteen countries are members of the European Conference of Ministers of Transport (ECMT), whose function is to co-ordinate and promote the integration of inland transport systems.

Finally, a few words should be said about sea routes and air transport in the EEC. For international movement, sea transport is important for the carriage of heavy bulky cargoes, especially non-perishable items such as coal, oil, mineral ores and timber where speedy transit is unnecessary. Most of the waterborne trade has its origin or destination in the manufacturing areas of the Community (*see* Fig. 32). In the case of the UK and Ireland, as intra-EEC trade has increased new cross-Channel ferry routes have grown up to

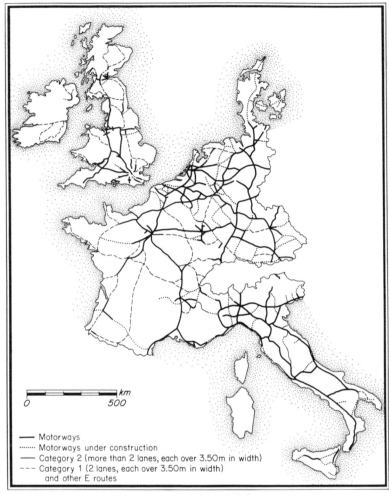

Fig. 31.—E routes and other major roads in the EEC.

accommodate the increased roll-on roll-off, and container cargo trade. In the 1970s there has also been a tremendous increase in the number of visits made by sea by U K residents for tourism purposes. Since the mid-1960s the market shared by British Rail's Sealink services and those of European Ferries has been challenged by other operators, e.g. P. and O., Normandy Ferries, Brittany Ferries and the Olau Line. New operators have developed routes from ports other than the traditional south-eastern ones, e.g. Plymouth, South-

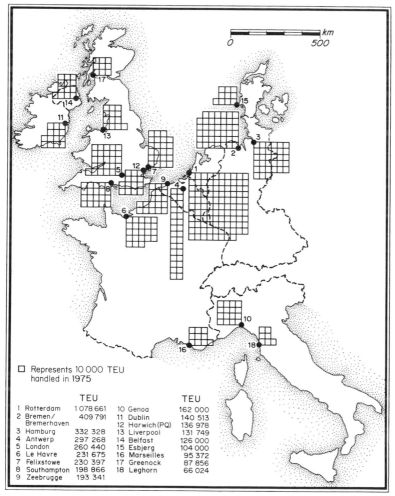

[*Source*: J. H. Bird & E. E. Pollock, "The Future of Seaports in the European
Communities", *Geographical Journal*, Vol. 144, March 1978.
FIG. 32.—Eighteen leading seaports of the E E C by numbers of containers handled,
1975. These seaports handled 88.9 per cent of the total of all containers handled
by E E C seaports with an annual throughput of more than 17,000 T E U
(twenty-foot (long) equivalent (container) units).

ampton, Portsmouth, Felixstowe and Hull. Hovercraft services have
developed and in most cases are able to provide cheaper crossings on
the shortest routes.

Although the E E C is a highly populated and economically advanced area, air travel is by no means as well-developed as in the

United States. Domestic and intra-EEC travelling distances are much shorter than in North America and political fragmentation has until recently hindered air transport development. Nevertheless, especially for those parts separated by water barriers, air travel can be promoted for business and non-business purposes. The spread of integration has prompted an increase in air transport for business use and there would seem to be much potential for air freight services.

Towards a Common Transport Policy

It is set out in Article 3 of the Treaty of Rome that the Community should establish "a common policy in the sphere of transport."[3] As explained above, such a policy was thought desirable in order to enable the free movement of people and goods over the national boundaries of member states. For the purpose of implementing a common transport policy, Article 75 states that the Council of Ministers shall establish:

(a) common rules applicable to international transport to or from the territory of a member state or passing across the territory of one or more member states;
(b) the conditions under which non-resident carriers may operate transport services within a member state;
(c) any other appropriate provisions.[4]

Other more specific requirements follow in Articles 76–84, although the actual policy content was left vague.

The provisions of the Rome Treaty were drawn up in the context of the Community of Six and excluded sea and air transport. Early efforts to align national policies in the late 1960s were directed towards rail, road and inland waterways. The enlargement of the EEC in 1973 meant that all member states were no longer linked by land so various proposals have been made to include sea and air transport in the common transport policy.

Transport policy should be an extremely important aspect of EEC affairs but as Thomson comments, "The development of a common transport policy has proved a slow, difficult business."[5] In 1961, the Commission produced guidelines for a common policy which included the elimination of price discrimination and subsidies, the abolition of frontier taxes and the removal of other obstacles to the establishment of a common market. A basic theme which emerged was that a Community transport policy should strive to create a healthy yet fair competitive situation in transport, backed by a certain degree of official regulation. In effect, the proposal was to base the common transport policy upon a commercial basis. This view was reinforced as late as 1971 when the Commission argued that "transport services should be operated on a free-market basis."[6] The problem of road and rail for goods transport was referred to in this report and it was argued that some intervention was needed in order to regulate competition between these modes. For example, rail companies, who maintain and provide their own infrastructure, might stand at a disadvantage for attracting freight when compared to road hauliers who use a road network not owned by them. A second basic principle to emerge in the late 1960s was the need to establish a common criterion on which to base investment decisions. This again requires a common system for each transport mode to be agreed by member states. As with the more general direction of transport policy, progress has been slow and the procedure of consultation unsatisfactory.

At an operational level, there is a common policy in the field of licensing and quotas for road transport, designed to adhere to the general principles referred to in the last paragraph. The aim of this system is to regulate cross-frontier flows and also restrict competition between hauliers in the various member states. Prior to 1968 a system of bilateral agreements operated, but a regulation of 1968 put into effect a system of E E C licenses enabling holders to make any number of journeys between any or all of the member states. The regulation established a quota of 1,200 annual permits, covering about 15 per cent of cross-frontier traffic. These licences were divided as follows: West Germany 286, France 286, the Netherlands 240, Italy 194, Belgium 161 and Luxembourg 33. It was planned that the number of Community permits should gradually increase and eventually completely replace the bilateral licences. In 1974 the Commission proposed that the total of Community licences should rise to 1,970—the U K received 227, considerably less than had been hoped for.

A second controversial issue as far as the U K is concerned has been the Community's attempts to harmonise the weight and dimensions of road vehicles. In May 1972 the Council of Ministers agreed that goods vehicles should have a maximum unladen weight of 40 metric tonnes and an 11 metric tonne axle limit as from the 1st January 1980. The U K, which applies 32 and 10 tonne limits respectively, has opposed the proposal on the grounds of the damage to the roads and to the environment that heavier lorries would cause. There has also been vociferous opposition from residents' groups in certain villages close to ports. An increase in allowable national weight limits of heavy goods vehicles now seems likely following the recommendations of the Armitage Enquiry, "Man, Lorries and the Environment" published in 1981. France, however, is unwilling to allow a further reduction in maximum axle weight as its motor industry currently produces vehicles with axle weights in excess of the new maximum. Also in road transport, the UK has been extremely reluctant to order that goods vehicles must be fitted with a tachograph in order to comply with EEC regulations on drivers' hours.

There has been very little progress towards a common transport policy for other inland modes of transport. Most developments have been of a general nature, often involving technical and commercial co-operation. In 1972 the European Parliament passed a resolution urging that there should be a seaport policy for the Community. As for other modes, the policy was to be firmly based upon free competition, with port charges being based upon costs. It was also intended that subsidies, particularly on new port investment projects, should be abolished. Bird and Pollock examined the case for a Common Seaports Policy and went as far as to suggest that such a policy could be financially linked with the EEC's regional policy.[7] In air transport there have also been proposals for a common policy. The proposed principles include a restructuring of the European aviation industry, an "airworthiness code", standardisation of aircraft equipment and common rules for the financial support of airline services in member states. As in other fields of transport policy, there has been very little positive action towards an integrated policy.

It would seem, therefore, that there has been a distinct lack of progress towards a common transport policy in the EEC. The main reason is undoubtedly the one which has held back other common policies—internal political considerations. Thomson talks of the conflict of transport philosophies, i.e. the conflict between regarding transport as a commercial service on the one hand and as a social service on the other hand.[8] He maintains that this conflict is present at both national and international level in the EEC. Additionally, he adds that "the strongly commercial philosophy was at odds with the growing concern for the environment, the quality of life and (after 1973) the conservation of energy. It was also at odds with the regional and social needs of the Community."[9] A similar conclusion is made by Gwilliam and Mackie. They agree that the EEC Commission is anxious to increase the momentum given to transport policy but comment, "What can safely be deduced from recent history is that there is many a slip between Commission cup and Council lip."[10] This tale is a most familiar one—in the case of transport, while it is agreed that a common policy is desirable, it is also true that some of the issues suggested for incorporation into such a policy will bring rather dubious benefits to member states.

NOTES
    1. *See* Robinson, H. and Bamford, C. G., *Geography of Transport*, Macdonald & Evans, 1978, Chapter III.

2. Bayliss, B. T., *European Transport*, Kenneth Mason Publications, 1965, p. 61.

3. *Treaty establishing the European Economic Community*, Cmnd. 4864, HMSO, 1972, p. 3.

4. *Ibid.*, p. 29.

5. Thomson, J. M., "Towards a European transport strategy", in Lee, R. and Ogden, P. E., eds, *Economy and Society in the EEC*, Saxon House, 1976, p. 278.

6. Commission of the European Communities, *Development of the Common Transport Policy*, 1971.

7. Bird, J. H. and Pollock, E. E., "The Future of Seaports in the European Communities", *Geographical Journal*, Vol. 144, March 1978, pp. 23–41.

8. Thomson, J. M., *op. cit.*, p. 277.

9. *Ibid.*, p. 279.

10. Gwilliam, K. M. and Mackie, P. J., *Economics and Transport Policy*, Allen & Unwin, 1975, p. 365.

Chapter IX

Migrations of People

Articles 48–73 of the Treaty of Rome

ARTICLES 48–73 of the Treaty provide for the Free Movement of Persons, Services and Capital. In the context of this chapter, however, it is Articles 48–51 concerning labour that really matter. These articles provide for the free movement of workers between member states (with the exception of those in the national public services). The Commission has sought to encourage such movement and there has been a remarkable degree of mobility of workers, although not all the immigrants into the EEC countries have come as a result of the Treaty.

It will be recalled that, during the inter-war period, with the growth of economic nationalism there had been restrictions on the movements of capital and labour between the countries of Europe. But there had, of course, been some politically motivated movements; for example, the break-up of both the Austro-Hungarian and Turkish Empires at the end of the First World War led to considerable population adjustments, and the persecution of Jews in Poland and Germany in the 1920s and 1930s resulted in substantial numbers seeking asylum elsewhere. Kosinski estimated that some 7.7m people were involved in intra-European demographic migrations associated with the First World War.[1] After these post-war adjustments, however, movements slackened except where expulsion occurred (as in the case of the Jews), or where people voluntarily returned to the homeland (as in the case of Germans who left Alsace-Lorraine and parts of Poland).

Freedom of Movement and Establishment

Articles 48–66 of the Treaty set out the principles for achieving the freedom for workers from the member countries to obtain employment anywhere in the Community, and the freedom of establishment for undertakings including subsidiaries, branches and agencies. The latter also extends to professional people, for example doctors and dentists, and the right to supply services such as insurance and banking, and wholesale and retail distribution. Freedom of establishment includes not only the right to engage in self-employed occupations, but also to set up and manage companies and other forms of business undertakings, subject to the national laws of the country in which the establishment is being effected.[2]

The first step taken towards making complete mobility of labour possible within the E E C was the adoption, on the 16th August 1961, of Regulation 15; it was applicable for two years only and included protection for indigenous workers in national labour markets during that period. But three and a half years later, on the 7th February 1964, Regulation 38 superseded Regulation 15 and one of its most important features was that it almost completely abolished priority for nationals in the labour markets of the Community (at that time the Six), introducing a rather complicated system for the notification of vacancies throughout member states through the intermediary of the European Co-ordination Office. However, in 1968, free movement of workers within the meaning of Articles 48 and 49 was attained by Regulation 1612 and in the first part of 1969 was implemented by the member states.

Excepting employment in public service, Regulation 1612 made it possible for the nationals of all E E C countries to enter another member country to seek work, or to take up a job, without a work permit and were entitled to the same treatment as nationals in every material respect and were given preference over nationals from non-member countries. For example, they had employment rights on the same terms as a member country's nationals in respect of pay, working conditions, tax treatment and social security benefits, including access to housing, and they were also granted the right to join a trade union and to hold office in it. A residence permit is still required for a worker, as well as for his dependants to live with him in the host country; only if a worker has reached retirement age or is permanently incapacitated, and has the stipulated length of residence, can he settle permanently in another country of the Community.

Articles 52–66 are concerned with the Right of Establishment and Services. The object of these articles is to ensure, so far as is possible, that there is freedom of establishment and freedom to provide services throughout the Community for companies and firms and for professional people such as doctors, architects, bankers, lawyers, etc. Much progress has, in fact, been made on the freedom of establishment with the removal of restrictions on nationals of other member countries from a number of professional, industrial and commercial activities, although there have been some difficulties and problems arising from the lack of mutual recognition of professional qualifications, e.g. the recognition of degrees, diplomas, certificates and other qualifications, and the co-ordination of conditions for engaging in specific occupations. Numerous directives based on Articles 52–66 of the Treaty are now in force, although they relate more especially to self-employed activities in commerce and manufacturing, craft industries and agriculture.

Progress in the mutual recognition of professional qualifications has been slower but this has tended to be inevitable since considerable difficulties have arisen with regard to the co-ordination of laws, regulations and administrative practices and the mutual recognition of qualifications. As a result of the enlargement of the EEC to ten members, and the possibilities of further enlargement, the Commission is continuing to study co-ordination of arrangements in member states.

The Commission and member states appear determined to achieve the objectives of Articles 52–66 and, while much progress has been made, the regulations enforcing freedom of establishment and the provision of services deal with the problem sector by sector and the task remains to be completed, although the Council has approved detailed programmes for the issue of directives.

Migration in Post-War Europe

The Second World War led to a dislocation of population but the end of the war witnessed the re-settlement of very large numbers of displaced persons. Here we are not so much concerned with the movements of these two groups of people as with the growth of international labour migration. Before looking at the numbers and movements of foreign workers, it will be useful to examine the reasons for this massive migration. There has, of course, been a long tradition of European nationals leaving their mother countries to seek work elsewhere in the Continent where better economic and social conditions were to be had: on the whole, however, the volume of such migrations was small. Since 1945, as Salt has commented, "the industrial countries of continental Europe, in their search for economic growth, have taken advantage of the long-established tendency for some migrants to better themselves by seeking job opportunities in other lands."[3] At first the flow was fairly small but as increasing prosperity developed amongst the countries of North-West Europe their doors were thrown open to migrant workers from their poorer neighbours; the flow of workers gradually accelerated and the gross annual movement of foreign workers was in the early 1970s, until late 1973, averaging between 2m and 3m per annum.

One important reason for the influx of "foreign" labour into North-West Europe has been the stabilisation of the populations in the north-west during recent decades and there are few signs that the indigenous populations will increase. As a consequence, the native labour force has scarcely grown at all; indeed, during the decade

1960–70 the European labour force as a whole expanded at merely 0.6 per cent per annum; some countries, such as the U K and West Germany had increases of an even lower order, 0.3 and 0.4 per cent respectively, and there were others, e.g. Austria and East Germany, which actually suffered a decline. Turkey alone (hardly a "European" country), with a 1.9 per cent growth in its labour force, showed a high growth rate. Since the indigenous labour forces of the countries of the Six failed to keep pace with their economic growth they had perforce to look elsewhere for additional workers and these were to be found in the Mediterranean countries (i.e. Portugal, Spain, Yugoslavia, Greece and Turkey) with their large numbers of unemployed and their much slower rates of economic growth. Thus, to quote Salt, "What could be more natural than for the countries of labour shortage to co-operate with those of labour surplus in bringing about greater equilibrium in the European labour market?"[4] (*See* Fig. 33.)

In many cases labour shortages have been of an occupational kind as a result of the indigenous population refusing, or being unwilling, to accept low-paid, monotonous and repetitious, or dirty jobs. For example, one can think of the large numbers of immigrant Pakistanis in the U K who became bus conductors, of West Indians who found

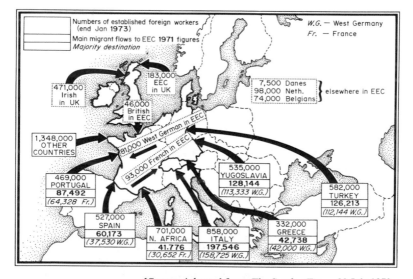

[*Source*: Adapted from *The Sunday Times*, 22 July 1973.
Fig. 33.—Origins of migrant workers to E E C up to 1973. (Bold figures refer to numbers of established foreign workers at end of January 1973; italic figures indicate main migrant flows to E E C for 1971 (majority destinations in brackets).)

jobs in the waste disposal service, or of black girls who became
hospital helpers and nurses. Again, in Belgium during the decade
after the war large numbers of immigrant Poles found work in the
coal-mining industry. Indeed, most of the countries of North-West
Europe which were enjoying economic expansion took advantage of
the abundant supply of cheap, low-skilled labour for the more menial
and unpleasant jobs. It must be recognised that these foreign immigrants often performed useful, even valuable, jobs and without their
help many essential service activities would have suffered acute
under-manning and been severely strained.

During the 1950s most of the immigrant workers were employed
in labouring jobs in agriculture, mining, construction and in the more
unpleasant and lower-paid service activities. During the 1960s there
was a perceptible change with agriculture, mining and services attracting fewer immigrant workers as larger and larger numbers entered the manufacturing industries; for example, Mayer drew attention to the fact that in Switzerland the number of foreign workers in
factories increased from 10 per cent in 1952 to 35 per cent in 1963,[5]
while in West Germany the proportion of foreign workers in the
metal industries increased from 25.6 per cent in 1960 to 35.7 per cent
in 1973. Gradually over the past quarter of a century there has been
an ever-growing penetration of foreign workers into all branches of
the economy.

The recent economic recession, largely following the energy crisis
with its concomitant growth in unemployment and inflation, together
with the constraints placed upon further immigration by such countries as the UK, France and West Germany, has led to a reduced
flow of immigrants. Nevertheless, as Salt has said, "it is undoubtedly
true that the migrants have become such an integral part of economic
growth in North-West Europe that their long term presence seems
assured."[6]

The Sources and Volume of Labour Supply

It would seem that about 6m foreign workers were employed in
Europe by the end of 1973, although estimates vary and are unreli-
able. As Table 38 shows, West Germany and France held dominating
positions as immigration countries, followed by Switzerland, Sweden
and Belgium (*see* also Fig. 34).

The dependence on foreign labour is more clearly brought out when
one considers the proportions of the total labour force accounted for
by alien workers: in the cases of Switzerland and Luxembourg almost
one-third of the total working population is made up of foreigners,
with West Germany and France depending substantially upon them
and even Belgium and Sweden needing appreciable numbers. Some-

TABLE 38

Foreign workers employed at the end of 1973

	Number ('000s)	Percentage of total labour force
West Germany	2,500	12
France	2,300	10
Switzerland	600	30
Sweden	220	6
Belgium	200	7
Netherlands	80	2
Luxembourg	33	30
Italy	33	0.3

what surprisingly Italy, traditionally an exporter of labour, absorbed 33,000 immigrant workers.

Notwithstanding the recessionary trend which has set in since the oil crisis of 1973–74, the numbers of foreign workers has continued to increase in most of the E E C countries and Table 39 gives the numbers of residents of foreign origin in some of the E E C countries.

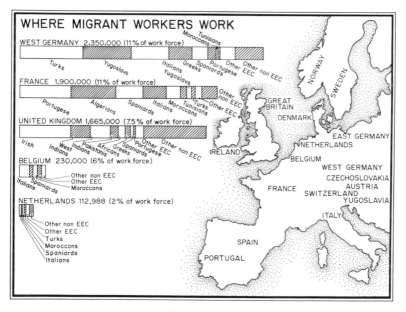

[*Source*: Adapted from *The Observer*, 2 May, 1976.
FIG. 34.—Destination and composition of migrant labour force, 1974.

TABLE 39

Residents of foreign origin, 1976

West Germany	3,925,400
France	3,422,000
UK	2,983,140
Switzerland	933,000

Although there is no precise figure of the expatriates earning some kind of living in the E E C, for some immigrant workers have returned home and some are illegal immigrants, it seems likely, according to the best consensus estimate that there is something of the order of 11m immigrant workers, including their dependants. Although perhaps 2m represent migrants between the E E C member countries, the vast majority of migrants come from North Africa, Turkey, Yugoslavia, Greece, Portugal and Spain but these form a non-union, cheap and easily cast-off labour force.

The Changing Flows of Migrants

The volume and geographical pattern of migration has markedly changed in the post-war period. During the war years the economies of many countries had been geared to the prosecution of the war and when, finally, hostilities ceased, large areas lay ruinous and exhausted and consumer goods were in very short supply. There was a need for industrial re-orientation and large-scale reconstruction. Once raw materials became available again, those countries such as Switzerland and Sweden, which had not been directly involved in the conflict and whose economies remained undamaged, attempted to meet some of the demand for the much needed goods and were prepared to accept immigrant labour in order to meet this demand. In 1946 Switzerland took in 50,000 foreign workers; this was the beginning of a continually growing number of alien workers which increased to nearly three-quarters of a million by 1964. Sweden accepted some 10,000 workers a year between 1946 and 1950, mainly Finns at first, but during the next twenty years the rate of immigration accelerated and by 1973 Sweden had 250,000 foreign workers. As normal industrial production recovered in the UK, France and Belgium, they began to experience shortages of labour and in the 1950s were accepting foreign workers at the rate of about 40,000 per annum respectively. At this time Italy supplied most of the migrant workers, who were especially welcomed in France and Switzerland. West Germany in these early post-war years was still busily reconstructing its industry after the immediate post-war pastoralisation policy and, moreover, was much concerned with resettling 8.5m refugees from East

Germany. There was, too, high unemployment in West Germany—
9 per cent in 1951—hence there was no need to import foreign
workers; it was not until the economic miracle got under way that
West Germany really felt the need to open its doors to foreigners.
Until the late 1950s labour migration remained fairly limited with
Italy providing rather more than half the total supply.

From about 1958 the situation changed. Growing economic prosperity among the industrial countries of north-west Europe, but
more especially that in West Germany, caused an augmented flow of
foreign workers. Whereas France and Switzerland had been the
principal host countries, in 1960 West Germany had become a major
importer of foreign labour, receiving a quarter of a million migrants
in that year. West Germany's miraculous economic recovery caused
her to become the focus of attraction for migrant workers, the
Gastarbeiter ("guest workers") as the Germans termed them. At first
the Italians provided the main flow and by 1960 more Italians were
going to West Germany than to France. The Italian source, however,
began to dry up as, in the early 1960s, the Italian economy began to
boom. Workers from further afield—Spain and Greece more especially—now began to seek work in the Federal Republic. In the late
1960s substantial flows of migrants from Yugoslavia and Turkey in
particular, but large numbers from Spain, Portugal and Greece also,
were going to West Germany. By 1970 labour migration to France
was chiefly from North Africa, Portugal and Spain. To sum up, it
will be clear that the chief sources of migrant labour by the early
1970s were the essentially rural countries of southern Europe and
North Africa where poverty and unemployment was rife and could
be relieved only by moving to the industrialised countries of the
north.

Notwithstanding the freedom of movement allowed to the nationals of EEC member countries, there have been relatively few migrants: up to 1973 the estimated figure was 1.75m. It is clear that
movements between EEC member states were of little consequence
when compared with the substantial flows from the poorer Mediterranean countries. One of the main reasons for the relatively restricted
movement between the member states of the EEC was that all the
member countries in the 1960s were experiencing rapid economic
growth and improving standards of living, hence there was little
encouragement for Community members to migrate.

The Imposition of Restrictions

Although among the EEC member countries there is freedom of
movement for workers, the onset of recessionary conditions following the oil crisis in the latter part of 1973 and the growth in

unemployment amongst the industrial countries of North-West Europe resulted in a curtailment of immigrant foreign workers. From 1974 a variety of measures were taken to check the immigrant flows from the Mediterranean countries, although the degree of restriction that was introduced varied between one country and another. To quote Salt:

> Luxembourg alone took no special restrictive measures. In contrast, West Germany imposed a ban on recruitment in November 1973, France in July 1974, and Belgium in August 1974. Other measures were also taken. In April 1975 West Germany decided to try to limit the size of the migrant labour concentration in any area to 12 per cent of that area's total labour force. France adopted a policy of no longer allowing illegal immigrants to regularize their positions; those caught by the authorities would be deported. Other countries tightened up their existing legislation; the Swiss government resolved in August 1974 to stabilize its immigrant population numbers by the end of the decade; the Netherlands, from 1974, has interpreted its immigration rules more strictly; in Denmark the general ban on immigration of 1970 had been eased in the summer of 1973 but was re-imposed the following November.[7]

The UK, too, imposed a clampdown on immigration.

These various measures had the effect of cutting back quite drastically the number of newly-entering foreign workers, but this did not stem immigration altogether; for example, in France the number of foreign workers entering the country in 1974 was reduced to half that for the previous year but 53,000 still came in and by 1976 the number of male labour immigrants had dropped to 20,000, while the number of Yugoslavs moving to North-West Europe fell by 90 per cent between 1973 and 1974. While the numbers of immigrant workers were severely curbed in all the industrial countries, there has been no real evidence of a great exodus of migrants returning back to their homelands; without doubt some have gone back home but the volume is hard to quantify. Unemployment amongst the foreign workers has grown as a result of the economic difficulties but since they qualify for unemployment benefit it seems likely that they are better off financially than they would have been by returning home where the prospects of employment were uncertain.

As recession hit the EEC economy in the mid-1970s, a point was reached where there became a net outflow of migrant workers. As Ogden notes, "In the receiving countries, the mid-1970s saw a halt of new arrivals, the return home of some and then latterly, a relaxation of some family movements (negative net balances in West Germany in 1974, 1975 and 1976 and then positive balances in 1977, 1978 and 1979). In France net migration has stood at nil in every year since 1974. In the sending countries (Italy and Greece, for example), out-migration gradually gave way to inward movement as migrants returned home. Yet it must be emphasised that all the receiving countries are faced with the challenge of a large permanent foreign population, the result of many "temporary" migrants becoming permanent, despite original intentions and of a high rate of natural increase in some foreign groups."[8]

The southern European enlargement of the Community presents a difficult problem for its policy of allowing the internal free movement of workers. Recognising this, the terms of accession agreed with Greece made provision for a seven-year transitional period before which full labour mobility could take place and similar terms have been agreed in principle for the integration of Portuguese and Spanish workers (see Chapter X for an analysis of this and other issues). The success of this policy will depend upon many factors, not least the performance of the EEC economy over the 1980s and the unemployment rates prevalent in member states. As full members of the Community, Greece, Portugal and Spain will continue to have living standards and wages considerably below those of West Germany, France, Denmark and the Benelux countries and natural economic forces would point to a substantial flow of migrant workers. It remains to be seen whether or not the attraction member states are prepared to stick to the terms previously agreed for the smooth absorption of such workers.

Social Problems

While freedom to work wherever one wants has become one of the great ideals of the EEC, throwing open the Community's doors to migrant workers from the poorer and much less industrialised countries of southern Europe was a very different matter. Immigrant labour assuredly was badly needed but the early in-comers were, as has already been pointed out, required for the more menial jobs although, in due course, many of the migrant workers sought and found better jobs in industry. The *laissez-faire* attitude towards immigration in the 1960s and early 1970s led to massive flows of workers into, especially, West Germany and France. The recession since the energy crisis of late 1973 brought a halt to this inflow but even before the onset of the economic recession governments were beginning to be embarrassed by the sizes of their immigrant communities and the problems they were likely to create. For example, racial intolerance was already beginning to make itself felt in some countries, more especially in the U K, France and West Germany, and in the U K the Government was constrained to pass laws against anti-racialism. The economic planners in West Germany, in 1973, estimated that by 1980 one in every six workers would be of foreign origin, but for the Government of the Federal Republic to endorse such an immigration policy seemed politically unthinkable. Thus, as Ogden has commented: "Incentives for migrants to leave have been introduced in West Germany, which has always seen foreign labour in terms of the notion *Konjuncturpuffer*: import when needed in a boom, re-export during a recession."[9] Again, in France, with its 3.4m official immigrants and half a million illegal immigrants (in 1973), a political issue was brewing. So, in July 1974 France stopped all immigration from outside the E E C and introduced further measures in October 1977, including financial inducements to encourage migrants to return home. In the Netherlands, too, which had already absorbed large numbers of Indonesians, the Government was worried that some 250,000 disaffected British Commonwealth immigrants might wish to move across into the Netherlands.

Anxiety about social tensions and problems of housing and accommodating migrant workers were beginning to manifest themselves. It should be remembered that in the labour migration process the first migrants were mostly young, single men seeking to escape from the poverty and unemployment of their homelands and hoping to find economic and social betterment in the prospering Community countries. Many of these workers were mobile, moving from job to job in an attempt to improve their lot and were short-term migrants. In the final stage, a migrant may become a more permanent resident in the host country and may send for his wife and family to join him. Bohning, in fact, has suggested that there is a changing pattern of emigration and discerns four stages as migrants' attitudes change and mature.[10]

One of the most serious social problems relates to the living conditions of the migrant workers. Attitudes towards housing vary considerably within the host countries: in West Germany many of the single immigrant workers are accommodated in hostels provided by the employers and, while the living conditions are quite good, segregation means the foreign workers are socially and culturally isolated; in the Netherlands immigrant workers, unless they are accompanied by their families, cannot rent publicly-owned housing and so are practically compelled to seek accommodation in the private sector, usually in inner city centres, for which they commonly have to pay high rents for inferior housing; while in France some workers dwell in overcrowded hostels and others—perhaps 100,000 or more—live in *bidonvilles* or shanty towns on the outskirts of the industrial towns.

It must be admitted that large numbers of the migrant workers are prepared to put up with sub-standard living conditions since their main concern is to earn money either to send back home to their families or to make life easier for them when they finally return home.

There are other serious social problems, especially where there are immigrant families with young children; as Ogden has said: "Particular difficulties have surrounded educational provision for migrants' children who by definition represent a wide range of linguistic and cultural origins."[11]

About one in ten workers from the Mediterranean countries earn their livelihood in the industrialised countries of north-west Europe but, as *The Sunday Times* survey (22nd July 1973) commented:

> The £1,000m a year these ambitious, hard-working, occasionally skilled migrants send home is a vital contribution to their underdeveloped home economies. Another £1,000m or more is even left by the migrants on deposit in Europe's banks. It could be vital capital for industrial investment but the migrants prefer to use it to enhance their own life in Europe. Yugoslavia has already begun to question the value of letting so many of its best workers—30 per cent of its emigrants are skilled—go off to produce for the rich men of Western Europe. Admittedly the remittances are badly needed but this flow of cash depends upon the migrants' keeping their links with home, and in the long term these could fade.

Social Policy and the Migration of People

There are certain aspects of EEC social policy that apply to the migration of people. Early guidelines were laid down through the work of the European Coal and Steel Community, with resettlement grants being given to workers obliged to move from areas of employment contraction. These heavy industries required an assured labour force, so it was thought desirable to promote the geographical mobility of workers. Such financial help has been a part of a much wider programme to accommodate the forces of change in these two important industries.

On a wider basis, the European Social Fund has provided some degree of help for migrant workers. Provision for a Social Fund was laid down in Article 123 of the Treaty of Rome, where it was stated that one of its objectives was to promote the geographical mobility of workers. Between 1960 and 1971, which marked the end of the first phase of the Fund's activities, over 700,000 workers received resettlement grants from the Fund. Under its rules, half the cost of this help was re-imbursed to member governments. Since 1972, the Social Fund has taken on a dynamic function—industrial change can now be anticipated and finance made available before workers actually become redundant. The reformed Fund is able to help workers in both regions of structural unemployment and in regions which could lose jobs as a result of continued integration. It is, as noted later (Chapter XII) an integral element of regional policies in the Community.

The Social Fund is directly financed out of the EEC Budget and, as expected, the poorer members have been the main beneficiaries. In 1974 a total of 164m u.a. was allocated towards helping the migration of workers within the Community. Italy received 65m u.a. and the UK 45m u.a. of this total. In addition, about 2m persons a year benefit from EEC regulations on social security for migrant workers. The aim of this aspect of social policy is to provide the freedom of movement for workers by co-ordinating social security systems in member states so that migrant workers are entitled to receive benefit irrespective of place of work in the Community.

In the late 1970s, the over-all size of the Social Fund increased steadily and by 1979 had reached just over 4 per cent of all payments to member states from the EEC Budget. Increased sums have been made available to train and assist migrant workers, but the over-all size and importance of the Fund goes nowhere near to meeting the demands of the governments of those member states with migrant worker problems. Of the Ten, West Germany and France are acutely aware of the social problems referred to earlier.[12] Given that freedom of movement of workers remains an essential part of the EEC's structure, there must be a very strong case for more resources to be devoted to this important aspect of the social affairs of the Community.

NOTES

1. Kosinski, L., *The Population of Europe*, Longmans, 1970.

2. Midland Bank Ltd., *Factual Guide to the Common Market*, November 1971.

3. Salt, J., "International Labour Migration: The Geographical Pattern of Demand", in *Migration in Post-War Europe*, ed. Salt, J., and Clout, H., Oxford University Press, 1976, p. 80.

4. *Ibid.*, p. 83.

5. Mayer, K. B., "Post-war migration to Switzerland," *International Migration*, 1965, 3, pp. 122–37.

6. Salt, J., *op. cit.*, p. 123.

7. Salt, J., Postscript, p. 220 in *Migration in Post-War Europe*, *op. cit.*

8. Ogden, P. E., "France adapts to immigration with difficulty", *Geographical Magazine*, June 1982, p. 319.

9. Ogden, P. E., "Smaller families in the Nine", *Geographical Magazine*, February 1979, pp. 321–2.

10. Bohning, W. R., *The Migration of Workers in the United Kingdom and the European Community*, Oxford University Press, 1972.

11. Ogden, P. E., "Smaller families in the Nine", *Geographical Magazine*, February 1979, pp. 321–2.

12. Ogden, P. E., "France adapts to immigration with difficulty", *Geographical Magazine*, June 1982, p. 319.

Chapter X

Aspects of the Geographical Enlargement and Future Functional Form of the EEC

As set out in the Treaty of Rome, the European Economic Community remains an unfinished structure. Functionally, the Community is best described as a customs union, to which have been added common policies of vastly differing weight and importance. The various aspects of its economic geography as discussed in Chapters III to IX do not therefore receive equivalent attention when viewed in terms of the current state of economic integration. In some areas there is much potential for co-ordinated action, while in others, decisions seem best left to individual member states.

Further integration can take place in a variety of ways. First, as envisaged by the Treaty of Rome, there is obvious scope for the development and extension of common policies in order to complete the whole. Equally, also provided for in the Treaty, the Community of Ten can be geographically extended and further links made with third parties. Finally, as implied by the Treaty of Rome, integration may be stepped up and widened through the acceptance of measures designed to ultimately create an economic union. Integration is a dynamic process and in the EEC at the present time, progress is being made in each of these ways. The future economic geography of the Community is inextricably dependent upon their combined outcome.

Twenty Years on from the Treaty of Rome

The first task of the EEC was to break down barriers which prevented the free movement of goods and people. As analysed in Chapters III and IX, the customs union between the Six was completed on the 1st July 1968 and for the enlarged Community of Nine on the 1st July 1977. Consequently, tariff-free trade exists between member states and there is a common external tariff on imports from non-member countries. The completion and subsequent success of the customs union, has been the EEC's most spectacular achievement (*see* Chapter III). There are, however, significant non-tariff barriers to trade; as Swann clearly illustrates, these can prevent and distort intra-Community trade.[1] For example, the taxation systems of member states are not yet fully harmonised and technical standards differ from country to country. It is therefore necessary to retain customs officers at frontiers and, in both the above cases, a great many detailed negotiations are required before the ultimate goal of a fully united common market can be reached. The free movement of labour was completed at the same time as the trade aspects of the customs union, although some restriction on the freedom to supply professional services still exists. For the free movement of capital, a completely free capital market does not yet exist—as with trade, there are significant national restrictions and taxation problems which inhibit the free flow between member states. In the future, work will continue in order to remove these remaining barriers.

The best developed of the Community's common policies is of course the Common Agricultural Policy (see Chapter IV). It has allowed the free movement of agricultural products between member states and in general, provided necessary support for Community agriculture. In a world where many still go short of food, it has guaranteed stable supplies. CAP has its critics—the cost of its positive achievements has to be met in terms of high consumer prices and over-production, so in the future the slow process of structural reform must continue. National interests are still plainly apparent in the field of agriculture and fisheries, but if progress is to be made, they must be replaced by much more of a Community spirit. This last comment must inevitably be made over the future development of other common policies, notably in the field of Regional Policy and Social Policy. Along with CAP, both can and must play an increasing role in the better geographical distribution of Community resources. The geographical enlargement of the EEC and movement towards economic union (see below) will give added weight to these areas of common policy.

Progress towards a common transport policy (Chapter VIII) and a common energy policy (Chapter V) has been even slower and the results more limited. It is agreed by member states that both should be an important part of Community affairs, although they suffer from being areas where national policies currently take an overriding precedence. Perhaps in the future, there may be more integration in these areas. Industrial policy is the least developed aspect of EEC affairs. The Commission constantly exercises its powers to prevent restrictive practices such as market-sharing and the operation of cartel agreements. It has also put forward proposals to help industries like aircraft manufacture, shipbuilding and textiles which face strong competition on international markets. Scientific and technological research has been promoted, but once again it is extremely difficult to reconcile the contrasting national interests of member states.

The Community has met considerable success in its economic relations with the rest of the world. As the world's largest trading unit, it has come to play a decisive role in international negotiations. In particular, the Lomé Agreement of 1976 (*see* Chapter I I I) and the Community's scheme of generalised preferences for all less developed economies have attracted much attention. Along with its various bi-lateral agreements with developing and developed economies, the EEC has lived up to its stated aim of trade promotion with the rest of the world. The negotiations have not always been easy, but the Community has emerged as a powerful force in world economic affairs.

The Six, and more recently the Nine, have therefore made substantial progress towards economic integration. As the EEC stands, twenty years or so on from the Treaty of Rome, it is nevertheless an unfinished structure. The startling rise in oil prices, the reality of widespread unemployment and, for the first time in 1975, a negative rate of economic growth all served to highlight the imperfect nature of the Community's unity.

From Nine to Twelve—the Economic Geography of Enlargement

Membership of the EEC at its outset, as discussed in Chapter I I, was open to all countries of Western Europe. Article 237 of the Treaty of Rome left the door open for the accession of new members, providing there was unanimous agreement by the Council of Ministers, and Article 238 made provision for a country to become an Associate Member of the Community. The attempts of the United Kingdom to join the EEC have been well analysed by Northedge.[2] About the same time as the UK's application in 1961, the Republic of Ireland, Denmark and Norway also gave notice they too wished to become full members. Greece was the first country to become an associate member in late 1962, with Turkey signing a similar agreement in the following year. Association requests were also received from Sweden, Switzerland, Austria and Portugal.

The UK's entry negotiations were finally concluded in mid-1972, following a series of lengthy discussions between the Heath government and the Community. As with the Republic of Ireland, Denmark and Norway, a five-year transitional period for membership was agreed, although in the case of the UK there were special additional concessions agreed. Following a national referendum, Norway withdrew her request for membership leaving an enlarged Community of Nine from the beginning of 1973.

The 1973 enlargement has posed many problems for the EEC as previous chapters have indicated. The UK has had to bear a considerable financial burden, not least due to the present stranglehold of the CAP in the Community's budget. As major agricultural producers, Denmark and the Republic of Ireland have not had to face this membership problem. The trade effects of integration, outlined in Chapter III, are also pertinent, with the UK being in a rather different position to the other 1973 accessionaries. Geographically, the distribution of funds and resources remain a key issue still unresolved in spite of the European Regional Development Fund. Finally, important administrative problems remain, which are not helped by conflicts in areas of national policy that are not fully integrated with those of the Community. Indeed, some would argue that further geographical enlargement can only accentuate and aggravate existing problems in the integration process.[3]

Even so, the 1973 enlargement gave encouragement to other potential members, notably the Mediterranean countries of Greece, Portugal and Spain, who all celebrated their return to democracy by making formal membership applications between 1975 and 1977. In May 1979 negotiations for Greece's accession were concluded, with full membership commencing on the 1st January 1981.[4] Negotiations between the EEC and the other two applicants are well advanced. The Commission have approved the entry of Portugal and made certain recommendations about the short-term restructuring of her economy. Spain's request is less advanced and there would appear to be more complications than in the case of Portugal. Spain hopes to become a member of the EEC at the beginning of 1984 though some existing members believe this is optimistic. It is no secret that powerful farming sectors in France and Italy favour a later date so as to postpone the impact of Spanish competition in wine and other agricultural products. Additionally, entry negotiations have not been helped by internal political problems in Spain and tensions over her external foreign policy. From the Community's point of view, it would seem desirable to admit Portugal and Spain at the same time, probably in 1985.

The southern enlargement of the EEC poses many issues and raises further problems. As Osborn notes:

> To list their names is almost to spell out the common problems. They are southern, poor, largely agrarian, and lacking in democratic traditions. Those may be the very reasons they should be welcomed with open arms into the Community, but to do so suggests a generosity of imagination and heart of which the Nine has not yet provided much evidence.[5]

Certainly the basic economic and cultural character of the EEC will change and hardened political positions will have to bend for the

Mediterranean economies to feel part of the Twelve. Everling leaves no doubt about these questions:

> Discussions about the second enlargement of the Community by the entry of Greece, Portugal and Spain are overshadowed by sorrowful concern about the future viability of the Europe of Twelve. The question, whether the aims of European integration can be realised under the new conditions, is at the centre of all considerations on Europe's future.[6]

There are five problems of enlargement common to Greece, Portugal and Spain. First, each has living standards below the EEC average. In 1978, the GDP per head for these Mediterranean economies was, in $ US, Spain 3,100, Greece 2,800, Portugal 1,700 compared with an EEC average of 5,700.[7] Spain and Greece have living standards more comparable with that of the Republic of Ireland ($ US 2,900) the poorest member of the Nine, but Portugal is considerably below. The implications are that intra-national disparities in the EEC will become greater and that it will be more difficult to reconcile the interests of Portugal and Greece on the one hand and West Germany and Denmark ($ US 8,400 and 9,000) on the other, by the application of the same Community policies.

A second group of problems arises from the character and importance of agriculture in Greece, Spain and Portugal. Each cultivates Mediterranean crops such as vines, olives, citrus fruits, vegetables, durum wheat, rice and tobacco, a similar range of products to the Mediterranean parts of France and Italy. The increased competition between producers is clear and, in some product groups, welcomed. In other areas of production (e.g. wine, vegetables and fruit), the EEC currently suffers from overproduction and hence prospects of stockpiles increasing would appear to be imminent. In general, also, agriculture in all the three countries is inefficient, with an average farm size considerably less than in northern Europe.

Geographical enlargement will bring into the EEC three member states where agriculture is an important part of their total activity and where employment in farming is considerably in excess of the EEC average (*see* Table 13 also). In 1978 agriculture employed 34 per cent of the labour force in Greece, 27 per cent in Portugal, and 21 per cent in Spain. These levels of employment can be compared with an EEC average of just over 8 per cent for that year. Moreover, "the number of persons engaged in agriculture in an enlarged Community context would, in fact, be more than doubled (i.e. would increase by approximately 5m), while over-all agricultural production would increase by only one fifth".[8] The implications of this situation are clear—a massive restructuring of agriculture in Greece,

Portugal and Spain is inevitably necessary and more non-agricultural jobs will have to be created in farming regions. In the early years of enlargement, increased unemployment and emigration from Mediterranean farming areas will be important issues, although, in time, the opening up of new market opportunities together with the higher guaranteed food prices under the CAP, could lead to increased production. Of the three new members, Spain has by far the greatest agricultural potential and also has the most suitable agricultural base to compete with France and Italy. Even so, the clear signs are that a long term strategy for Mediterranean agriculture within the CAP will have to be developed as a matter of urgency. The terms agreed for the application of the CAP to Greek agriculture clearly supports this view.[9] A major question still to be answered is whether or not the internal politics of the CAP will permit a satisfactory solution.

Thirdly, problems arise on industrial goods. Remaining Greek tariffs on trade with the EEC will be eliminated in a series of stages over a five-year transitional period to 1986. As with the first geographical enlargement, this phasing is designed to give Greek industrialists a sufficient breathing space to adjust to competition from other Community producers. Unlike the UK and Denmark, Greece, Portugal and Spain are semi-industrialised economies at an intermediate/take-off stage of development and so do not have complete industrial structures. As Ferreira observes, although dependence exists:

> while the Community accounts for almost half of the foreign trade of the Applicants, the share of the Applicants either in supply of imports to the Nine, or foreign demand for their exports, is small ... the consequences of enlargement for aggregate trade are obviously much more crucial for the Applicants than for the Community.[10]

He later attempts to apply the dynamic trade models of integration (*see* Chapter III) to the case of Greece, Spain and Portugal. Two possibilities exist. First, the applicants may compete for the northern markets of the EEC and, secondly, they may develop intra-regional flows of trade between themselves (especially Spain and Portugal) in order to offset the likely competition from established industrial producers within the Nine. As in agriculture, adjustment and restructuring is necessary. Some industries and firms will benefit from free access to a much larger market, while others (e.g. in steel, textiles and shipbuilding) will face serious problems of adjustment. As empirical studies have shown, the process of integration will favour those industries which are highly productive and in a position to compete. Others will struggle to survive.

Fourthly, enlargement raises an important social issue relating to the freedom of movement of labour. As Chapter IX indicated, in the 1960s the EEC countries provided an essential source of employment to migrant workers from Greece, Portugal and Spain. The subsequent downturn in the EEC economy since 1974 has increased pressure on regions which have traditionally regarded emigration as a safety valve to relieving internal pressures of unemployment and underemployment. By 1976 there were only 1.25m migrant workers from the three countries in the Nine and the present signs are that the Community cannot absorb any substantial increase in numbers of migrant workers. Consequently, in the accession terms agreed with Greece, there were restrictions on the free movement of workers until the end of a seven-year transitional period, although Greeks employed in the Nine qualified for full social benefits from 1981. Negotiations with the two other applicants point to a similar period of transition. Even if full freedom had been granted earlier, uncertain economic prospects in the EEC economy make renewed migrant flows unlikely.

Finally, the above agricultural and industrial trends will generate new regional problems for Greece, Portugal and Spain, in addition to the present basic GDP disparities. There will be problems of decline in certain agricultural and industrial regions which will necessitate a restructuring and conversion of regional economies. Weaker regions, particularly along the Mediterranean, are currently in a difficult situation and will encounter even more serious problems with enlargement. Intraregional disparities seem likely to widen as the benefits of integration will most certainly not be evenly distributed. Such problems are not aided by the weak period of economic growth currently being experienced by the Community as a whole. New industries and jobs will have to be attracted to such regions through effective national and Community regional policy measures. Unless appropriate measures are pursued "differences in the level of development between countries and regions in the enlarged Community could well grow ... and would be bound to compromise gravely the indispensable cohesion of the future Community of Twelve".[11]

The second geographical enlargement of the EEC is beset with many problems. At the present time, one can merely outline the likely impact of Greek membership and the potential accession of Portugal and Spain. Geographically, the EEC's centre of gravity, if not economic potential, will shift much more towards the Mediterranean; culturally, the basic character of the Community will be altered. For enlargement to succeed, there must be a massive geographical transfer of resources through established EEC policies and institutions, which will further test the political will to integrate the economies of Western Europe.

What are the prospects beyond a Community of Twelve? Turkey remains an Associate Member of the E E C and must be a plausible, if distant, candidate for full membership.[12] The E E C Commission are well aware that a Community of Twelve raises a "Mediterranean dilemma", i.e. to take care that enlargement does not create too much adverse friction with countries who have traditionally had special relations with the Community. Turkey is a case in point, along with the Maghreb countries of Algeria, Morocco and Tunisia and the island economies of Malta and Cyprus, who have both been suggested as future full members. Enlargement could also cause problems for Yugoslavia, although negotiations are currently under way for a new preferential trade agreement. In the 1980s it seems certain that the E E C will develop a much stronger policy of Mediterranean co-operation. In some cases, this could be seen as the next stage towards the third geographical enlargement of the Community.

Economic and Monetary Union

"Economic and Monetary Union (E M U) represents the state of fusion between countries where there is a common budget, a common taxation system, a common banking system and capital market, and a common currency."[13] Although there is no explicit reference to E M U in the Treaty of Rome, it is a logical next stage from the successful completion of the customs union. It should also be stated that E M U is a powerful lever and involves the greater political integration of member states, in keeping with the federalist approach to integration (*see* Chapter 11). Geographically E M U has various implications tied up with the transfer of resources—if achieved, it would allow the complete freedom of movement of firms, capital and savings so increasing the attractiveness of core regions. To be politically successful however, it would have to be accompanied by a geographical re-allocation of resources in favour of the less prosperous member states and regions. It is this question of political feasibility which stands firmly in the way between aim and reality.[14]

The chequered path and commitment to E M U is clearly analysed by McRae and Cairncross.[15] In short, following the Hague Summit of December 1969, the Council of Ministers examined a series of alternative plans and decided to set up a group of experts under the chairmanship of Luxembourg's Prime Minister, M. Pierre Werner. It soon became clear that a basic disagreement existed within the Werner Committee—West Germany, the Netherlands and Italy felt that monetary union should be preceded by the harmonisation of economic policies, while France, Belgium and Luxembourg favoured

an early co-ordination of monetary exchange rates in order to oblige governments to move towards economic union. Both groups of member states were of course seeking to protect their own interests. The Werner Report (published in late 1970), was the now familiar attempt to provide a compromise, with the principle of parallel progress towards both goals being put forward. Werner envisaged that monetary union (with fixed exchange rates or even a common currency) should be completed by 1980. In March 1971 the Council of Ministers passed a resolution calling for the gradual achievement of EMU. During the first stage to the 1st January 1974:
the following measures must be taken:

(*i*) strengthening of co-ordination of short-term economic policy and monetary and credit policy;

(*ii*) accelerated introduction of free movement of persons, goods, services and capital; measures to include certain harmonisation of some taxes;

(*iii*) Regional Policy: establishment of Regional Fund;

(*iv*) efforts to achieve common position in monetary relations with third countries and international organisations;

(*v*) narrowing of the margins of fluctuation of the currencies of member states (maximum margin between rates, 2.25%);

(*vi*) possibly, establishment of European fund for monetary co-operation.[16]

Werner's strategy was based firmly upon a system of fixed exchange rates, (*v*) above being popularly referred to as "the snake in the tunnel", a device to limit the spread between the strongest and weakest currencies. The new Community applicants, including the UK, took part in the snake agreement when it was launched in April 1972. It was, however, an experiment doomed to failure, lasting only a matter of weeks. The British pound came under severe pressure when it was realised that the par value agreed in the world-wide Smithsonian discussions of the previous December was an overvaluation. Within a matter of weeks, the UK, the Republic of Ireland, and Denmark withdrew in rapid succession from the snake, allowing their currencies to float freely against the US dollar. France later withdrew and as Tsoukalis remarks, "In a world of generalised floating, the EEC snake was both left without a tunnel and seriously mutilated."[17] The snake ultimately became a Deutschmark zone with the currencies of West Germany, the Benelux countries and Denmark being linked together.

The international economic and political environment on which EMU was to be built changed further with the energy and subsequent balance of payments crises of 1973 and 1974. The movement towards EMU received a further setback as a result of internal political wranglings over regional policy (*see* Chapter XII). So, by the mid-1970s the issue of EMU had become buried under the weight of other EEC problems. It was forcibly raised again in December 1975, with the publication of the controversial "Report on European Union" drawn up by Mr Leo Tindemans, then Belgian Prime Minister.[18] Presented to fellow Heads of Government, this report aimed to seek ways of gradually transforming relations between member states and broadening the base of their collective action.

In addition to providing suggestions for the Community's future, the Tindemans Report also heeded a warning. It stated that "The European Community is an unfinished structure that must be completed or it will collapse."[19] Tindemans further warned that it was partly a victim of its own successes and that it had lost its *parfum d'aventure*. His view was that the crisis was so great that in the immediate future, member states must take a drastic leap forward. "The price of inaction would be a weakened, divided and increasingly impotent Europe."[20] To achieve a more united Europe, Tindemans suggested a new approach—there should be a common economic and monetary policy, the further development of common policies, a more effective transfer of resources to less prosperous regions and an overhaul of the Community's institutions with more power being given to the European Parliament. In the Community's state of economic and political disarray, Tindemans argued that little could be achieved. A particularly controversial part of his Report was the suggestion that the stronger member states should forge ahead to achieve greater unity, leaving the weaker countries like the UK to catch up later. This was implicit in his statement that "The speed of the EEC convoy should not be held back to the speed of the slowest vessel".[21] The Report was not without its critics—some commentators said it was too modest, while paradoxically others argued that it was too ambitious. The President of the EEC Commission, S. Ortoli, rejected the idea of a two-speed Community and also took a dim view of the Tindemans suggestion to give more power to the European Parliament.

More recently, there has been a further upsurge of activity in calling for the relaunching of EMU. In January 1977, President Giscard d'Estaing of France called for a special meeting of the Council of Ministers to consider this question and his view was later supported by West Germany. Roy Jenkins, the President of the Commission, subsequently backed the case for EMU and gave new arguments in its favour.[22] He argued that monetary union was vital in order to restore business confidence and promote growth in the economies of the Community. It would also provide a stable exchange rate system, a means for controlling inflation and release currencies from their traditional dependence on the US dollar. Progress was made in July 1978 when at the Bremen summit West Germany and France jointly proposed that a zone of monetary stability should be created through a new European Monetary System (EMS). Agreement on the new system was reached in early December 1978, although the UK declined to take part. Italy and the Republic of Ireland had some initial hesitation but later decided to join the scheme linking exchange rates of member states.

Full details of the EMS were published in a White Paper.[23] The central element was the European Currency Unit (ECU), which is valued at the same rate as the European unit of account. Each currency of the participating member states has a central rate against this ECU and a rate against each other. The margin of fluctuation of participating currencies is 2.25 per cent (as in the snake), but with provision for a 6 per cent fluctuation margin for currencies formerly floating (Italy). Intervention is compulsory once the limits of the permitted margins of fluctuation are reached. A credit support mechanism also operates and within two years of the introduction of EMS, it was planned to set up a definitive European Monetary Fund. The UK declined to join the system for various reasons, the principal one being that domestic deflation was feared.[24] Greece, like the UK, is not a member of the EMS.

The launching of EMS once again raises the issue of full Economic and Monetary Union. Like the snake, it is an effort to stabilise internal exchange rates, so reducing the uncertainty for intra-EEC transactions. If successful, it should promote trade between member states and give a major stimulus to employment and growth. The UK has various fears concerning both EMS and EMU and remains to be convinced that either will bring benefits to the poorer members of the Community. Geographically, therefore, there is a need to improve the flow of EEC funds in order to improve the regional distribution of work and wealth in the Community. The poorer regions will need an assurance that their economic difficulties will not be aggravated by further steps towards union but, as yet, the richer member states do not seem willing to pay this price for the advantages they are receiving.

NOTES
    1. Swann, D., *The Economics of the Common Market*, Penguin, 1975, Chapter 4.
    2. Northedge, F. S., "Britain and the European Communities, 1945–72", in The Open University, *The European Economic Community: History and Institutions*, 1974, pp. 13–34.

3. Everling, V., "Possibilities and Limits of European Integration", *Journal of Common Market Studies*, Vol. X V I I I, No. 3, March 1980.

4. For details, see *European Community*, No. 7, July 1979, pp. 12–13.

5. Osborn, A., "Poor queue at Common Market gate", *The Daily Telegraph*, 14 February 1977.

6. Everling, V., *op. cit.*, p. 217.

7. *O E C D Observer*, March 1979.

8. *Commission of the European Communities*, "Enlargement of the Community: Economic and Sectoral Aspects", Supplement 3/78, p. 32.

9. *European Community*, *op. cit.*, p. 13.

10. Ferreira, A. D. S., "The Economics of Enlargement", *Journal of Common Market Studies*, Vol. X V I I, No. 2, December 1978, p. 121.

11. *Commission of the European Communities*, *op. cit.*, p. 36.

12. Burrows, B., "A Community of Thirteen? The Question of Turkish Membership of the E E C", *Journal of Common Market Studies*, Vol. X V I I, No. 2, December 1978.

13. McRae, H. and Cairncross, F., "Economic and Monetary Union", in *The European Economic Community: Economics and Agriculture*, The Open University, 1974, pp. 48–55.

14. *See* Tsoukalis, L., "Is the re-launching of economic and monetary union a feasible proposal?", *Journal of Common Market Studies*, Vol. X V, No. 4, June 1977.

15. McRae and Cairncross, *op. cit.*, pp. 48–55.

16. The European Parliament, *Europe Today*, 1976, section 4.162.

17. Tsoukalis, *op. cit.*, p. 244.

18. For a summary, see *European Community*, No. 1, January 1976, pp. 6–8.

19. *The Daily Telegraph*, 8th January 1976.

20. *European Community*, *op. cit.*, p. 6.

21. *The Daily Telegraph*, *op. cit.*

22. *European Community*, No. 3, March 1978, pp. 3–6.

23. *The European Monetary System*, Cmnd. 7419, H M S O, December 1978.

24. *See* "Economic Progress Report", No. 106, January 1979.

Part Three

REGIONAL ISSUES

Chapter XI

The Regional Problem in the EEC

DURING the 1960s the "regional problem" came into geographical usage to describe the noticeable differences in regional living standards and well-being prevalent in many developed economies, particularly in Western Europe.[1] Today, all member states of the EEC have their own regional problem and regional diversity is now a matter of European concern since the realities of economic integration have served to promote a growing awareness of the problems facing the least privileged Community regions.[2]

Traditionally, the regional problem applied to a persistent and deep-rooted imbalance in prosperity between regions in a particular country. In the UK peripheral regions such as the North, Scotland, and Wales, have lagged behind more prosperous regions such as the South-East when looked at in terms of earnings levels, job prospects and social infrastructure. In Italy a type of "regional dualism" has existed for many years—the seven southernmost states, the *Mezzogiorno*, could still almost be described as having many symptoms of a less developed economy, while the rest of Italy, the Centre-North, has prospered from the benefits of post-1945 industrial expansion.[3] Spatially, the French economy has a rather different regional problem—it possesses a "core-periphery" type of structure, with the Paris region exhibiting considerably greater prosperity than all other regions. Regional problems have attracted the greatest attention in these member states but as this chapter indicates, each country of the EEC is currently faced with its own peculiar regional problem.

At Community level any reference to regional problems cannot be divorced from the variations in prosperity which exist between member states. In a sense there is a type of regional problem existing between EEC members—West Germany and Denmark are clearly the most affluent, with the UK, Italy, the Republic of Ireland and Greece the poorest member states. In general, the problem regions of these poorest member states are the least prosperous regions in the entire Community, with living standards considerably behind those of the most prosperous regions.

The emergence of the regional problem at member state level is in general a function of economic growth in the post-war economy. Problem regions have not been able to adapt to change in the same way as more favourably placed regions. Frequently their economic

base lacks modern industrial and service activities, and geographically they are poorly placed to serve major markets. At a European
level the growth of economic integration has favoured centrally
placed locations such as the Rhine Valley and Paris Basin. Regions
within these areas have exerted considerable attraction for new industrial development, with investment coming, not only from within
the EEC, but also from the USA, Japan and the rest of Europe. As
the EEC moves towards greater unity, this spatial polarisation will
continue, giving even less hope for peripheral regions such as Scotland, Wales, Northern Ireland, the Republic of Ireland and the
Mezzogiorno.

This chapter analyses the EEC's regional problem both within
and between its member states. To a certain extent such an analysis
is restricted by data availability. The quality of information at regional level in the EEC varies between member states and it must
also be recognised that variations in the geographical nature of
administrative units can sometimes conceal important variations.
The Commission is clearly aware of such data problems and is
currently seeking to introduce a more consistent system of regional
data collection between member states.[4] In spite of this reservation,
it is possible to draw up a profile which clearly shows significant
differences in regional living standards within and between member
states.

Finally, in this introduction, it should be emphasised that the
regional problem is currently a central issue in EEC affairs. The
problem is Community-wide as Clout indicates: "Demonstrations of
cultural identity and even of autonomist sentiment have emanated
from Basques and Bretons, Cornishmen and Corsicans, Walloons
and Welshmen, and members of many other minority groups who
are concerned about their economic well-being, their cultural survival
and the nature of their relationship with central administration."[5]
Indeed, it goes much deeper and concerns the Community itself; for
if the spirit of Article 2 of the Treaty of Rome is to be achieved, it is
essential that there should be a more equitable distribution of benefits
from economic integration.

Regional Variations in Living Standards

Regional variations in living standards can be looked at in a variety
of ways. The central indicator in any analysis is *regional GDP per
head*, which in simple terms represents the volume of goods and
services available for consumption per head of population. More
specifically, it represents the value per head of economic activity
taking place within a region and has been widely used to show
disparities in economic development between the regions of a parti-

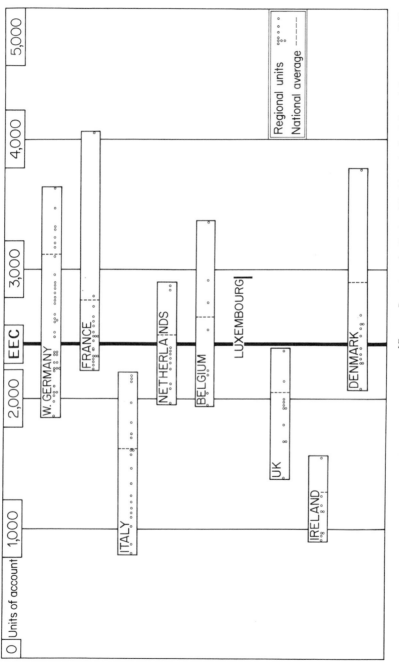

FIG. 35.—Distribution of GNP per head in the EEC 1970. (Note in the case of Luxembourg the national and the regional average are coincident.)

[*Source: Report on the Regional Problems in the Enlarged Community, 1973.*]

cular country. It has been suggested too that such an indicator should be used to determine those regions where regional policy should intervene to provide aids to development. The first official attempt to analyse variations in regional living standards in the E E C was contained in the Thomson Report published in 1973.[6] This report had been produced by the Commission in response to a request from the Heads of Government for more information on regional problems within the enlarged Community of Nine. At that time the Report was seen as a first stage to the setting up of a European Regional Development Fund (see Chapter X I I) and an important information collection exercise prior to embarkation upon the second phase of the road to Economic and Monetary Union (see Chapter X).

Figure 35 from the Thomson Report, provides much evidence of variations in regional income per head.[7] It indicates that in two member states, Denmark and the Republic of Ireland, only one region (that containing the capital) had an income per head above the national average; in France, only two out of the twenty-one régions were above the average. In contrast, all other regions in these countries fell below the national average. The graph also clearly shows significant variations in average living standards between the Community members in 1970. In particular, for the U K, Italy and the Republic of Ireland, not only is the national average but also the average of all regions below the Community average income per head. Living standards in the South-East, the U K's most prosperous economic planning region, fail to match those of the Community average. This fundamental divergence between member states has been behind the attempts of poorer members to secure a more equitable Community regional policy (see Chapter X I I). In contrast, the national average of the richer member states is above the Community average and only a few of their regions are below.

A further analysis of the Community's regions was published by the Commission in early 1981.[8] In many respects, this report is in line with the findings of the earlier Thomson Report. It does, however, contain much more detailed information and analysis of regional problems and has a particularly significant chapter devoted to the problems of enlargement (see Chapter X). As distinct from the Thomson Report, the First Periodic Report analyses trends in the intensity of regional problems at a time of recession in the E E C economy.

Figure 36 shows regional variations in G D P per head in 1977.[9] As for 1970 (Fig. 35), all regions in the U K, Italy (except Valle d'Aosta) and the Republic of Ireland have a figure below the E E C average. Comparatively, living standards in the whole of the Re-

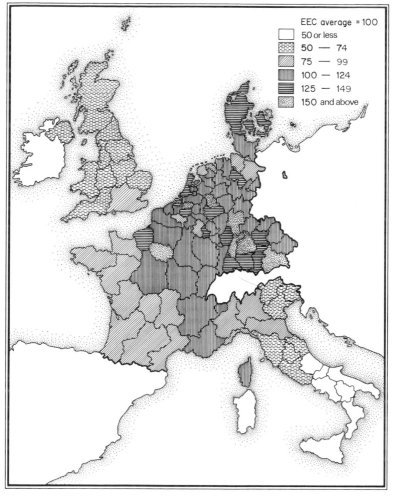

EEC average = 100
- [ ] 50 or less
- 50 — 74
- 75 — 99
- 100 — 124
- 125 — 149
- 150 and above

[*Source*: *The Regions of Europe*, COM (80) 816, Commission of the European Communities, 1981.

FIG. 36.—Regional levels of economic development (GDP per head), 1977.

public of Ireland and the Italian *Mezzogiorno* are only around 40 per cent of the EEC average measured in these terms. Significantly, more Community regions in other member states have fallen below the average in 1977 than in 1970. Geographically, such regions are concentrated in the west and south-west of France but also include Lüneburg (West Germany), Friesland (Netherlands), Luxembourg and Hainaut (Belgium). At the other end of the scale, the prosperous

regions of 1970 remain the prosperous regions of 1977. Hamburg
and Bremen in West Germany have the greatest levels of affluence,
although geographically, the Île-de-France, covering most of the Paris
Basin, is the most populous of regions in this top category. Most of
the main cities of the central and northern parts of the EEC have
living standards of more than 150 per cent of the Community average. In between these extremes, the greatest number of Community
residents live in regions where the GDP per head is up to 25 per cent
above the average—this category covers most of the remaining parts
of France, West Germany, the Benelux countries and Denmark.

The 1981 Report provides clear evidence that the post-1974 recession has had a more than proportionate impact upon the poorest
regions and member states. Comparing the 1977 position with that
of 1970, it states that "the deterioration in the position of the UK
and Italian regions as well as Ireland will be noted. Regional disparities between weaker and stronger regions widened considerably in
the 1970s".[10] The Commission's analysis clearly shows, therefore,
that the Community regions now distinctly fall into clear groupings
essentially encompassing the rich and poor member states. Within
member states, although regional income divergences are very much
lower, they remain particularly wide in Italy and France.

At national level, the gap between living standards in the rich and
poor member states continues to widen as Table 40 indicates.
Although this information is presented in a different way to the 1981
Report on problem regions, it does show continued divergence.
Denmark is now the most affluent EEC member state, marginally
ahead of West Germany. The UK's average living standard has
deteriorated to around 78 per cent of the EEC average, compared
with 85 per cent at the time of the Thomson enquiry.

TABLE 40

GNP per head of member states, 1979

	£	Index
Denmark	6,100	139
West Germany	6,000	136
Belgium	5,500	125
Luxembourg	5,400	123
Netherlands	5,200	118
France	5,050	115
EEC-9	4,400	100
UK	3,440	78
Italy	2,700	61
Ireland	2,200	50

Source: The Daily Telegraph, 10th November 1980.

There is, therefore, clear evidence of variation in living standards within and between E E C member states. Such evidence has been central to the claims of the poorer members for a fairer distribution of Community resources. With the second geographical enlargement the gap between the richest and poorest member states will widen further, adding to the Community's already serious regional problems.

Other Measures of Regional Inequality

The regional problem can be analysed in other ways as well as G D P per head.[11] Historically, variations in the level of unemployment have been used to denote less prosperous regions within a country and crudely used for the allocation of regional development assistance. In the U K, for example, peripheral regions such as Scotland, Wales, the North and Northern Ireland have traditionally had unemployment rates above other regions and clearly lack comparable job opportunities. They also have comparatively lower activity rates (i.e. proportion of the workforce of employable age in employment). In other E E C countries similar regional variations have been recorded for many years.

Figure 37 shows the regional unemployment position in 1977, when the average unemployment rate in the Community was 5.3 per cent. Clearly, as with G D P per head, some regions were better off than others. The map indicates that the worst unemployment rates are to be found in parts of the *Mezzogiorno* and Belgium, although, in general, the peripheral regions of France, Italy and the U K (along with the whole of the Republic of Ireland) have levels well in excess of the average. The peripheral regions, of course, have a G D P per head below the E E C average, as Fig. 36 illustrated. Not unexpectedly, there would seem to be a good relationship between these two indicators of the regional problem.

The Commission's report on *The Regions of Europe* which analyses changes in unemployment rates between 1970 and 1977, provides additional information to that of Fig. 37. "Increases of registered unemployment were steepest both as regards numbers and percentages in the stronger regions of the Community. Unemployment growth was most severely felt in a belt of stronger regions covering mainly North-Eastern and Central France, Belgium and South Germany."[12] While it must be remembered that such regions still have unemployment rates below those of peripheral regions, recession in the E E C economy has affected job prospects in all regions. Recession has also had an impact on the attitude of member states towards migrant labour (*see* below and Chapter I X). Currently, Belgium has the highest unemployment rate of all member states (12.4 per cent in 1980), and in traditional problem regions such as Limburg and

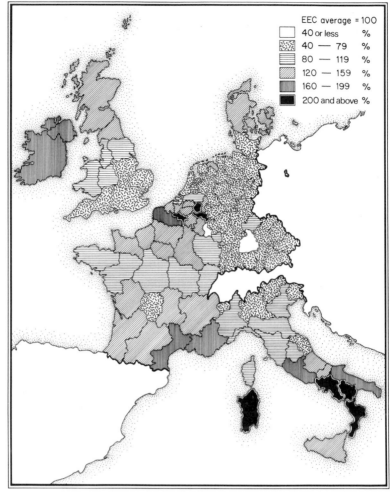

[*Source*: "Labour Force 1979", *Eurostat*, published in *The Regions of Europe*,
COM (80) 816, Commission of the European Communities, 1981.
FIG. 37.—Regional unemployment rates in 1977.

Hainaut this rate is exceeded. In general, though, the stronger regions
are finding it easier to adapt to recession and will be the first to
benefit from a general upturn in the EEC economy.

Migration into or out of a region is a third indicator of regional
prosperity. Due to the free movement of labour between member
states, the net migration rate of a particular region is arrived at
through a consideration of various factors such as population move-

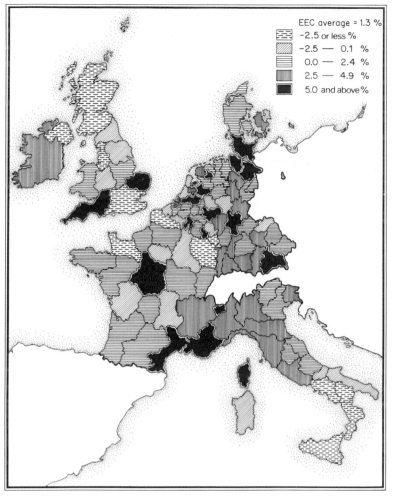

EEC average = 1.3 %
-2.5 or less %
-2.5 — 0.1 %
0.0 — 2.4 %
2.5 — 4.9 %
5.0 and above %

[*Source*: *The Regions of Europe*, COM (80) 816, Commission of the European Communities, 1981.

FIG. 38.—Average annual rates of net migration, 1970–78 (%).

ment from other regions within that member state, from other EEC member states or from outside the Community itself. Figure 38 shows the average annual rates of net migration for EEC regions from 1970 to 1978. A negative rate indicates that a region is losing population to other regions in that member state or, in some cases, to other parts of the Community. Migration patterns at regional levels have not been uniform as Fig. 38 shows.

The migration of population from the *Mezzogiorno*, particularly to northern industrial regions, has been a traditional economic safety valve (*see* Chapter XIII). During the 1960s, when the Italian and EEC economies were in a period of sustained growth, net out-migration was over 11 per cent per annum. During the 1970s this rate has fallen dramatically and was as low as 0.5 per cent per annum during the period 1975–8. Correspondingly, the growth in the number of migrants into northern industrial regions also fell in this period due to a reduction in the number of migrant workers from the South. In the case of West Germany, the net losses of population indicated in Fig. 38 are due to a virtual halt in recruitment of labour from non-EEC countries. In France and the UK there was net out-migration from crowded prosperous regions such as the Île-de-France, Champagne–Ardennes and South-East regions. So, it is not necessarily true that out-migration is always associated with problem regions, although historically, this has generally been the case.

Towards an Explanation of Regional Inequalities

The Thomson Report stated that "the fundamental cause of regional imbalances stems from the absence of modern economic activity or the overdependence of a region on backward agricultural or declining industrial activities".[13] Although the time period differed, these factors would seem to be responsible for the regional inequalities shown in Figs. 36 to 38. According to Thomson, a cause of differential development in the EEC was the predominant position of agriculture in certain regions. As shown in Chapter IV, the Community's agricultural workforce has shown a consistent decline yet in many regions there remains a problem of low productivity and underemployment of resources. Backward agricultural regions such as the *Mezzogiorno*, parts of the Republic of Ireland, the Highlands and Islands of Scotland and many parts of France have an economic base still heavily dependent upon agricultural incomes. It is not uncommon for agriculture to employ one in five or more of the region's workforce and, despite help from the CAP, such regions have a low GDP per head, an ageing population structure, and lack new job opportunities. Within the EEC, backward agricultural regions are significant problem regions.

Similar problems face depressed industrial regions, although for different causes. Regions such as the Northern region of the UK, Alsace, Lorraine and Nord-Pas-de-Calais in France and Limburg in Belgium are good examples of such regions, the traditional recipients of regional aid. The economic base of these regions is still heavily dependent upon activities like iron and steel, coal-mining and textiles.

Unfortunately for their regional incomes, these are not activities which are growing in importance in their respective domestic economies. With specific exceptions they lack certain types of new infrastructure and are poorly placed for the attraction of modern activities. Once again, both national and E E C sources of regional aid have been available for many years but their economic prospects remain dull, particularly at a time of recession.

Within the above framework, the Thomson Report was a unique attempt for the definition of problem regions in the E E C. It laid down the criteria that to qualify for regional aid, a region should have:

(*i*) G N P per head below the Community average; and *either*

(*ii*) the percentage of the working population employed in agriculture higher than the Community average *and* the percentage of the working population in industry lower than the Community average; *or*

(*iii*) at least 20 per cent of the population must be employed in declining industries such as coal-mining and/or textiles.

On this basis, proposed beneficiaries from a European Regional Development Fund would include the whole of the Republic of Ireland, Northern Ireland, Wales, Scotland and the North of England in the U K, the *Mezzogiorno* and many other parts of Italy, the whole of western and south-western France, plus smaller areas in other member states, generally peripheral to the main centres of economic activity. By many yardsticks these are the Community regions most in need of regional development assistance. For political reasons, though, the Thomson scheme never materialised (*see* Chapter X I I). A real opportunity was lost to get deliberately E E C aid to its main problem regions.

The Thomson Report had its limitations in identifying the Community's problem regions. It did not recognise that in many cases core regions had a particular type of regional problem associated with prosperity rather than poverty. In regions such as the Île-de-France, South-East England and the Randstad, social overhead capital is strained and the quality of life suffers from over-crowding and congestion. The negative side of regional development policies seeks to check their development in order to aid the prospects of poorer regions. To this extent agreement had previously been reached between member states in 1972 to limit the scale of financial assistance available to such regions. It was to have been the first stage in the evolution of an effective Community Regional Policy.

The processes of integration referred to in earlier chapters have in themselves led to a "new" type of EEC problem region, the frontier region. There is growing evidence that frontier regions between member states or adjacent to the Community's external frontier are being handicapped by inadequate cross-frontier infrastructure, currency problems and legal differences not satisfactorily explained by the type of analysis employed above. As integration has progressed, these regional nerve spots have tended to be obstacles to the more general unity sought by their countries. Some such regions, as Fig. 39 shows, have suffered from history on various occasions, but others are modern in origin. As Burtenshaw says:

> Western Europe abounds with examples of problem regions in a national context that are also frontier regions. The Bayerisches,

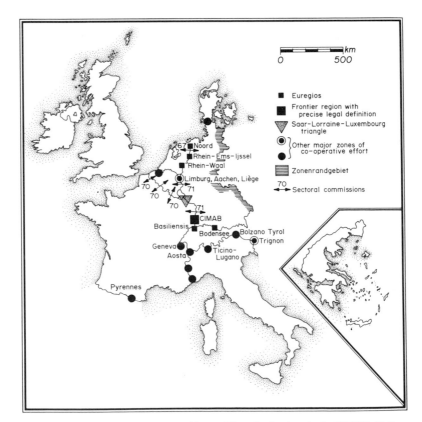

[*Source*: D. Burtenshaw, "Problems of Frontier Regions in the EEC" in R. Lee & P. E. Ogden, *Economy and Society in the EEC*, Saxon House, 1976, p. 219.
FIG. 39.—Major frontier regions in the EEC.

Wald, the Eifel mountains and Emsland have been recognised for over twenty years as problems regions in West Germany: all are marginal to the state as is the Saarland which was recognisably a depressed region from its return to West Germany. With France, Alsace and Lorraine are peripheral as are northern Schleswig, Savoy, Limburg and Luxembourg within their respective states.[14]

In all cases, these regions are nationally peripheral and adjoin frontiers with other EEC member states. Where a region adjoins the Community's external frontiers, its lack of prosperity is invariably greater. Frontier regions complicate an already complex regional problem.

Finally, some comment should be made on the analysis contained in the Commission's 1981 Report. It recognises that the reasons for an increase in regional disparities during the period 1970–77 "are many and complex."[15] In particular, the changed migration situation referred to above is used to partly explain the divergent situation between this and previous periods. Even so, there are a whole series of structural factors which can be used to explain regional variations in living standards. These include differences in regional factor endowments and infrastructure, the accessibility of a region to EEC markets, the nature and structure of its activities, social attitudes, and regional policy incentives. Clearly the Commission has revised its thoughts since the more simple (though convenient) Thomson explanation.

Geographically, the 1981 Report would seem to be particularly significant in its recognition of the role of peripherality and centrality in regional development. In a similar analysis to that of Clark (*see* Fig. 25), the Report contains a map showing an index of peripherality for each Community region from the most central situation, Rheinhessen-Pfalz in West Germany. Not surprisingly, wide differences exist. The *Mezzogiorno*, Northern Ireland and all regions of the Republic of Ireland are locationally the worst-placed of all EEC regions. The peripheral regions of the UK, most of Denmark, parts of western and southern France, and further parts of Italy also have a high degree of locational disadvantage compared with the Community's centre. In contrast, the most accessible regions of the EEC are concentrated in a small triangular-shaped area with corners at Stuttgart, Hamburg and Lille. The Île-de-France and South-East England are important peaks outside this plateau. Complementary to Clark's earlier analysis, the relative accessibility of peripheral and central regions has widened over the last twenty years, providing further evidence of the disadvantages of integration for problem regions.

As this chapter has indicated, the regional problem in the EEC is
a complex one and can be analysed in various ways. It is appropriate
therefore to conclude with a synthesis of the relative intensity of
regional problems as contained in the 1981 Report (*see* Fig. 40).
Following a factor analysis, the Commission Report stated that

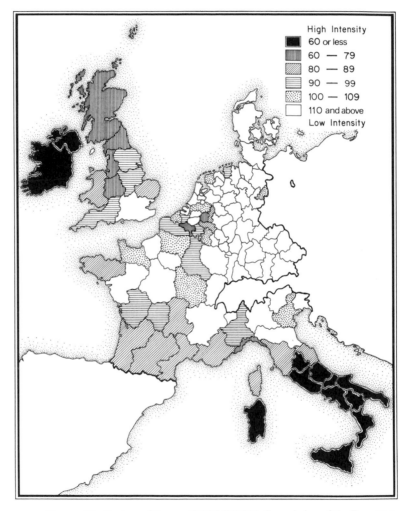

[*Source*: *The Regions of Europe*, COM (80) 816, Commission of the European
Communities, 1981.

FIG. 40.—Relative intensity of regional problems, 1977. Indicators used: GDP per
capita (current prices, current exchange rates) (EUR = 100); long-term (6
months) unemployment rate (labour survey) (EUR = 100).

statistics on regional GDP per head and the long-term unemployment rate were the best indicators of regional imbalance and could be combined into an index of relative intensity of regional problems. Once again, it can be seen that the *Mezzogiorno* (plus Lazio and Umbria), Northern Ireland and the whole of the Republic of Ireland are those parts of the Community with the lowest GDP per head and highest rates of structural unemployment. In the category above them, 60–79 per cent the average, fall four problem regions of the UK, Liguria in Italy and Hainaut and Limburg in Belgium. The poorest French and Dutch regions, along with others, fall in the 80–89 per cent category. Regions with the lowest intensity of regional problems are in the whole of Denmark and West Germany, the two most prosperous member states, and the core parts of France, the UK and Italy.

Looking ahead, the Commission see little change in this state of affairs during the 1980s. The regions with the most intense regional problems in the 1970s seem destined to remain the worst off over the next decade. Despite the call for a European regional directive, the problem regions of the EEC have living standards which considerably lag behind those of the more favourably located central regions. Further integration and the second geographical enlargement can only serve to aggravate this difference.

NOTES

1. For example, see Hemmings, M. F., "The Regional Problem", *National Institute Economic Review*, Vol. 35, 1963.

2. See Clout, H., ed., *Regional Development in Western Europe*, John Wiley & Sons, 1975, Chapter 1.

3. Podbielski, G., *Italy—Development and Crisis in the Post-War Economy*, OUP, 1974, Chapter 9.

4. Commission of the European Communities, *The Regions of Europe*, COM (80) 816 Final, 1981, Sections 1.6, 1.8 and 4.1.

5. Clout, H., ed., *op. cit.*, p. 3.

6. Commission of the European Communities, *Report on the Regional Problems in the Enlarged Community*, COM (73) 550, 1973.

7. *Op. cit.*, p. 124.

8. Commission of the European Communities, *The Regions of Europe*, COM (80) 816 Final, 1981.

9. *Ibid.*, Map 4.1.

10. *Ibid.*, Section 4.2, para. 2.

11. See Clout, H., "Unequal Shares in Prosperity", *Geographical Magazine*, March 1979, pp. 385–95.

12. Commission of the European Communities, *The Regions of Europe*, COM (80) 816 Final, 1981, Section 3.2.2, para. 2.

13. Commission of the European Communities, *Report on the Regional Problems in the Enlarged Community*, COM (73) 550, 1973, p. 9.

14. Burtenshaw, D., "Problems of Frontier Regions in the E E C", in Lee, R. and Ogden, P. E., eds, *Economy and Society in the E E C, 1976*, Saxon House, p. 221.

15. Commission of the European Communities, *The Regions of Europe*, C O M (80) 816 Final, 1981, Section 4.3.1, para. 1.

Chapter XII

Regional Policies in the E E C

The Case for Regional Policies

THE spatial disparity in regional development as analysed in the previous chapter has formed the *raison d'être* for regional policies in the various member states of the Community. Unemployment problems in particular have been a long-standing motivating factor although it is now widely accepted that not only economic but also social, environmental and political reasons make it necessary to close the gap between richer and poorer regions. To this end, each member state of the E E C has pursued some form of regional policy which until recently has been independent of any Community-wide policy.

Government economic policy, through fiscal and monetary control, provides little or no help for problem regions and may even exaggerate their weakness. In a simple way this is explained in Fig. 41. In theory, where one region (the South) has higher wage rates than another region (the North), capital should be attracted to the lower wage region and labour should be tempted to migrate from it. Regional disparities are short term—given time, the system will be in equilibrium. In the real world, however, this does not happen. As shown by the persistence of regional problems, the market mechanism fosters the concentration of capital due to the existence of external economies of scale. Labour is also by no means as mobile as the theory suggests, with certain groups of the workforce not being prepared to migrate from their home regions. So, lower wage regions remain and tend to have unemployment rates in excess of their more prosperous counterparts. It is necessary, therefore, to have a separate regional policy to counteract the natural workings of the market economy.

The above general model is certainly applicable to most E E C member states, although geographically their regional problems are not necessarily of a north–south nature. The traditional objective of regional policies has therefore been to foster conditions which are conducive to job creation in problem regions. In this way, it is hoped to counteract the natural forces of polarisation shown in Fig. 41. In the late 1960s and the 1970s there has been a growing recognition of the social character of regional problems with regional policies being necessary to promote environmental and infrastructural improvement in addition to job creation. As Coates has emphasised, social

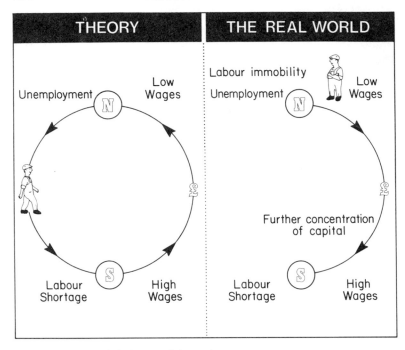

FIG. 41.—Regional imbalance and the market economy.

overhead capital is unevenly distributed between regions and he, moreover, questions whether or not personal access to such capital should be determined purely on the basis of where one lives.[1] Equally, from a social viewpoint, it has been recognised (especially in the UK, but also in other EEC countries) that it is unacceptable to ask a worker to move from his home location in search of work purely on the basis that no jobs are available for him. Regional political pressures have also been significant (especially in Italy) in promoting the need for regional policies. In all, there are strong economic, social and political grounds for regional policies, and in EEC member states, there has been a distinct "gearing up" of resources devoted to regional policy programmes over the last fifteen or so years.

Finally, it should be stated that the case for regional intervention, especially on economic grounds, has been reinforced by integration. With the creation of a customs union between EEC members, regional specialisation has been further promoted and the problems of depressed regions increased. As Buck says, "Policies for the adaptation of industrial structures of depressed regions will now be even more necessary if the consequences of trade liberalisation are not to prove cumulative."[2] As geographical employment proceeds and the Community moves towards its goal of Economic and Monetary Union (*see* Chapter X), the pressures on problem regions will increase. This thinking was undoubtedly prevalent at the 1972 Paris Summit Conference, when Mr Heath, then the British Prime Minister, succeeded in getting agreement on the need for a Community regional policy. Monetary integration also poses risks for member states, since currency rate changes can no longer serve to keep the inefficient in a competing position. The impact of E M U would seem to be to further improve the productivity of regions and states that are already ahead.[3] In short, it serves to increase regional disparities, so reinforcing the case for effective regional policies to set out reducing the gap between rich and poor regions.

National Systems of Regional Aid

Each member state of the E E C has defined its own problem regions and introduced a variety of measures for dealing with regional imbalance. Such policies have evolved at different speeds and above all, developed in an unco-ordinated manner. As Clout recognises, diversity is obvious and continues to be a major stumbling block towards reaching agreement on an effective Community-wide policy.[4] The only common thread stems from the very nature of regional policies, i.e. financial incentives are provided in order to encourage job creation and infrastructure improvement in the designated problem regions. The significant contrasts come in the form of differences in the geographical designation of regions to receive aid, in the scale and approach of regional policies and in the function of disincentives. These contrasts will be discussed briefly, since they form an important background to more recent efforts to promote a Community Regional Policy.[5]

In four member states, the U K, France, Italy and the Republic of Ireland, there is a wide delimitation of regions to receive aid. The Assisted Areas (before 1979) covered around 60 per cent of the surface area of the U K, and in France the complex graded system of assistance for industrialisation is available over most of the country. In Italy, the *Mezzogiorno* covers around 40 per cent of the geographical area, while in the Republic of Ireland, the maximum development incentives are available throughout the whole of the west and south-western parts of the country. In the five remaining member states the regions qualifying for assistance are geographically less significant.

Each member state pursues a regional policy of taking "work to the workers" in its depressed problem regions. A whole range of financial incentives is offered in many member states, usually on a graded basis. In certain countries of the Nine, this aid is available for assisting the growth of existing industry as well as for the encouragement of new firms. In others, notably West Germany, help is only for new developments in the designated regions. Table 41 gives a detailed summary of the diverse system operating in the late 1970s. As can be seen, the more general system of regional development incentives is backed up by a variety of other measures in most member states. In four member states regional policy is of a "carrot and stick" variety in so far as the policy of creating growth in designated regions is backed up by disincentives to growth in core regions. The most extensive disincentive system in operation is in France, where a whole range of measures are at the disposal of central government. These of course reflect the dominance of the Paris region in the modern French economy. Jarrett makes out a strong case for this other side of regional development policy. He says that "one must ask whether to counteract the attraction of the developed areas, it is enough simply to offer investment aids elsewhere."[6] With growing integration in the EEC, this would seem to be a neglected area of regional development strategy. As he later agrees, there is nevertheless a strong case against such controls, especially for poorer member states. If they are not careful, development may be diverted to other member states, so increasing the competitive nature inherent in regional affairs. Recognising this aspect, in 1972 the EEC members agreed to limit help to core regions to a maximum of 20 per cent of the capital cost. The first (and just about only) agreement on harmonisation should not be overstated since the limit set was rather high and it was envisaged that it would be progressively reduced (*see* below).

Within the framework of Table 41, most member states have adopted a growth pole/development point approach to their regional problems. The logic of this approach can be traced back to the French economist Perroux, who in the early 1950s observed that economic growth within regions came from certain "propulsive industries" concentrated within a small number of locations. The rapid growth of these industries generated further development through component activities, and given time, Perroux argued that regional growth could be self-sustaining. In a spatial context Perroux's ideas imply that urban centres should be designated; this is precisely what has happened in France, where all urban agglomerations except Paris have been designed *métropoles d'équilibre*. In Italy this pattern has not been entirely followed, although existing urban centres were coincidental with the growth pole designation of the Naples–Salerno area

TABLE 41

A summary of regional policies within the Nine (c. 1977)

Member state	Regions designated	Incentives	Disincentives
UK	Assisted Areas e.g. North, North-West, Wales and Scotland	Regional Development Grants on buildings, plant and machinery; Discretionary Payments.	Industrial Development Certificates outside Development Areas; Office Development Permits for London and SE
France	Most of country, but with concentration in the NW and SW and the *métropoles d'équilibre*	Regional Development Grants; cheap loans; discretionary tax relief; special help for coal and steel areas	"Agrément" system for development in Paris region and parts of Oise *département*; redevance and traiset taxes on Paris region
Italy	Mezzogiorno, including specifically designated growth poles	Grants; investment allowances; social security refunds; state directives	Scrutiny of all major investment plans of all companies
Netherlands	Stimulation areas in Northern region, the SW and SE plus 26 development points, mostly within these. Restructuring areas in South Limburg and around Tilburg	Financial help; industrial estates; labour retraining schemes	Congestion tax on new buildings in Randstad; other legal limitations
Belgium/ Luxembourg	Coal-mining and old industrial regions (e.g. Wallonia, S. Kempenland, Borinage)	Grants for industrial modernisation; new factory construction; infrastructure schemes	—

TABLE 41—*continued*
A summary of regional policies within the Nine (c. 1977)

Member state	Regions designated	Incentives	Disincentives
W. Germany	Border zones with E. Germany, Czechoslovakia and Austria plus many small development points	Financial aid for investing in new industry	—
Denmark	Outlying regions such as NW, NE, Southern and Central Jutland, Lolland-Falster and Bornholm	Grants for new factory construction; transport infrastructure	—
Ireland	Over half the country included in the Western underdeveloped region and selected Gaeltacht areas; other development points	Financial aid for industrialisation; selected industrial zones	—

and the Catania-Siracusa-Palermo poles in Sicily (*see* Chapter XIII). More recently, development points have been established in the Netherlands, West Germany and the Republic of Ireland. In practice, therefore, the regional incentives referred to in Table 41 have been geographically concentrated in small selected locations. Not all EEC member states have followed a growth pole strategy. The UK, notably, has pursued a growth area policy for the last forty years or so, and in other member states a growth pole policy has been intermixed with this wider type of regional policy. The consequence, once again, is diversity, both in the policy type and strategy.

In spite of around thirty years of operation, in general terms, regional policies in member states have only met with a limited degree of success. In the UK the problem regions of today are the traditional problem regions of the 1930s. In France Paris still dominates, although about 0.5m new jobs have been created elsewhere over the last twenty years or so. In Italy the job loss in the *Mezzogiorno* has continued in spite of massive sums of financial aid. In West Germany and Belgium regional policies have helped the problem mining regions, yet there is still progress to be made. In short, regional policies at national level have had no more than a holding effect, ensuring that regional imbalance does not increase further. One of the main tasks of the E E C's Regional Commission therefore should be to find better ways of monitoring the effectiveness of regional aid so as to provide a more coherently planned framework for its future distribution. The alternative, as Jarrett warns is that "governments concerned can accept that a major instrument of policy will become ineffective as integration proceeds; or they can refuse further integration in certain fields at least. Clearly neither is in the Community interest."[7]

Regional Aid from the E E C

Agreement on a European Regional Development Fund (E R D F) was eventually achieved in December 1974 after a series of protracted arguments and discussions between member states and the Commission. Although a working regional policy has resulted, the outcome has been a great disappointment, particularly to the less-favoured regions and poorer member states.

There have been many difficulties in creating the E R D F. Initially, no regional policy was developed by the Community since there was no specific provision in the Treaty of Rome for a common regional policy. It is, however, accepted that if the spirit of Article 2 is to be met (*see* Chapter II), some sort of regional policy is necessary to ensure the harmonious development of the Community. To have vast differences in prosperity between member states and between regions within those member states is a recipe for disharmony rather than increased integration. On this basis, the spatial concentration of the benefits from economic growth in the first decade or so of the E E C's lifespan has reinforced the basic need for a regional policy. There have been other difficulties, which are related to the analysis of previous chapters. Chapter X I diagnosed a variety of regional problems facing member states—to devise a common policy to cover all of these is not easy. Further, all member states have pursued their own forms of regional policy. As the previous section showed, these policies are diverse, so it is very difficult to see a single Community policy replacing them. At the best, harmonisation should be attempted in the early years of a common policy. A further and final complication is that other Community policies and institutions work in a regional context.

The financing of the Common Agricultural Policy (*see* Chapter I V) provides help for problem farming regions. The huge payments from the Guarantee section of E A G G F help to provide "a living wage" to poor inefficient farmers, especially in parts of France, Italy and West Germany. The compensatory payments, too, recognise particular problems of farming in difficult regions. The Guidance section of EAGGF, although considerably less important, is progressively striving to upgrade the quality of agriculture in problem regions. This is clearly shown in Fig. 42. The European Coal and Steel Community (ECSC) provides finance to assist in the retraining of workers who have lost their jobs in coal-mining. It also provides help for the training of workers in regions where the steel industry has expanded, e.g. Taranto in southern Italy and Fos in the south of France. A third form of established Community regional aid is from the European Investment Bank (EIB). This institution was set up to finance both projects in less developed regions and projects which could not satisfactorily be financed by member states. As Fig. 43 indicates, such aid is significantly directed to the Community's problem regions.

Since its establishment in 1960, the European Social Fund (ESF) has provided financial support for the training, rehabilitation and retraining of the Community's workforce. In particular, it has tried to combat the forces of structural employment prevalent in problem agricultural regions and in industries such as textiles and clothing. More recently its functions have been extended to include a wider range of workers and finance has been made available to help increase employment opportunities in all member states. As expected, the poorer member states are the main beneficiaries—in 1978 Italy was allocated £157m and the UK £75m out of a total fund of £382m. In size, however, the ESF is only small, taking up around 4 per cent of the Community Budget. So, regional aid from the EEC comes from a variety of sources in addition to the common regional policy. Table 42 indicates their total significance up to the end of 1977. In volume, these four sources are substantial and should be seen as complementary to the ERDF.

In October 1971, the first step towards establishing a Community-wide regional policy was taken with the agreement to limit the level of financial support for "central" regions. The Community was divided into "central" (approximating to "core") and "peripheral" regions, the latter group, of course, being the least-favoured. Aid for "central" regions was limited to a maximum of 20 per cent of the capital cost of projects and it was hoped to reduce this level in due course. Some harmonisation of the type of assistance was also agreed. This first step should not be overrated, for in practice the limit set was within the scope of policies that were operating in the "central" regions. More recently, limits have been agreed for "peripheral" regions and poorer member states. The highest limits are for a maximum of 35 per cent of the value of investment in the

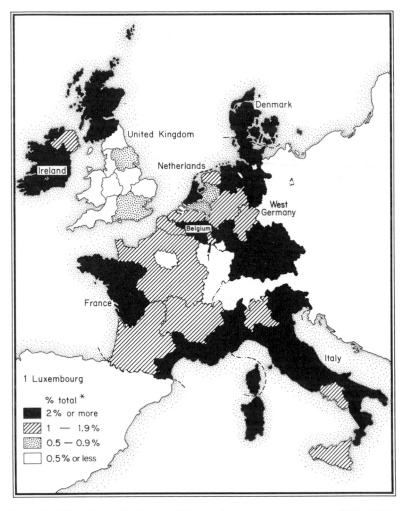

FIG. 42.—The regional distribution of finance from the guidance section of EAGGF, 1979. (*Note that this excludes finance to overseas départements of France, Greenland and projects in more than one region.)

Republic of Ireland, Northern Ireland and the *Mezzogiorno*. There are also 30 per cent and 25 per cent limits in other problem regions, with the 20 per cent limit remaining in other more favoured regions.[8]

The establishment of an ERDF has been a slow and painful process. National politics rather than the well-being of the less-

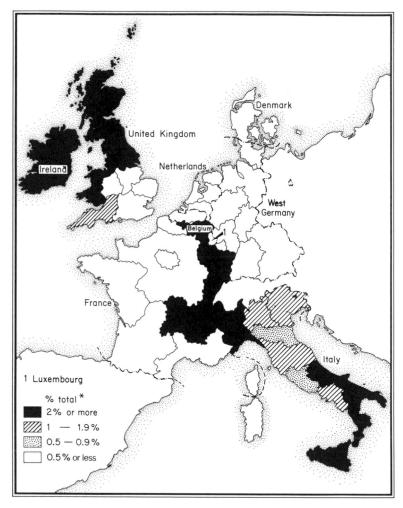

FIG. 43.—The regional distribution of finance from the European Investment Bank,
1979. (*Note that this excludes finance to Greenland and projects in more than
one region.)

favoured regions has been an overriding consideration. The basis for
the political arguments has arisen out of the mechanics of financing
the Fund—as with all common policies, member states contribute
through their payments into the Community Budget, while disim-
bursement is a direct consequence of the agreed policy. Like the
CAP, there is a built-in danger of competition in regional aid. As
Hallet says:

The question what kind of regional policy, if any, the Community should adopt has not been discussed solely in terms of what would be inherently desirable. A major consideration in recent discussions has been Britain's desire to do in regional policy what France so brilliantly accomplished in agricultural policy—getting more out of the kitty than she puts in.[9]

Since Hallet wrote this, the respective position of member states has hardened. The poorer nations, with the EEC's major peripheral regions, are seeking a significant fund to be allocated primarily to themselves. West Germany, on the other hand, has always been in favour of a very small fund; France is both determined not to lose out, while at the same time questioning the whole desirability and need for a community regional policy. To complicate matters, the

TABLE 42

Regional aid from the EEC to the end of 1977

Source	Total to date (£m)	Total in 1977 (£m)	Function
ECSC	3,334	594	Loans for the modernisation of coal-mining and steel industries and new employment creation schemes
EIB	4,664	1,000	Loans for a variety of projects, mostly in less prosperous regions
EAGGF	1,066	n.a.	Grants for the modernisation of agricultural production
ESF	1,000	n.a.	Grants for the retraining and resettlement of $3\frac{1}{2}$m workers

n.a. Not available.

Source: European Communities Information Service.

Commission seeks an effective policy, but sees that compromise is necessary. In all, therefore, the size and distribution of the ERDF have been the main bones of contention.

The initiative to get an ERDF off the ground came at the Paris Summit of Heads of State or of Government in October 1972. The UK, who had shortly before signed the Treaty of Accession, and Italy, jointly proposed a fund of £1,250m per annum. They anticipated that this sum would be distributed exclusively on projects in the less-favoured regions. So, along with the Republic of Ireland, the proposers would be the major beneficiaries. France and West Germany were not too impressed—they favoured a much smaller fund (£250m), which could be used to reimburse national governments towards the financing of existing policies. So, a third issue, that of "additionality", came to light at this meeting. At the time, the dis-agreement was overshadowed by the impending enlargement of the Community and the communiqué from the Summit asked the Com-mission to produce a report analysing the regional problems in the Nine (*see* Chapter XI).

The Thomson Report was an attempt to reach a compromise in order to ensure that the ERDF got off the ground at the beginning of 1974. It favoured a reasonably significant Fund, although the Commission decided not to lay down a precise size. Instead, it pro-posed that the required size of fund should figure in the annual budgetary estimates of the Community and so be based upon the Nine's available resources. As Stabenow notes, "The Commission proposed that 500 millions of units of account (about £200m) should be credited to the Regional Fund for 1974. It is thinking in terms of 750 millions of units of account for 1975, rising to one milliard of units of account for 1976."[10] On the question of distribution, the Thomson Report contained a map of proposed beneficiaries—these regions covered over half of the Nine's geographical area and about one-third of its population. In national terms, the percentage of eligible population is given in Table 43.

TABLE 43

Thomson Report: proposals for percentage population to benefit from
a ERDF

Ireland 100%, Italy 51%, UK 36%, France 33%, Denmark 32%, Belgium 17%, Netherlands 15%, West Germany 12%, Luxembourg 11%

On the basis of the above formula, the three poorest member states would be the greatest beneficiaries from a Fund. France, notably, would receive as much from a Fund as she paid into it, as too would Denmark. The four remaining member states would all be net contributors.

Stewart and Begg provide various criticisms of Thomson's attempt at compromise.[11] In particular they say that "the absence of clearcut proposals increased the likelihood that prolonged bargaining would undermine the coherence of the policy as a whole." Furthermore, as they discuss, the Report did not answer the key questions of size and distribution referred to earlier. Consequently, the Commission's plan for a Fund of 2,250m units of account (u.a.) over three years was counteracted by proposals from the UK for a Fund of 3,000m u.a. and from West Germany for a Fund of 1,000m u.a.

The proposed starting date for the ERDF went by, while trying negotiations continued between member states. Agreement was finally reached at the Summit of December 1974. Thomson's behind-the-scenes efforts were obviously a factor, but the return of a Labour government in the UK (and its persistent anti-EEC murmurings) helped to promote a compromise of sorts. The size of Fund agreed for the period 1975-7 was 1,300m u.a. (£540m). This was much smaller than the proposals from either the Commission or the poorer member states—in fact, it was only marginally in excess of West Germany's earlier proposal. The distribution to member states is shown in Table 44. This represented rather more of a compromise, although France was to receive a significant share. Italy and

TABLE 44

The European Regional Development Fund, 1975-77

	% share	Size of distribution (m u.a.)
Italy	40.0	520.0
UK	28.0	364.0
France	15.0	195.0
West Germany	6.4	83.2
Ireland	6.0	78.0
Netherlands	1.7	22.1
Belgium	1.5	19.5
Denmark	1.3	16.9
Luxembourg	0.1	1.3
	100.0	1,300.0

1975—300m u.a. to be allocated
1976—500m ,,   ,,   ,,
1977—500m ,,   ,,   ,,

the UK, two of the poorest member states were to receive over two thirds of the sum available. The question of additionality also involved compromise—aid from the Fund is paid directly to national governments, although they *may* decide to use the money to provide additional regional assistance.

The ERDF provides aid for two types of project, infrastructure, and industrial and service sector investment. The eligible categories of infrastructure are listed—they are items directly linked with industrial or service sector development (e.g. industrial estates) or certain items required for farming in mountain and hill or other less-favoured areas. The contribution from the Fund varies from 10-

30 per cent depending upon the size of investment. Qualifying investment projects are also stipulated—they must be projects already benefiting from regional aid or in the service sector, or must be concerned with tourism or be based on services that have chosen to settle in the region in question. The Fund's contribution is 20 per cent of the investment cost or 50 per cent of the aid paid from public funds under national regional policies. The rules of the Fund are, therefore, rather complex, with only a certain degree of uniformity between member states. In the U K, resources from the Fund have enabled an extension of the advance factory programme and help for infrastructure projects has been transmitted to the local authorities involved. There has been a clear adoption of the principle of additionality. The Commission however, has noted, and is concerned about, the contrasting situation in other member states.

From January 1977 one of the Regional Commissioners, Signor Antonio Giolitti, was given specific responsibility for co-ordinating the various forms of structural help for the poorer regions. In September he outlined the Commission's hopes for the next three-year period. He said that "if the Community is to go farther along the road of economic integration (and engage the loyalty of its citizens), it must have a comprehensive and active regional policy. Although it must be co-ordinated with, and complementary to, national regional policies, it must have its own distinct character."[12] He then made out a strong case for a change of emphasis and outlined the Commission's future plans. The main points were, first, that the new Fund should be 750m u.a. in 1978, rising by 100m u.a. in 1979 and 1980. Secondly, the new provisions should oblige all member states to clearly demonstrate that their receipts from the Fund were used as an additional contribution to national aid programmes. Thirdly, the Commission asked for 100m u.a. of the Fund to be available to finance specific Community measures, so providing a second and innovative side to the E R D F. Finally, there should be greater co-ordination of all forms of Community regional aid.

As in 1974, the full Commission plan was not accepted by the Heads of State or of Government. In December 1977 they agreed to a total Fund of 1,850m u.a. for the period 1978–80 and 580m u.a. was allocated for 1978, rising to 620m u.a. in 1979 and 650m u.a. in 1980. The quota allocations are roughly as Table 44, with a marginal increase for French overseas *départements*. (*See* Fig. 44.) The definition of project types has been made more flexible, particularly in the field of infrastructure. The Commission's proposal for a non-quota section of the E R D F has also been accepted, but at the level of 5 per cent of the Fund's total resources. The Council of Ministers stipulated as a condition of acceptance that every project financed in this

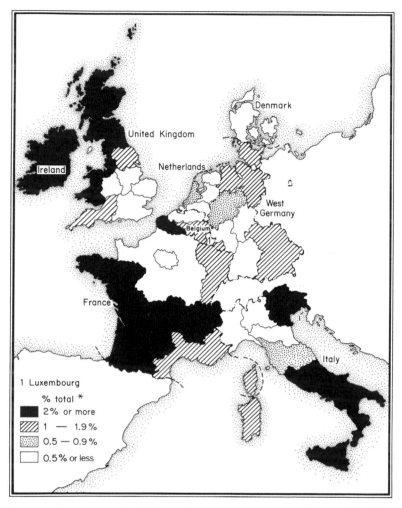

FIG. 44.—The regional distribution of finance from the European Regional Development Fund, 1979. (*Note that this excludes finance to Greenland and projects in more than one region.)

manner must be unanimously approved by themselves. The question of additionality has, however, still not been fully resolved.

The Commission's current thinking on regional policy is that the size of E R D F should be increased and concentrated on the regions in greatest need. In 1981, the Fund was 1,165 E C U (about 870m u.a. for comparisons with earlier years) but this seems pitifully small at a time when all regions are suffering from recession. Social Fund spending has also increased significantly. The E R D F and E S F are both under review at the present time and there is a strong feeling in the Community that a new directive on regional policy is required although this could be delayed until after a general meeting of European Regional Development ministers in Madrid planned for 1982. It remains to be seen whether or not an improved E R D F will be the outcome.

Even with more resources and greater flexibility, it is not claimed that the E R D F will resolve regional problems overnight. The national experience is such that this would be a foolhardy suggestion. The scale of problems of the poorer regions is indeed great; the fact remains that, with increased economic integration, the gap between rich and poor regions will widen. Although recent modifications to the E R D F provide a better basis for dealing with regional problems, the Fund must remain a disappointment to the Community. The danger is that, through becoming a victim of political circumstances, the bitter experience of the E R D F has cast a grey cloud over the whole future of economic integration in the E E C.

NOTES

1. Coates, B. *et al.*, *Geography and Inequality*, OUP, 1977, Chapter 3.

2. Buck, T., "Regional Policy and European Integration", *Journal of Common Market Studies*, Vol. XIII, No. 4, 1975, p. 373.

3. *The European Economic Community: Work and Home*, The Open University, Unit P933 7–8, 1974, p. 120.

4. Clout, H., ed., *Regional Development in Western Europe*, John Wiley & Sons, 1975, p. 15.

5. For fuller details, see Clout, H., ed., *op. cit.*

6. Jarrett, R. J., "Disincentives: the other side of regional development policy", *Journal of Common Market Studies*, Vol. XIII, No. 4, 1975, p. 379.

7. *Ibid.*, p. 386.

8. For details, see Stewart, J. A. and Begg, H. M., "Towards a European Regional Policy", *National Westminster Bank Quarterly Review*, May 1976, pp. 35–6.

9. Hallet, G., "Regional Policies in the European Economic Community", in *Regional Policy for Ever?*, Institute of Economic Affairs, 1971, p. 123.

10. Stabenow, W., "Regional Policy in the EEC", in Sant, M., ed., *Regional Policy and Planning for Europe*, Saxon House, 1974, p. 78.

11. Stewart, J. A. and Begg, H. M., *op. cit.*, p. 38.

12. Speech to North of England Development Council, Newcastle upon Tyne, 9th September 1977.

Chapter XIII

Problem Regions of the EEC

As we saw in the last two chapters, no country in the Community is entirely free from problems and all, to a greater or lesser degree, have problems of regional imbalance. We saw, too, that regional imbalance is very much a matter of geographical conditions and an unequal endowment of natural resources but there are also factors of an historical and cultural kind which have exerted an influence. There is not space to discuss all the regional problems of every member country of the EEC (which could easily constitute a book in itself) hence our intention is to describe and discuss some sample problem regions under the following headings: problem agricultural regions, problem industrial regions, problem frontier regions and problem congested regions. These will help us to understand the problems of regional imbalance, highlight the difficulties inherent in attempting to redress the balance, and, in some cases, illustrate how the problems may be assuaged and corrected. Figure 45 shows the EEC's principal administrative regions.

The problem regions within the EEC constitute a very substantial proportion of the whole area and some 40 per cent of the total population lives in these regions. The Community's problem areas include Scotland, northern England, Wales, Northern Ireland, Republic of Ireland, western France, most of peninsular and insular Italy, much of Jutland in Denmark, parts of the northern and eastern areas of the Federal Republic of Germany, along with some small areas in the Netherlands and Belgium. According to the Thomson Report "the regional problem encompasses the whole range of economic evolution from excessively agricultural regions to areas that have experienced their first industrial revolution and are facing unemployment as a result of structural changes necessary to change those industries and bring them up to date."[1] As the Thomson Report showed it is possible to group problem regions into the various functional categories noted in the first paragraph above. At the same time we should note that the problems of the regions are seldom due to a single condition, e.g. depressed agriculture, declining industry, marginal location, etc.; often several factors contribute to the regional problem though one may override the others.

Let us first enumerate the different functional problem categories.

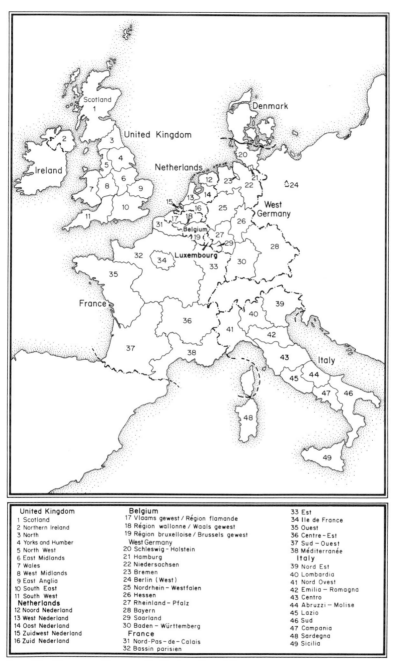

United Kingdom	Belgium	33 Est
1 Scotland	17 Vlaams gewest / Région flamande	34 Ile de France
2 Northern Ireland	18 Région wallonne / Waals gewest	35 Ouest
3 North	19 Région bruxelloise / Brussels gewest	36 Centre-Est
4 Yorks and Humber	West Germany	37 Sud-Ouest
5 North West	20 Schleswig-Holstein	38 Méditerranée
6 East Midlands	21 Hamburg	Italy
7 Wales	22 Niedersachsen	39 Nord Est
8 West Midlands	23 Bremen	40 Lombardia
9 East Anglia	24 Berlin (West)	41 Nord Ovest
10 South East	25 Nordrhein-Westfalen	42 Emilia-Romagna
11 South West	26 Hessen	43 Centro
Netherlands	27 Rheinland-Pfalz	44 Abruzzi-Molise
12 Noord Nederland	28 Bayern	45 Lazio
13 West Nederland	29 Saarland	46 Sud
14 Oost Nederland	30 Baden-Württemberg	47 Campania
15 Zuidwest Nederland	France	48 Sardegna
16 Zuid Nederland	31 Nord-Pas-de-Calais	49 Sicilia
	32 Bassin parisien	

FIG. 45.—European Community Regions (Level 1).

(*i*) The depressed agricultural regions are those characterised by the fact that the economic base of the region is heavily dependent upon farming and where productivity is low and employment opportunities are rather limited. Such regions are also generally typified by their ageing population structure and high levels of migration. The Scottish Highlands, mid-Wales, western Ireland, Brittany, parts of Aquitaine, the Massif Central, the French Jura, south-eastern Bavaria, the Alpine hill country of Italy and southern Italy could be classified in this way. At EEC level, the Common Agricultural Policy has aimed to assist such regions by, for example, granting compensatory allowances to hill farmers and ensuring generally high target and intervention prices.

(*ii*) The depressed industrial regions are those characterised by an economic base heavily dependent upon declining heavy industries such as coal-mining and shipbuilding and, also, the traditional textile industries. Central Scotland, North-East England, the South Wales coalfield, and the Sambre–Meuse coalfield are examples of former flourishing industrial areas which are now largely depressed and centres of high unemployment. Help for such regions has been and still is, available from the European Coal and Steel Community and the European Social Fund as well as national and regional aid.

(*iii*) Peripheral regions are those which are geographically located around the extremities of the Community and, in some instances, close to international frontiers. As regions, they are apt to be losing out largely because of the "pull" of the core areas. Some of these marginal regions are also mainly agricultural regions but, as a group, it was hoped that the Community's Regional Policy would provide them with assistance although, unfortunately, it has not worked out this way. Regions such as northern Scotland, western Ireland, Brittany, Aquitaine, Schleswig–Holstein, south-eastern Bavaria and southern Italy may be said to fall into in this category of depressed peripheral areas.

(*iv*) The core regions have all attracted migrants by virtue of the fact that economic activities and developments are largely concentrated in them; as a result, the social overhead capital is strained and costs of living are high. Regions such as South-East England, the Paris Basin, the Randstad, the Rhine Valley, Copenhagen and northern Italy will continue to be centres of attraction for people and economic development, but in order to ensure that the gap between them and the rest does not widen, agreement has been reached in limiting the scale of assistance available for new developments. In 1972 mutual agreement was reached between the members of the EEC on a maximum limit of financial assistance to core areas. It is hoped that eventually this level will be reduced. This was the first stage in the projected harmonisation of regional policies and the evolution of a Community Policy. Alas, not much else by way of agreement has been forthcoming.

Individual countries in Western Europe have pursued their own policies within their own territories. For the E EC member countries this makes moves towards a Community policy even more difficult to achieve. At national level each country has defined its own type of problem region and introduced a variety of measures to cushion these regions from the increasing reality of modern economic growth. As in the United Kingdom, the "carrot and stick" type of policy is more generally favoured by France, the Netherlands and Italy. Other countries, however, have not introduced policies to provide a disincentive towards development (for details *see* Chapter XII).

Depressed Agricultural Regions

The Scottish Highlands and Islands

This region, lying north of the Highland boundary fault which runs from Helensburgh to Stonehaven, occupies some two-thirds of the total area of Scotland. Apart from the Plain of Caithness, the Moray Lowlands, the Buchan Peninsula and the west coast fringe and islands, the Highlands form an extensive inland plateau split into two unequal parts by the tear fault of Glen More. Most of the inland plateau lies over 460 m but in parts of the North-West Highlands and the Grampians it lies over 914 m. In the west the annual rainfall is high, usually well over 2,540 mm, with much snow and a frost-free period of only about 90 days. The short summers are cool and often cloudy and rainy with little sunshine. Since the glens are more sheltered, they are drier. In the east the plateau is drier but it is very cold in winter with north-easterly winds bringing heavy snows. In the Great Glen, for instance, rainfall decreases from 2,905 mm in the south to 762 mm in the north. In summer, valley floor temperatures average about 15° C (58° F) or a little less in the North-West Highlands. While most of the inland plateau has a mean daily average of under 3.5 hours of sunshine, the eastern coastal belt averages around 4 hours. Briefly, the interior plateau has the worst climate in the British Isles but oceanic conditions characterise the western and northern islands since winters are mild and summers cool, although exposure causes them to be wet and windy.

The Highlands have only 8 per cent of the total population of Scotland spread over a vast rural hinterland. This is not surprising since, at least from the eighteenth century, emigration has been a characterising feature; furthermore, the Highland population continues to decline. Indeed, the entire region has suffered as a result of its remoteness, isolation, difficult geography and very limited resources. Since cultivation becomes unprofitable in the Scottish Highlands above 182 m such farming as is carried on consists of pastoral farming, the rearing of hardy Blackface sheep in heather and cotton grass areas and cattle, now mainly Shorthorns rather than long-haired Highland cattle. In some of the more sheltered glens and straths there are small acreages of oats, potatoes, turnips and rotation grasses.

Along the western seaboard, among the Hebridean islands and in the Shetlands crofting is practised. King writes:

> Crofts account for about a quarter of the agricultural output in Orkney, Shetland and the five Highland counties, and there are approximately 20,000 holdings of up to 75 acres run by these tenant farmers. Rent is comparatively low, little more than £50 per holding, but the crofter has not, up to the present, any right to a share in the increased value of the croft which may be due to his husbandry. This lack of incentive and the highly complex crofting laws hold back the development of nearly (2 million acres) of scenically attractive land.[2]

On the sides of lochs and on raised beaches the crofters wrest a hard living from the land, growing oats and hay for fodder, potatoes, turnips and vegetables for domestic consumption and cattle feed, and pasturing sheep and horses on common grazings. The croft is seldom self-supporting and the crofter usually has to supplement his income by some fishing or the making of hand-woven tweed or undertaking seasonal employment.

The east coast lowlands lie in the rain shadow hence rainfall varies between approximately 635–762 mm; although summers are cool there is a fair amount of sunshine and days are long. Land use is concerned with crop cultivation, principally barley, oats, turnips and other roots, but not wheat or potatoes for it is too cool, and with wide-scale stock raising, chiefly cattle.

Largely because of the strictly limited possibilities and partly because of the lack of alternative resources, traditionally the Highlands and Islands have exported their sons and daughters who have moved into the few coastal towns or southwards into the Central Lowlands and England in search of work. In agricultural rural areas resource management is principally equated with farming, the traditional activity of the countryside but in marginal fringes and what Alice Coleman termed *wildscape* areas resource management has wider implications involving water catchment, forestry, keepering

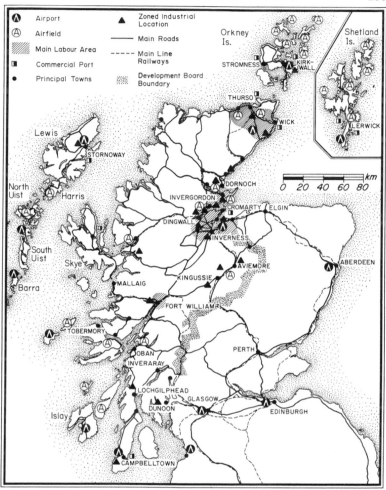

[*Source*: The Highlands and Islands Development Board.
Fig. 46.—The Scottish Highlands and Islands.

for shooting sports, and other forms of recreation in addition to
limited agricultural production. In the Highlands of Scotland the
generation of hydro-electric power has provided some jobs while
afforestation schemes have helped to maintain some viable rural
communities. Although tourism and recreation tend to be seasonal
and susceptible to changing demands, there is no doubt that they
provide an important input into local economies.

House has commented:

Redevelopment and growth in the Highlands and Islands is almost an "act of faith" for many Scots and it is impossible to ignore the substantial achievements of the Development Board created for that region in 1965. These have been equally impressive whether one considers the many disseminated improvements in fisheries, tourism, manufacturing and land development or the larger scale proposals to create growth areas: on the Moray Firth, in the Wick–Thurso region or around Lochaber (Fort William)."[3] (*See* Fig. 46.)

Even so, development strategies have tended to be piecemeal and to lack an over-all integrated approach for, as Strachan has said, "the provision of a job is not enough, it must be the right kind of job, and it must be backed up with an attractive social environment. Good housing, adequate services and improved accessibility are as important as work."[4] Perhaps this, however, was expecting too much in such a large, thinly-populated area. Furthermore:

The case for the diversion of investment to the Highlands and Islands, in the face of overall Scottish priorities is not universally accepted, and indeed there are those who argue that even north of the Central Lowlands there is a better case for investing in the modernised agrarian structure, manufacturing base and growth prospects of N E Scotland.[5]

The exploitation of North Sea oil has brought jobs and prosperity to the eastern littoral, although this has only served to attract more people to the east coast as the growth of many of the towns demonstrates.

Summing up, it may be said that the traditional activities of the Highlands are incapable of providing an adequate and satisfying livelihood for those, especially the younger folk, dependent upon them and, notwithstanding the attempts of the Development Board to revitalise the region, continued outmigration is likely to continue as people are attracted to the better economic and social environment of the east coast.

The Central Plateau of France

The Massif Central is a tilted Hercynian horst block; in its essentials, it is a tableland, roughly bounded by the 300 m contour, which has an average elevation of some 900 m and consists of varied rocks although basically it is made up of ancient crystalline rocks such as granite and gneiss. By Tertiary times the area had suffered severe planation and the old crystalline basement rocks had been covered by Mesozoic rocks. The Alpine orogeny, in addition to uplifting and tilting the region towards the north-west, resulted in fracturing, producing faults, along the eastern and southern margins and also in the centre, gave rise to volcanic activity, producing volcanoes and lava flows, and caused the rejuvenation of rivers resulting from changes in base-level. Subsequently, erosion stripped off many of the Mesozoic rocks and eroded the volcanoes. As a result of its geological history the Massif Central is, in detail, structurally complex and exhibits a variety of landforms. Climatically, the Central Plateau has a measure of continentality but it is its altitude which is largely responsible for the severe conditions which in the winter part of the year make it bleak, wet and windy.

Seven sub-regions can be distinguished within the Central Plateau: Morvan–Beaujolais in the north-east, the Cevennes in the south-east, the Grands Causses in the south, the south-western Uplands, Limousin in the north-west, the Basins of Bourbonnais in the north, and the Auvergne in the centre. Except in the Basins of Bourbonnais, there is little in the way of arable agriculture, and pastoral farming, involving the rearing of cattle, sheep, goats and pigs, is dominant. In the Morvan the soils are acidic and there is little cultivation, farming being concerned with livestock, especially store cattle and pigs. In the Cevennes sheep and goats are reared but their numbers are decreasing and the traditional practice of transhumance is decaying. The lowest south-eastern slopes are terraced and there is tree-culture, mainly of olives and stone fruits and, where water is available for irrigation, there is some market-gardening. On the dry limestone plateaus of the Causses the economic mainstay is sheep-rearing. Lack of soil, vegetation and surface water militate against human occupation and activity. The Grands Causses are a difficult area and in the department of Lozère a mere 10 per cent is classed as arable. In the Causses of Quercy in the west conditions are rather better and though the plateau tops are bare the intervening valleys are quite fertile. The climate is not as extreme as it is in the Grands Causses, the pastures are richer, and farming is more rewarding and productive. The south-western Uplands are made up of the crystalline plateau of the Ségalas and the massifs of Lacaune and Montagne Noire. Traditionally the Ségalas has been a region of poor subsistence agriculture but in more recent times soil improvement by liming and fertilising has led to a more varied and rewarding agriculture with the production of wheat, potatoes, and fodder crops with fruit in the more sheltered areas; cattle are also reared for veal and for dairy produce. The enclosing higher crystalline uplands of Lacaune and the Black Mountain are largely ill-drained moorland and heath but in the more sheltered valleys there is some cattle-rearing and a little cultivation of cereals. Limousin is an almost level, featureless granite plateau rising from about 300 m in the west to nearly 900 m in the east. In the higher eastern areas it is cool, cloudy and wet in summer and there is some snow in winter. It is an area of heath and rough grazing with peat-bogs in waterlogged hollows; it is, accordingly, poor country and the people depend mostly on cattle breeding. To the west, where the land is lower, conditions are kinder: winters are not as severe, summers are much warmer, rainfall is less and more equitably distributed, while the soils are deeper and more fertile; consequentially there is more arable farming with cereal cultivation and the production of potatoes, sugar-beet and root crops. Even so, cattle-rearing is the dominant branch of farming. The Basins of Bourbonnais in the centre north of the Central Plateau mainly comprise the valleys of the Allier and upper Loire. The Allier depression forms the fertile plain of Limagne where rich crops of wheat, sugar-beet and fodder crops are grown together with apricots, peaches and pears as orchard crops. Viticulture is practised on the lower valley slopes and in the vicinity of towns there are market gardens. The Loire valley is less productive, largely because the soils are poorer. Although the two valleys are mainly arable areas, considerable, and increasing, numbers of livestock, especially cattle, pigs and poultry are raised. Finally, the Auvergne lies in the centre of the Plateau; here are eroded volcanoes and basaltic lava flows. Farming is the basis of the livelihood of most people in the Auvergne but the emphasis is on livestock rearing. Although some sheep are reared in the more southerly parts of the Auvergne, it seems likely that cattle-rearing for meat and milk (mostly processed into cheese) will remain the dominant factor in the economy of the Auvergne (*see* Fig. 47).

Summing up, it may be said that, apart from the rich and productive Limagne, farming is something of a struggle as a result of the altitude, generally poor soils and often inclement climate which generally prevails in the Central Plateau. It is a somewhat niggardly and impoverished region and not for nothing has it been called *le pole repulsif* of France. Traditionally, it has exported its people. Population continues to move from the central mountainous areas and the limestone plateaus of the south, especially from the *départements* of Haute-Loire, Cantal, Aveyron, Lozère, Corrèze and Creuse.[6] As George has commented:

The intensity of the exodus and its effects on rural life varied. In a few extreme cases it resulted in a real run-down of human resources on a regional scale. Once the majority of the young adult population had left, the ageing of the population structure soon sterilised the regions of exodus, as in . . . certain parts of the Massif Central.[7]

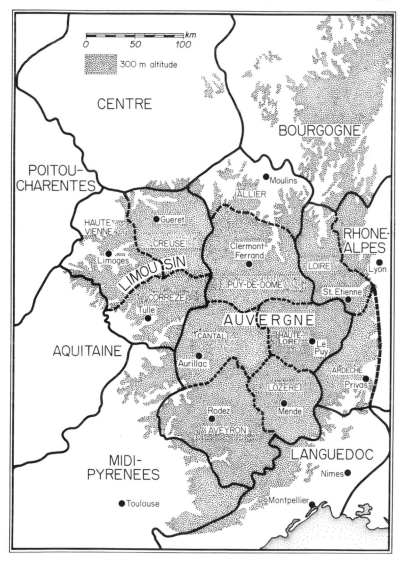

[*Source*: H. Clout, *The Massif Central*, OUP, 1974.
Fig. 47.—The central plateau of France (Massif Central).

In many areas, as, for example, in the Morvan, ruined farmsteads and deserted hamlets testify to the considerable depopulation which the area has suffered.

In an attempt to stem the drift and to turn what natural advantages it has to good account, a company *La Société pour la Mise en Valeur de la Région Auvergne-Limousin*, known in short as S O M I V A L, was established in 1964, to undertake rural development and improvement. S O M I V A L is organised into three sections which are concerned with agriculture, forestry and tourism. The company concerned itself not with the already established centres of tourism but rather with the extension of tourism into the lesser known rural areas which were undeveloped and unspoiled; it is hoped that, once enticed by the physical attractions of the country, tourism will become more widely dispersed and that this, in turn, will augment the income of those dependent upon a not very rewarding agriculture. In its attempts to diffuse tourism more widely throughout the Auvergne, S O M I V A L has undertaken some forty development projects:

> The type of development favoured is that of holiday villages, consisting of individual chalets and secondary homes, in some instances aligned round artificial lakes, possessing communal services. The objective is to afford inexpensive holidays in quiet surroundings as compared with the more animated and expensive established resorts. In this way tourism is seen as the final stage in integrated rural development, absorbing some of the produce of an improved agriculture and employing a proportion of the labour displaced through agricultural improvement schemes.[8]

Southern Italy: the Mezzogiorno

Nowhere within the E E C is the problem of regional imbalance more acute than in Italy. Although Italy has benefited enormously from the processes of integration and made great progress, the "economic miracle" has also emphasised that the national economy is beset with many structural problems. The major problem is that of regional dualism, for whereas the North has a flourishing agriculture, is highly industrialised and has standards of living approaching the Community average, the *Mezzogiorno*, the seven southernmost provinces along with Sicily, is barely at the take-off stage of development while living standards are only around 50 to 60 per cent of the Italian average and are the lowest within the E E C. Although great advances have been made since the 1950s, the basic problem of a gap between the North and the *Mezzogiorno* has remained.

The problem of the *Mezzogiorno* differs from that of other depressed regions of the Community in various ways. First, there is the scale of the problem for the *Mezzogiorno* covers about 40 per cent of the total area of Italy and has over one-third of the population, while the disparity of income differences, referred to above, is greater than in any other country. Secondly, the *Mezzogiorno* has never been, even remotely, a prosperous part of Italy. Geographically, the shape and position of Italy are both against the *Mezzogiorno* and, historically, these factors have combined to favour disunity. The distance between industrial Lombardy and Sicily is around 1,500 km and, bearing in mind the centrifugal tendencies at work within the E E C, the *Mezzogiorno* is well away from the industrial heart of the Community. In short, the *Mezzogiorno* is geographically peripheral both to the rest of Italy and the rest of the E E C and lacks the natural stimulus to foster economic development. Finally, the *Mezzogiorno* does not possess the resources which could form a basis for development: topographically, it is mostly mountainous or hilly, with limited lowland areas; climatically, it is semi-arid; its soils are thin, stony and dry; and the region is deficient in energy resources and important minerals.

The *Cassa per il Mezzogiorno* (Fund for the South) was established in 1950 to synchronise economic policies for the promotion of Southern development. In its early years, much energy and finance were directed towards the structural reform and commercialisation of agriculture and to economic and social infrastructure to aid development. It must be recalled that the traditional agriculture was based upon the *latifundia*, large estates owned by absentee landlords and worked by peasants under a system little removed from medieval serfdom. A monoculture, based upon wheat-growing alternating with fallow was practised together with transhumant cattle- and sheep-rearing. Such a method of extensive farming, which underutilised the resources of both the land and the workers, persisted until well into the present century. In addition to the *latifundia* there were the *minifundia*, the tiny holdings, often with scattered plots, which had arisen through the increasing subdivision of land holdings. Minshull comments that "In 1950, 45 per cent of all agricultural workers in the south owned no land at all; 28 per cent were sharecroppers who surrendered up to 60 per cent of their crop to the landowners as rent; only 27 per cent owned their own land."[9] Clearly such an out-moded system of agriculture had to be changed and the *Cassa* felt it necessary to break up the large agricultural estates largely farmed by share-cropping tenants and to develop production and marketing co-operatives. About one-third of the *Cassa*'s funds was spent on infrastructure. Transport development was the first priority, along with water, electricity and hospital services. In spite of these early efforts, however, there was a continued outflow of labour to the North where, as a result of an expanding national economy, industrial production was booming. There were doubts as to the benefits of this early agriculture/infrastructure strategy prom-

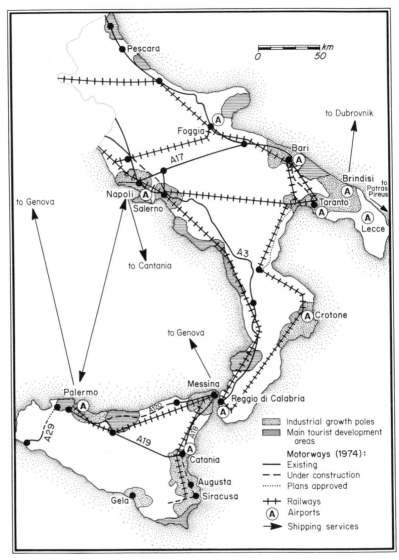

FIG. 48.—The Mezzogiorno.

oted by the *Cassa.* The planners had hoped that their policy would
lead to industry being attracted to the *Mezzogiorno*, but this was not
so. It was feared that a continuation of this initial strategy would
waste further public investment and hence, around 1957, there took

place a major change in development policy which resulted in greater emphasis being placed in the direction of industrialisation (*see* Fig. 48).

Investment through the *Cassa* has been principally in agricultural improvement, industrial development, tourism development and infrastructural improvement. Here we are only concerned with the changes and improvements in agriculture in the *Mezzogiorno*. Let us, therefore, attempt to summarise these and to assess their impact. As was indicated above, emphasis in the early 1950s was on the rehabilitation of agriculture which involved 56 per cent of the active population in the South and was the principal economic activity. Seventy-seven per cent of the initial fund of £600m was assigned to agriculture. "The chief items of intervention were river and erosion control, marsh reclamation, afforestation of uplands, road, aqueduct and sewer construction and, in support of the land reform, the building of farmhouses and service villages."[10] Altogether 535,000 ha (70 per cent of the total land expropriated from the large landowners) was in the South and this was redistributed to the landless and semi-landless peasants. 91,000 families in the *Mezzogiorno* benefited from this land reform. The land reform went beyond mere expropriation and redistribution, since it also involved land improvement, irrigation schemes, land-use planning, the establishment of co-operatives and marketing centres as well as the building of farmhouses and service centres and, as King has commented, "This conversion of bare *latifondo* land to a landscape of intensive farming with regularly planned farmhouse settlement is perhaps the most visible post-war geographical change in the rural South."[11] Output per hectare on expropriated land increased two- or three-fold as did *per capita* incomes, although it must be acknowledged it varied regionally and land reform was least successful in Calabria and central Sicily. Perhaps the most important effect of the land reform was the breaking of the social and economic power of the great land-owning class. Although the land reform could count some successes, it was costly and not wholly successful and the growth in the *Mezzogiorno*'s population did not halt the substantial drift of people to northern Italy. Yet it may be, King writes:

> that the most important effects of the reform are those which are not immediately apparent or measurable. To the downtrodden peasantry, who before 1950 lived in a hopeless world of poverty and unemployment, it brought some relief and the hope of better things to come; viewed in the long term structural growth sense, the reform fulfilled, albeit partially, the important function of stabilizing the peasants on the land to provide a point of departure

for future development; even in the short term it probably averted a disorder whose costs could have been immeasurable. It was inevitable, however, that such a one-dimensional programme should have serious limitations as a regional development policy. If the reform had been more sensitive with regard to differing geographical areas, to changing conditions over time and to the all-important human frailties of the South, it would have been more effective and less costly.[12]

Depressed Industrial Regions

North-East England

The industrial area of the North-East, roughly between the rivers Blyth and Tees, and primarily based upon the Northumberland and Durham Coalfield, grew to importance upon its coal-mining, iron and steel, and shipbuilding industries, but by the time of the Great Depression, 1928–35, the decline of these basic industries had set in and the Depression merely aggravated the economic dilemma of the area and brought massive unemployment. The area suffered acutely, largely because its economy was too firmly based upon coal-mining and the heavy industries; there were few light industries or activities employing female labour to ease the distress. The Second World War brought a temporary recovery but by the mid-1950s it became obvious that the existing industries—coal, engineering and shipbuilding—were in irreversible decline. Teesside suffered less in the post-war years because of the expanding iron and steel and chemical industries, but the traditional heartland of the North-East, i.e. the new county of Tyne and Wear, became industrially weakened, and socially and psychologically demoralised. This "depressed area" was recognised by the Government as a "development area" and a series of measures, including the creation of trading estates and the diversification of industry along with the establishment of new towns, e.g. Killingworth, Peterlee, Washington, Cramlington and Newton Aycliffe, were activated (*see* Fig. 49).

Prior to the First World War the Northumberland and Durham Coalfield had an average annual output of 54.4m tons, between 1931–5 it had decreased to 42.3m tons, and in 1967–8 to 26.6m tons. The coalfield has suffered a dramatic rundown in employment since the late 1950s, declining from 156,000 mining jobs in 1951 to 118,000 in 1961 and to 36,600 in 1976.[13] The older, shallower workings, which were situated on the Pennine flanks in the west, have mostly become exhausted or were uneconomic to work with the result that many of the collieries in west Durham have been closed down and since many of the villages were more or less solely dependent upon

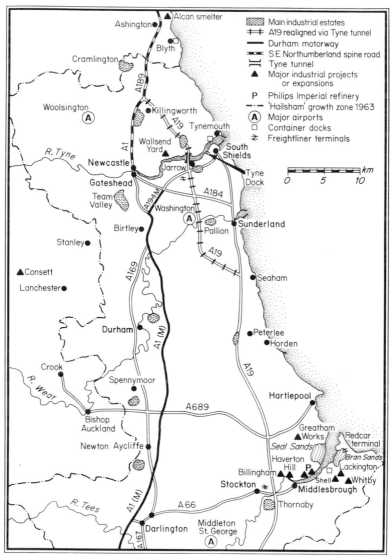

Fig. 49.—North-East England.

mining, there has been acute unemployment. Increasingly, the coal-mining industry has moved to the east where the large modern collieries mine the deep seams in the concealed portion of the coalfield. Since the coalfield was conveniently situated for the export of coal by sea, it has traditionally been a coal-exporting field and in the inter-war years rather more than a third of its output was exported. Because of this dependence upon the export trade, the field felt the effects of the Great Depression more than any other British field. In post-Second World War years it has also had to compete with the cheap exports of Polish coal. House has commented: "as pits close it is accepted that districts may lose their *raison d'être* and both regrouping and decline by out-migration of people may be the logical answer, as it seems to be for West Durham."[14]

The estuaries of the Tyne, Wear and Tees have a long history as an important shipbuilding and repairing area but during the past decade the industry has undergone an acute decline in part due to the savage competition from Japanese construction, in part to the energy crisis of 1973–74 which led to a severe cut back in tanker-building, and in part to union troubles. The loss of employment in shipbuilding and repairing over the past decade has been of the order of 50,000. In the North-East region the characteristic engineering industries are the making of marine and locomotive engines especially on Tyneside and the production of constructional steelwork (plates, girders, rails, etc.) centred on Teesside. Marine engineering is naturally associated with shipbuilding and as the latter industry is now in great difficulties so, too, marine engineering is in difficulties.

The North-East has been hit badly by the recession of the late 1970s and early 1980s. Unemployment has been consistently well above the national average and in January 1982 stood at 16% of the region's working population.

The Belgian Coalfields

The Belgian coal deposits occur in two basins:

(*i*) the Southern Basin which lies in the Sambre–Meuse trough (*see* Fig. 50 (*a*)) and which comprises two main sections,
(*a*) the Western Section, where the chief mining areas were the Borinage, centred on Mons, the Central Basin around La Louvière, and the Charleroi Basin (*see* Fig. 50 (*b*)) and
(*b*) the Eastern Section, around Liège; and
(*ii*) the Northern Basin in the province of Limburg which is known as the Campine or Kempenland Field.

The coal deposits of the Sambre–Meuse fields, though badly contorted and faulted formed the sole source of Belgium's coal until the First World War. Mining in the four basins was difficult and mechanisation was often not practicable, hence output *per capita* was low. In 1917 the rich reserves, which had been discovered beneath

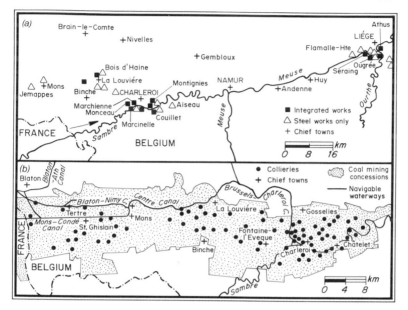

[*Source*: F. J. Monkhouse, *A Regional Geography of Western Europe*, 1974.
FIG. 50.—The Sambre-Meuse Coalfield: (*a*) Western and Eastern Sections; (*b*) detail
of Western Section.

the Kempenland sands, began to be exploited. The Kempenland
seams which are workable lie at depths of between 450 and 900m;
they are thicker and much less faulted and twisted than those of the
Sambre–Meuse fields. Modern mines, using mechanised equipment,
were sunk in and around the mining centres of Genk, Eisden, Ber-
ingen and Hasselt.

During the past twenty-five years the Belgian coal-mining industry
has undergone drastic changes. When the Coal and Steel Community
came into being in 1953 Belgium was producing 30m tonnes of coal
mined by 160,000 miners.[15] At that time two-thirds of the output
came from the Sambre–Meuse fields, more particularly the Charleroi
basin, and only one-third from the Kempenland field. Since that time
the decline in coal-mining has been dramatic and in 1976 total output
had dropped to a mere 7.2m tonnes. This decline is a reflection, in
part, of the geological conditions, out-dated equipment, low productivity and the high cost of coal and, in part, the change over from
solid to liquid fuel. In the early 1950s there was a coal crisis resulting
in the piling up of coal stocks at the pitheads to the tune of 6.7m
tonnes.[16] The outcome of this was the reorganising of the industry
and in the process numerous poor and unprofitable pits in the

Western Section of the Sambre–Meuse field were closed down and 30,000 miners dismissed while production in the Southern Basin as a whole was drastically reduced, and limited, in 1961, to 11.9m tonnes. In the Sambre–Meuse coalfield is to be found an industrial landscape highly reminiscent of those in many areas in Britain: a scene of pit-heads, spoil heaps, derelict factories and industrial slums. Five main towns form the foci of industrial concentrations since the industrial belt does not form a single conurbation. The industrial zone tends rather to be broken up by rural stretches; nevertheless, around each focal town there are satellite villages thereby creating wide-spreading industrialised urban areas.

The locality to the west of Mons, known as the Borinage field, and the neighbouring Centre field focusing on La Louvière have been characterised by roughly similar problems. Both areas in the postwar period have suffered economic decline. The Borinage area traditionally had been chiefly concerned with coal-mining and had never developed any manufacturing activities of any significance. Between 1948 and 1950 there were 28 pits employing 30,000 miners and "in 1953 coal-mining accounted for 56 per cent of employment" but after this date there was a drastic closure of pits—to 9 in 1956, 5 in 1965, while by 1974 only one colliery remained producing 500,000 tonnes of anthracite a year.[17] As F. J. Gay has commented: "The task of bringing replacement jobs to such areas as Mons and the Borinage, with little or no industrial tradition, has proved particularly difficult."[18] Nevertheless, since 1960, the E C S C has provided aid to the Borinage area and some 48 new factories have been established providing 8,000 new jobs. But, as a result of chronic unemployment the Borinage suffered out-migration while several thousand daily commute to other towns. Although the Borinage area suffered considerable hardship in the late 1950s and throughout the 1960s, there has since followed a substantial measure of industrial diversification, including the development of three large industrial estates concerned with the production of consumer goods and light industries. La Louvière and its area has likewise got over its traumatic period and the economic situation is much healthier. The other towns further to the east, Charleroi, Namur and Liège had a much broader industrial base and, accordingly, suffered much less.

Peripheral Regions

The Republic of Ireland

The Republic of Ireland is a peripheral, underdeveloped nation which in the Thomson Report qualified for aid under the Community's Regional Development Policy. The Republic of Ireland suffers from an essentially rural subsistence economy characterised by low productivity, a large proportion, 25 per cent, of the workforce engaged in agriculture, a limited development of manufacturing industries which are constrained by the small domestic demand and a limited export market, a small population of 3.162m with the lowest density, 45 per km², in the EEC, a traditionally high level of emigration, a low level of urbanisation with an underdeveloped urban hierarchy, and endemic poverty in most of the western areas.

Although the Republic's location, geography and resource endowment strongly militate against its development, Johnson says: "The key to many of the State's social and economic attributes lies in the size, distribution and history of its population."[19] Emigration, particularly of the young people, during the time of the Famine, a falling marriage rate and the delayment of marriage led in consequence to a reduction in the birth rate:

As a result of the combined effects of reduced fertility and emigration, the population of what is now the Republic of Ireland fell from 6.5m in 1841 to about 3.2m in 1911. Urban growth during this period of population decline was extremely modest, rural depopulation devitalised life in the countryside and, during a period of rapidly developing nationalism, emigration was seen as a process by which the nation's life blood was being drained away, although the economic advantages that migration brought to the individuals involved were too often overlooked.[20]

The whole of the Republic of Ireland qualifies for aid under the Community's Regional Development Policy, but the western part (see Fig. 51), which is hilly, even mountainous in parts, very moist and equable, is a truly underdeveloped region. Although there is little frost, rain normally falls on 225 days or more, it is commonly windy, and in summer spells of fair, warm, dry and sunny weather are rare. Consequentially commerical farming in the western region is severely handicapped and between a third and a half of the population are dependent upon a marginal subsistence agriculture. Wide areas of highland and poorly-drained bogland are devoid of settlement, while elsewhere rural settlement is often one of dispersed crofts with infrequent villages and such towns as there are are characteristically very small with frequently no more than about 1,500 inhabitants. Cork (125,000), Limerick (60,000), and Galway (27,000) are the only towns in western Ireland of any size and function as regional centres.

The Atlantic margins of the Republic consist of small "cottage" farms of usually under 16 ha and sometimes under 4 ha; in these areas which environmentally are difficult for farming and which are remote from commercial markets, the farmers are seldom able to

FIG. 51.—The Republic of Ireland.

support themselves and are compelled to rely on government assistance or on remittances from members of the family who have moved
away. In the west-central area—the counties of Sligo, Roscommon
and Galway—there are small farms, again usually under 16 ha with
some emphasis on the keeping of store cattle and sheep, while in the
south-western counties of Clare, Limerick and part of Tipperary,
there are small farms with some emphasis on dairying.

Minshull has made a useful summary of the farming situation in
western Ireland:

TABLE 45

Percentage employment in regions of Republic of Ireland, 1973

	Agriculture	Industry	Services	Workforce Total
East	6	39	55	415,000
South-East	34	27	39	121,000
North-West	51	18	31	30,000
Donegal	44	24	32	43,000
Mid-West	34	28	38	102,000
TOTAL (Whole of Republic of Ireland)	25	31	44	1,139,000

Poor soils, small and fragmented farms, lack of capitalisation and co-operative organisation, characterise a subsistence-oriented rural economy. Although total population decline has now been arrested in the Republic generally, many parts of the west are still threatened with decline. This is because of selective migration by young people, which adversely affects the birth rate and causes stagnation in many rural communities. The farm population is relatively old, and in the western region nearly 60 per cent of the farmers are over 50 years of age, representing a major obstacle to change.[21]

By the 1950s it was becoming abundantly clear that existing economic policies were totally inadequate and that there was a need for a new employment strategy. The Republic's small population of 3.2m is too restricted a base for a programme of industrial expansion supported only by the demands of the home market. In late 1950s several schemes for economic and social development were launched. It was recognised that one of the most pressing regional problems was to maintain a viable population in the western underdeveloped area; it was also realised that some more widely-based economic development was necessary. Although agricultural productivity might feasibly be increased, this could not be expected to create a demand for more labour and so attention was turned to the greater promotion of tourism and to attracting manufacturing industry.

The Republic of Ireland is not a major tourist country since the total number of visitors in 1971 was only around 2m but, from the viewpoint of its economy, tourism was of exceptional importance since it was the country's biggest money-earner after agriculture and played a vital role in the balance of payments. Receipts for 1971 totalled £103m. The Government, through the Irish Tourist Board, had done much to develop further the tourist industry. However, the troubles in Northern Ireland have had a crippling effect upon the Irish tourist industry and 1972 was a very bad year for Irish tourism: there were 212,000 fewer British visitors, earnings dropped by one-fifth, and there was a total loss of revenue amounting to £25m. This setback, from which the Republic has still not fully recovered, was unfortunate since in the attempts to revitalise the economy tourism had a very important role to play—for, perhaps more than anything else, it can facilitate and develop the spatial re-distribution of economic activity in the country. It is in western Ireland that the major areas of tourism growth and potential lie; development in the west "has the outstanding merit of providing employment in areas traditionally dominated by a declining farm economy."[22]

The Government of the Republic of Ireland, largely through the Irish Development Authority (IDA), has introduced a variety of measures to stimulate industry.

(*i*) incentives have been offered to encourage industrial investment, more especially for export-oriented industries;

(*ii*) restrictions upon foreign ownership of Irish companies have been rescinded;

(*iii*) the Underdeveloped Areas Act (1952) specified that western Ireland should be an "Underdeveloped Region" and made industries set up within the region eligible for preferential aid;

(*iv*) the Shannon Free Airport scheme provides advantages for companies producing for export markets, permitting them to import and export free of customs duties;

(*v*) the Small Industries Act 1969 aimed at assisting the modernisation and enlargement of local craft industries in the small towns in the west;

(*vi*) a number of factories have been established in areas which are continuing to lose people through migration, e.g. the towns of Donegal, Sligo, and Tralee where light industries have been introduced;

(*vii*) following recommendations by Professor Colin Buchanan, a number of regional development centres, e.g. Sligo, Galway, Ennis, Shannon and Athlone, have been designated.

These and other measures aim to re-vitalise and develop the poor, isolated and economically marginal Western Underdeveloped Region.

Brittany

Professor George, reviewing the western region of France, has said:

the most frequently mentioned problem is that facing Brittany.

Neither agriculture nor maritime activities can guarantee employment for its population, which is still large. Industry is only found in a few towns with, moreover, a basis of State creations, like the arsenals of Brest and Lorient, or enforced transfers, like the Citroën factories in Rennes.[23]

The peninsula of Brittany developed a strong individuality which it still largely retains. Its comparative remoteness and isolation from the rest of France (it was in fact the last region to come under the French monarchy) engendered a certain aloofness and helped to make the Bretons a people apart, much like the Welsh are in Britain today. The persistence of the Celtic tongue, Breton, together with traditional ways of life and ancient customs, account in part for Brittany's distinctive character. Relative isolation bred a spirit of independence and encouraged conservative traits so that Brittany became a province where "the past is preserved in the present".

Nature has not been particularly bountiful and it is very much a "region of difficulty"; assuredly, the environment, if not harsh, is by no means an easy one in which to live. In fact, the very difficulty of getting a living from the land has, on the one hand, driven the Bretons to the sea to augment their livelihood, and, on the other, caused them to migrate across the seas. This intimacy with the sea persists to this day since the Bretons are still the chief fishers of France and form the most numerous element among the sailors of the French navy and mercantile marine.

From the human geographical viewpoint, there is a distinction—now slowly but gradually becoming blurred—between the coastal zone and the interior areas. This distinction was recognised by the Bretons themselves who distinguished between the *armor*, or land of the seaboard, and the *arcoët*, or the land of the forest, i.e. the wooded hinterland. The coastal lowlands, though rugged, rocky and cliffed in places have many sheltered bays and fine ria harbours where ports have developed. The sea is the dominating influence in the coastal zone for not only does it serve as a medium of communication linking the various parts together but it provides a means of livelihood for fishing is an important resource. In the inshore waters shellfish are collected, as also is seaweed which is used as a food and fertiliser. Many Breton fishermen also join in the long-range cod fisheries around the Grand Banks and in northern waters. Many fishermen combine fishing with farming but the former subsistence type of farming has undergone drastic changes and the characteristic farming in the *armor* today is the large-scale growing of primeurs, i.e. early fruits, vegetables, and flowers, especially in sheltered areas around St. Malo, St. Brieuc, Roscoff and Quimper. Climatically, the coastal zone differs slightly from the *arcoët* in that it is more pronouncedly maritime: it is milder, completely frostless, and enjoys more sunshine and less rain. The early springs have fostered a highly developed and prosperous horticulture. Since the war, more especially, tourism has provided an increasing source of income. The wild, sea-fretted coast and its sheltered coves with small picturesque ports has attracted the holiday-maker so that many Bretons have found catering for tourists a more lucrative and easier business than fishing (*see* Fig. 52).

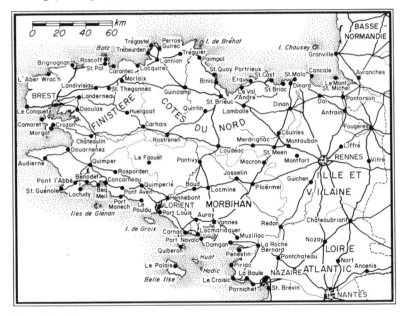

F IG. 52.—Brittany.

The *arcoët* was once thickly forested but almost all the forest has gone, yet much of the countryside possesses a wooded aspect; this is due to the fact that the numerous small fields are separated by hedgerows while here and there are clusters of trees, and wooded country of this kind is termed *bocage*. The interior is a land of gentle ridges and furrows which suffer from the double handicap of a bleakish and damp climate and generally poor soils; these have militated strongly against its development and it is an area where self-sufficient farming was, and to a large extent still is, characteristic, and where a dispersed settlement pattern of small, isolated farmsteads prevails. The peasants—poor, conservative, clinging to their local customs, and often superstitious—live a hard life and from time to time they have voiced their dissatisfaction. The uplands, now largely moorland and heath, support nothing save a few sheep, and are almost totally devoid of settlement. The valleys and more especially the basins, such as those of Châteaulin and Rennes, are areas of comparatively rich agricultural land where cereals, potatoes, sugar-beet, and fruit-trees are grown and where cattle-rearing, dairying and pig-keeping are practised.

"The control of Paris weighs heavily over much of the western regions, which for several generations have supplied labour to the industries and services of Paris, with the result that in the last twenty years there has been a certain demographic exhaustion, expressed in an appreciable ageing of the population structure, especially in Brittany."[24] Brittany has suffered a measure of inaccessibility because of its poor communications, but in more recent years funds have been provided to improve the poor road network, helping thereby to reduce the isolation of Brittany. Brittany has also suffered from lack of investment in industry, a situation which was aggravated by the crisis situation in the shipbuilding industry. Brittany ranks for only medium rates of assistance for regional industrialisation; nevertheless, between 1954 and 1968 some additional 20,730 entered manufacturing employment, a 15.9 percentage change; even so in 1968 the total numbers employed in manufacturing amounted to only 151,300 in the whole of Brittany. Under the Fifth Plan the town of Nantes was given the status of a *métropole d'équilibre* but "the creation of a metropolitan region is difficult, particularly as Rennes is the established trustee of Breton tradition and regionalism."[25] It will be clear that Brittany has many problems and that it continues to remain relatively poor, neglected and relatively remote and isolated. It is type-cast as a peripheral region.

Schleswig-Holstein

The border province of Schleswig-Holstein lies between the North and Baltic Seas at the base of the Jutland peninsula. The isthmus, some 75 km wide, historically was of great importance since it served as a link between the two seas, short-circuiting the long sea passage around Jutland. The two political provinces of Schleswig, to the north, and Holstein, in the south, have existed for a thousand years, "but they have had varied relations with each other and with Denmark to the north and with the German lands to the south."[26] The Eider river formed the traditional boundary between Denmark and Germany but both provinces were annexed by Prussia in 1864.

The province forms part of the North German Plain. It is covered by a thick spread of glacial and post-glacial deposits and only in a few places, chiefly in western Holstein, does the underlying chalk reach the surface. Physically, three fairly distinctive areas can be discerned: the marshes in the west, the product of a long struggle between man and the sea when dyking and silting took place to effect land reclamation; the central upland of *geest* which in the west consists of sandy plains crossed by streams with wide flat floors and which in the east comprises fluvio-glacial deposits with flat alluvial fans where streams carved their way through the north-south trending moraines; and the eastern morainic hill country which has a hummocky relief of uplands and hollows. On the western coast are salt mud-flats, known as *Watten*, which are exposed at low tide; on the eastern coast there are long, deeply-penetrating embayments known as *Förde* which are submerged melt-water eroded channels.

The *geest* uplands of the interior are poor with areas of bog and peat, now mostly drained, while the heath has been partially afforested with conifers. Although in the north there are meadows and pasturelands supporting cattle, the poverty-stricken soils will only support "occasional fields of rye, oats, potatoes and buckwheat, that alternate with occasional clumps of stunted oak wood (*Kratt*), peat, bog and coniferous woods."[27] The peripheral zones are more productive. In the *Marschen* zone in the west, where it is cool and damp, some summer wheat, beans and cabbages are grown, but the economy is mainly pastoral for most of the land is under grass. Apart from cattle-rearing, some sheep and geese are kept. In the eastern morainic uplands where there is less rainfall and areas of good loessic and brown forest soils farming is rather more rewarding with grain and oil seeds being cultivated; there are also some gardens and orchards, while in the meadow lands cattle are raised and fattened (*see* Fig. 53).

The "marsh" village is characteristic of the North Sea coastlands and the banks of the Elbe; in the geestlands compact villages are dominant; while in the east settlement is mainly one of isolated farmsteads and small hamlets. Apart from Kiel and Lübeck, which are the only sizeable towns, the remaining towns, e.g. Schleswig, Rendsburg, Neumünster, Flensburg, are small, with populations of less than 100,000. The total population of Schleswig-Holstein is around 2.25m giving an over-all density of about 144 persons per km², although density in the rural areas is between 50 and 75 persons per km². Dickinson comments:

> The result is rural overcrowding which even the subdivision of large holdings cannot absorb. Industry might absorb the extra hands, but here there are small prospects of expansion, and it

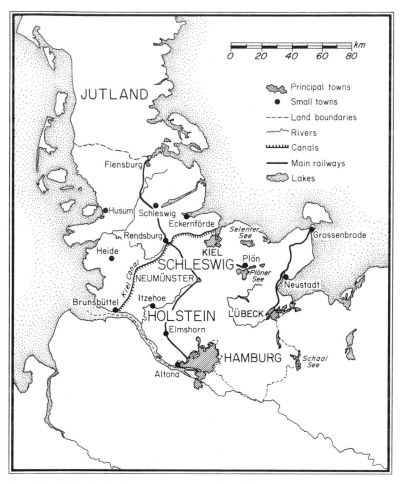

FIG. 53.—Schleswig-Holstein.

would seem that about half a million persons cannot be employed in the province and must go elsewhere.[28]

Schleswig-Holstein is but one of a whole series of development areas running along West Germany's eastern borderlands. This eastern frontier zone constitutes a problem area; as Parker has said; "Since the division of the country there has been a movement of population and economic activity westward leaving a sort of 'cordon sanitaire' along the frontier which it has proved very difficult to revitalise."[29]

Problem Congested Regions

The Paris Region

Like the London region, the Paris region poses a problem of definition: clearly it does not refer to the municipality, notwithstanding its population of 2.59m, but does it refer to the *agglomération parisienne* with its population of 8.5m, or the Région Parisienne embracing three *départements* and extending up to 90 km away from the city, or to the Paris Basin Planning Region? Perhaps the area covered by the master plan (the *Schéma Directeur d'Aménagement et d'Urbanisme de la Région Parisienne*) of 1965 provides the clearest indication of the Paris region.

The functions of Paris are multifarious: above all, however, it is the political capital but, besides being the seat of a highly centralised administration, it is a major industrial town, a great commercial centre, a great cultural focus, and a tourist centre. Paris is a city of the world as well as *the* city of France. Beyond the limits of the municipality there are a number of satellite towns, such as St. Cloud and Versailles to the west, which are residential areas, and Suresnes, St. Ouen, St. Denis to the north-west, which are industrial areas, and Aubervilliers–Bobigny to the north-east together with the banks of the Seine around Argenteuil.

The continuing growth of Paris is creating problems and it is estimated that by the end of the century Greater Paris will have a population of at least 12m. In view of this growth a Master Development Plan has been drawn up which involves a linear extension downstream. New zones of urban development are to be developed along two preferential axes: on the northern axis will be Noisy-le-Grand, Bry-sur-Marne, Beauchamp and Cergy–Pontoise; on the southern axis Evry, Trappes and Sud de Mantes. While the City of Paris has lost population as a result of migration, the outer suburbs are experiencing phenomenal rates of increase, e.g. at Mantes-la-Jolie, Creil and Melun. George comments: "The development of the Paris region seems to be directed in the future towards multiplying the nuclei of urban life within a very large agglomeration, dominated by the symbol of Paris, but less and less by the core area of the old Paris alone"[30] (*see* Fig. 54).

Since the Paris agglomeration employs about one-fifth of the total French labour force—some 4m workers—an inadequate transport system has to cope with 3m daily commuters and there is frightful congestion. In early morning, at lunchtime and at teatime the traffic on the *peripherique* has to be seen to be believed. Since about one-third of the workers travel by private car, the parking problem is acute. The Paris Metro, i.e. the underground system, only extends to

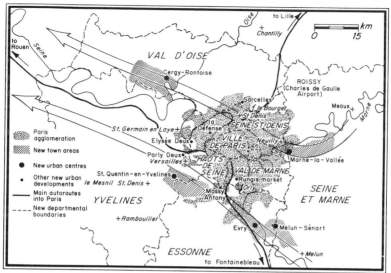

[*Source*: J. Ardagh, *The New France*, Penguin, 1979.
FIG. 54.—The Paris Region. The eight départements of the new "Paris Region"
showing the two parallel axes of the new urban centres.

the inner suburbs, but there are plans to extend the Metro system
with new rapid transport proposals.

A measure of industrial decentralisation has been attempted within
a 250 km radius around Paris concerned more particularly with the
metallurgical and general engineering industries, the electrical, electronic and precision engineering industries, the chemical industry,
textiles and clothing, and the wood and furniture industry. But, says
George, "The term 'industrial decentralisation' applies more to an
intention than to an objective reality."[31] Between 1945 and 1962,
1,280 decentralisation operations were effected which involved the
creation of 114,500 jobs and a further 231,000 jobs forecast. Most of
the decentralisations appear to have gone to the smaller towns of
from 15,000 to 50,000 inhabitants to the west and north of Paris, and
especially to places with easy and rapid contacts with Paris.

As long ago as 1947 J. F. Gravier's book *Paris et le désert français*
described France in terms of a core/periphery model and indicated
that Paris had accrued to itself an excessive share of the country's
population, economic activities, decision-making, cultural and higher
education facilities. It was clearly apparent to Gravier that provincial
France was gradually becoming a cultural and economic "desert"
and that if a halt was not called to the continuing growth of the core

area, the peripheral regions would be further weakened. Only by a policy of decentralisation and vigorous regional development could the overweening power and influence of Paris be halted and the problems of the provinces assuaged. Notwithstanding the development of *métropoles d'équilibre* to serve as regional growth poles and magnets for migrants, the Paris Region remains the great pole of attraction in France.

The London Region

The London region lies within the larger South East Economic Planning Region, over which, however, it exerts a strong influence. Within the planning region one can discern a threefold zonal structure:

(*i*) Greater London, the built-up area almost all of which is administered by the Greater London Council;

(*ii*) the encircling Outer Metropolitan Area, with a population of some 5.5m, which makes up most of London's city region outside the metropolis; and

(*iii*) the Outer South-East comprising the peripheral areas of the planning region.

The term "Metropolitan Region" is used to embrace the Greater London Area and the Outer Metropolitan Area.

South-East England is the largest, most populous, most economically important, and most prosperous region in Britain. The huge concentration of population in the South-East is in part a response to, and in part a cause of, the largest concentration of economic activity and jobs in the country. Greater London and the surrounding towns constitute the country's most important manufacturing area with some 2.5m workers engaged in a very wide range of industries. In spite of the importance of these, they are even surpassed by the service activities which employ over 5m people or some 39 per cent of the British total. The latter are absorbed by the national government administration, local government, medical and hospital services, education, electricity, gas and water services, and the building industry; in addition, there are numerous other service activities grouped as professional, scientific, hotel and catering, and the entertainments industry.

The highly concentrated development of a very wide range of manufacturing industries and service activities in the South-East owes much to the demands of the capital itself with its 7.3m inhabitants enjoying relatively high incomes and to the region's unrivalled nodality in terms of communications. Population growth in London and its region—from 10.5m at the beginning of the century to 17m today—and its remarkable economic development during the past fifty years have led to a host of problems relating to housing, land shortages, water supplies, transport, waste disposal, pollution and tourism growth.

Over the past 150 years London has grown from a city of rather more than 1m people into a great conurbation of nearly 8m. Greater London is the centre of a region containing a further 9m people. The continued growth of Greater London in the inter-war years, together with the bomb and fire damage of the Second World War, made it necessary to plan for some measure of decentralisation of people and industry. It seemed desirable, too, to halt the urban sprawl and the institution in the post-war years of the "green belt" effectively restricted this outward migration since it prevented new industrial building and created a much needed recreational zone. Industrial expansion has been encouraged to site itself in the development areas to promote decentralisation, although this has not been easy to achieve since London possesses too many geographical advantages for industry to move away without strong incentives or compulsion. The decentralisation of population has been promoted in three different ways:

(*i*) by the building of "out-country estates" on the borders of the Greater London area;

(*ii*) by the construction of eight new towns; and

(*iii*) by the expansion of existing towns which lay well away from London.

As a result, London has continued to lose population whereas the areas outside the conurbation have gained population, especially in areas to the north of the conurbation which have experienced increases of around 4 per cent annually[32] (*see* Fig. 55).

Pressure on land resources for houses, shops, offices, industry and transport is acute. While competition for urban land, as between, for example, large departmental stores, office blocks, markets, factories, etc., tends to sort itself out in economic terms because of differential land prices, the situation is different when it comes to housing, for housing provision must take into consideration social as well as economic factors. Lower-paid workers, for instance, cannot afford to live far from their place of work because of high commuting costs. In London many jobs are in or near the city centre where, of course, land values are high and, as a consequence, it becomes almost impossible to provide reasonably priced housing without a large measure of public subsidy. There appears to be a shortfall of around 150,000 houses but Keeble has commented that "the successful elimination within the not-too-distant future of London's long-standing and serious housing problem must remain in doubt."[33]

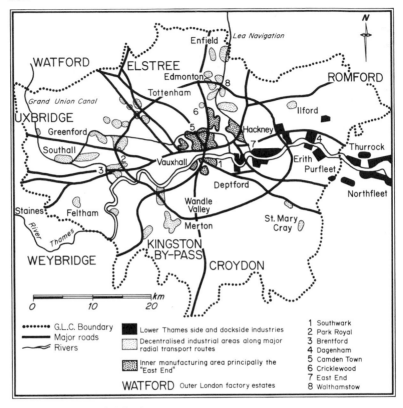

FIG. 55.—The London Region.

The provision and maintenance of transport facilities, in both the public and private sectors, has created acute planning problems. London's public transport system—suburban railway, underground and bus services—has been faced with serious and growing problems over the past fifteen years. There are, perhaps, two main problems: the massive growth in motor-car ownership and the consequent congestion to which it has given rise has become self-defeating, since the vast amount of traffic clogging the highways has slowed down movement in central London, especially at peak periods, and in spite of the introduction of traffic management schemes, the road network is inadequate to meet the growing volume of traffic; the second main problem relates to the financial problems facing London's public transport services: the services have to cope with a marked peak demand between 07.00 and 10.00 hours in a morning and 16.30 and 19.00 hours in the evening in connection with journeys to work;

accordingly, the public transport systems (rail, underground and buses) have to meet the costs of vehicles, track, equipment and staff which are economically used only during the two peak periods of the day. In order to be viable, constant increases in fares have been imposed, although this has merely encouraged the loss of off-peak traffic to private transport. It would seem that the fundamental financial problems of London's public transport system cannot be overcome other than by some form of massive subsidisation. Another major transport problem relates to London's airports: the rapid growth in air traffic, both passenger and goods, has focused attention upon the need for a third London airport. Again, the amount of business carried on by the Port of London has fallen severely and it now accounts for only 17.5 per cent of the total national trade. Once Britain's largest port, it is now struggling for its life and is operating at a heavy financial loss—£16m in 1978. Without doubt many of its difficulties arise from the industrial decline of Britain and changes in world trading conditions, but many more arise from conditions in the docks themselves particularly associated with a militant labour force. In consequence the long-term future of the Port of London is not bright.

Earlier reference was made to the 17m people living in the South-East Region and to its economic growth. This demographic and economic expansion, together with the improvement in social conditions, is placing stresses and strains upon the region's, and especially Greater London's, water resources. Municipal and industrial needs are clearly going to require increased amounts of water. It would seem there will be no escape from the necessity to find greatly increased volumes of water. Currently London's water supply is provided by three principal sources: the artesian bores which tap the Chalk aquifer, though this yield is gradually declining; the Thames itself upstream from London, the abstracted water being filtered and stored in large reservoirs such as the four at Staines and the four near Walton-on-Thames; and the string of reservoirs in the Lea Valley which stretch all the way from Waltham Abbey to Walthamstow. Gregory writes: "the predicted population expansion indicates a potential deficiency of some 500 million litres (1100 million gallons) per day by the end of the present century."[34] How is this deficiency to be made good? The more immediate solution is to exploit further the two main sources of supply—the groundwater resources and surface storage in reservoirs. In the long term, however, it appears that it will be necessary to import water from outside the region by transferring water from river to river by a measure of environmental engineering. Alternatively, desalinisation may have to be resorted to if sufficiently economic methods could be adopted.

The growth of the overseas tourist trade to Britain grew from 6m in 1970 to 12m in 1977. During the course of the latter year probably some 9m tourists visited London. It is unfortunate that in the summer holiday season, especially, too many crowd into London and this brings with it many disadvantages. The great influx of overseas tourists in summer exacerbate the congestion on the capital's thoroughfares and underground system. A more serious objection to the growth of London as a tourist centre is that houses and flats in the centre of the city are frequently turned into hotels, thereby aggravating the already acute housing situation. A further complaint is that the tourist industry, especially its hotel and catering side, employs large numbers of foreigners who compete with the indigenous population for jobs and accommodation. Another important issue is the problem of conservation, since the flood of summer tourists means that London's ancient buildings, historical monuments, parks and other places of interest must bear the impact (in terms of wear and tear, litter, disfiguration, vandalism, etc.) of the tourist. Finally, the greater the influx of foreign tourists, the greater the inconvenience and loss of amenity and facilities for those resident in London.

The problems of land and its allocation in relation to the population, employment, housing and transport problems outlined above demand land-use control and regional planning. Planning proposals for the London region date from the early years of the present century and Ebenezer Howard, Sir Raymond Unwin and Sir Patrick Abercrombie all advanced ideas and strategies to help solve the problems of London and its region. Abercrombie's concentric zone plan became the basis of post-war planning but the growing pressure upon land led to a comprehensive rethinking of regional policy for the South-East. The *South East Study 1961–1981* was the initial investigation into the problems of the region but in its approach it tended to be rather orthodox and was strongly reminiscent of Abercrombie's plan on a larger scale.[35]

In 1966 the new economic planning regions were delimited and introduced and economic planning councils were set up to act as advisory bodies to the government in connection with physical and economic planning. The Council of the South-East region quickly produced a long-term physical plan for its area which departed markedly from earlier ideas. The Council's plan suggested a developmental pattern based upon sectors related to the principal radial routes diverging outwards from London. Each of these sectoral developments led urban and industrial developments outwards to proposed future growth areas: the South Hants area, the Aldershot–Basingstoke area, the Reading to Newbury area, the area between Luton, Bedford and Milton Keynes, the area south and north of

Biggleswade, the area roughly between Chelmsford and Colchester, north Kent between Chatham and Deal, the area between Ashford and Folkestone, and the area north of Brighton to Redhill. There have since been modifications to these proposals. Whatever the final outcome it is, as Thomas has commented:

> too much to expect that all the planning problems of London and its surrounding region will finally be solved. At best a new plan will impose a fresh order, will reduce land-use conflict, and will go some way to maximising the personal welfare of the population of the region. In an area where such dynamic social, economic, and geographical forces interplay this would be achievement indeed.[36]

NOTES

1. Commission of the European Communities, *Report on the Regional Problems in the Enlarged Community*, COM (73) 550, 1973.

2. King, W: A., *The British Isles*, 2nd edition, 1976, Macdonald & Evans Ltd, p. 113.

3. House, J. W., *The UK Space: Resources, Environment and the Future*, 2nd edition, 1977, Weidenfeld & Nicolson, pp. 53–4.

4. Strachan, A. J., "Scotland—The Highlands, Islands and Southern Uplands", in *An Advanced Geography of the British Isles*, Hulton Educational Publications Ltd, 1974. p. 354.

5. House, J. W., *op. cit.*, p. 53.

6. Minshull, G. N., *The New Europe*, Hodder & Stoughton, 1978, p. 144.

7. George, P., *France: A Geographical Study*, Martin Robertson, 1967, p. 61.

8. Thompson, I. B., *Modern France: A Social and Economic Geography*, Butterworths, 1970, p. 382.

9. Minshull, G. N., *op. cit.*, p. 233.

10. King, R., "Italy", in *Regional Development in Western Europe*, ed. Clout, H. D., John Wiley & Sons, 1975, p. 98.

11. King, R., *op. cit.*, p. 97.

12. *Ibid.*

13. House, J. W., *op. cit.*, p. 47.

14. *Ibid.*

15. Robinson, H., *Western Europe*, 5th edition, University Tutorial Press Ltd, 1977, p. 309.

16. *Ibid.*

17. Minshull, G. N., *op. cit.*, p. 191.

18. Gay, F. J., "Benelux", in *Regional Development in Western Europe*, *op. cit.*, p. 149.

19. Johnson, J. H., "The Republic of Ireland", in *An Advanced Geography of the British Isles, op. cit.*, p. 211.

20. *Ibid.*, p. 212.

21. Minshull, G. N., *op. cit.*, p. 245.

22. Aalen, F. H. A. and Bird, J. C., *Tourism in Ireland—East, Guidelines for Development*, Eastern Region Tourism Development, 1969, p. 3.

23. George, P., *op. cit.*, p. 191.
24. *Ibid.*
25. *Ibid.*
26. Dickinson, R. F., *Germany: a regional and economic geography*, 2nd edition, Methuen & Co. Ltd, 1964, p. 603.
27. *Ibid.*, p. 606.
28. *Ibid.*, p. 611.
29. Parker, G., *The Logic of Unity*, 2nd edition, Longmans, 1975, p. 86.
30. George, P., *op. cit.*, p. 221.
31. George, P., *op. cit.*, p. 210.
32. Thomas, D., "The South East", in *An Advanced Geography of the British Isles*, *op. cit.*, p. 154.
33. Keeble, D., "The South East and East Anglia", in *Regional Development in Britain*, 1972, p. 81.
34. Gregory, K. J., in *An Advanced Geography of the British Isles*, *op. cit.*, p. 66.
35. Thomas, D., *op. cit.*, p. 163.
36. Thomas, D., *op. cit.*, p. 164.

Appendix

The Treaty of Rome: An Outline of its Principal Provisions

Article 1—By this Treaty, the High Contracting Parties establish among themselves a EUROPEAN ECONOMIC COMMUNITY.

Article 2—The Community shall have as its task, by establishing a common market and progressively approximating the economic policies of member states, to promote throughout the Community a harmonious development of economic activities, a continuous and balanced expansion, an increase in stability, an accelerated raising of the standard of living and closer relations between the States belonging to it.

Article 3—For the purposes set out in Article 2, the activities of the Community shall include, as provided in this Treaty and in accordance with the timetable set out therein:

(*a*) the elimination, as between Member States, of customs duties and of quantitative restrictions on the import and export of goods, and of all other measures having equivalent effect;

(*b*) the establishment of a common customs tariff and of a common commercial policy towards third countries;

(*c*) the abolition, as between Member States, of obstacles to freedom of movement for persons, services and capital;

(*d*) the adoption of a common policy in the sphere of agriculture;

(*e*) the adoption of a common policy in the sphere of transport;

(*f*) the institution of a system ensuring that competition in the common market is not distorted;

(*g*) the application of procedures by which the economic policies of Member States can be co-ordinated and disequilibria in their balances of payments remedied;

(*h*) the approximation of the laws of Member States to the extent required for the proper functioning of the common market;

(*i*) the creation of a European Social Fund in order to improve employment opportunities for workers and to contribute to the raising of their standard of living;

(*j*) the establishment of a European Investment Bank to

facilitate the economic expansion of the Community by opening up fresh resources;

(k) the association of the overseas countries and territories in order to increase trade and to promote jointly economic and social development.

Articles 4-8—These lay down the institutional structure of the Community, the obligations of member states and a detailed programme for the twelve year establishment of the common market.

Articles 9-37—These set out in detail the means and timetable for the establishment of the customs union.

Articles 38-47—These list the three main principles for a common agricultural policy, i.e.

(*i*) free trade in farm products between the Member States with common price levels;

(*ii*) the joint financing by the Community of the costs of market support for farm produce and the subsidising of exports to non-member countries, and the cost of modernising agricultural economy;

(*iii*) a common policy for trade in agricultural products with third countries.

In addition, it is stated that another aim of the policy is to raise the level of farming efficiency throughout the Community, particularly in the less-favoured areas.

Articles 48-73—These lay down the principles for achieving the free movement of people, capital and services. The first set of articles lay down the freedom for workers from Member States to get employment anywhere within the Community. Similarly, there is provision for the freedom of establishment for firms' branches, agencies etc., as well as for professional persons like lawyers and doctors. The right to supply services is also covered and applies to activities like wholesale and retail distribution, insurance, and banking. Finally, a programme for the removal of restrictions on the movement of capital is outlined and also the basis for harmonising company laws.

Articles 74-84—These provide for a common transport policy but only for rail, road and waterways transport.

Articles 85-94—These lay down rules of competition which are deemed necessary to ensure a free market in trade between Member

States. Specific articles in this set cover restrictive practices, policy towards monopolies and mergers and aid to State industries.

Articles 95-99—These deal with taxation policy and intend to ensure that Member States do not impose taxes on each other's produce which are higher than those levied on their own. Taxation harmonisation is the stated longer-term intention.

Articles 100-102—These provide for the harmonisation of national laws to the extent necessary to further the objectives of the Community.

Articles 103-109—These cover the objectives of economic policy to be adopted by the Community, especially the measures to be taken in case of balance of payments crisis.

Articles 110-116—These articles lay down the basis for the adoption of a common commercial policy to be adopted by the Community in its relations with third countries.

Articles 117-128—These are a series of social policies designed to promote better conditions of living and work. The European Social Fund is to be an important agent of this policy, and in the longer term it is hoped to harmonise various social security schemes. Specific provision is made for the equal payment of men and women.

Articles 129-130—These state the purpose of the European Investment Bank in contributing to the balanced and steady development of the E E C in the interest of the Community.

Articles 131-136—These provide for arrangements to be made for the association of countries with special relations with the Member States.

Articles 137-198—These lay down the composition and functions of the Community's Institutions, viz.

137-144 The European Parliament
145-154 The Council of Ministers
155-163 The Commission
164-188 The Court of Justice
189-192 Provisions common to several institutions
193-198 The Economic and Social Committee

Articles 199-209—These set out financial provisions relating to the contribution of member states to the Budget and European Social Fund and the procedure and basis for monetary transfers.

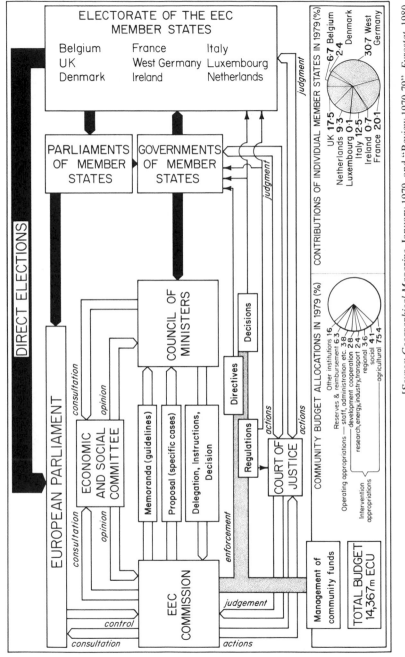

ELECTORATE OF THE EEC
MEMBER STATES

Belgium	France	Italy
UK	West Germany	Luxembourg
Denmark	Ireland	Netherlands

DIRECT ELECTIONS

PARLIAMENTS OF MEMBER STATES

GOVERNMENTS OF MEMBER STATES

EUROPEAN PARLIAMENT

ECONOMIC AND SOCIAL COMMITTEE

COUNCIL OF MINISTERS

COURT OF JUSTICE

EEC COMMISSION

Memoranda (guidelines)

Proposal (specific cases)

Delegation, Instructions, Decision

Directives

Decisions

Regulations

consultation

opinion

opinion

consultation

control

consultation

enforcement

judgement

actions

actions

actions

judgment

judgment

Management of community funds

TOTAL BUDGET 14,367m ECU

CONTRIBUTIONS OF INDIVIDUAL MEMBER STATES IN 1979 (%)

Belgium 6·7
Denmark 2·4
West Germany 30·7
France 20·1
Ireland 0·7
Italy 12·5
Luxembourg 0·1
Netherlands 9·3
UK 17·5

COMMUNITY BUDGET ALLOCATIONS IN 1979 (%)

Other institutions 1·6
Reserves & reimbursement 6·3
staff, administration etc. 3·8
development cooperation 2·8
research,energy,industry,transport 2·4
regional 3·6
social 4·1
agricultural 75·4

Operating appropriations

Intervention appropriations

[Source: Geographical Magazine, January 1979, and "Review 1970–79", Eurostat, 1980.

FIG. 56.—The Treaty of Rome: Institutions of the European Economic Community.

The relationship between the five Community Institutions referred to in Articles 137–198 is shown in Fig. 56. In simple terms, this structure has been established in order to oversee the implementation of the various articles of the Treaty of Rome and also, the Euratom and European Coal and Steel Community treaties. In practice, the process of decision-making is slow and involves a great deal of consultation. As a general rule, within the framework of the above treaties, the Commission makes proposals and produces memoranda, seeks the advice of the European Parliament and the Economic and Social Committee and finally, acts on the instructions of the Council of Ministers. The Court of Justice only intervenes if decisions are involved, e.g. the dispute over lamb imports between the U K and France in October 1979. The Council of Ministers is the most important cog in the decision-making wheel—in general, any decision must be taken by a unanimous vote unless a member state which is opposed agrees to let itself be outvoted. Where this occurs, a majority vote is accepted, although the weighted system of voting means that it is still impossible for the four largest member states (France, West Germany, Italy and the U K) to dictate to the rest.

Figure 56 also indicates the allocation of Community funds and the Budget contributions of member states. The latter is based upon a complex formula relating to G N P, customs duties, agricultural levies and a small share of total V A T revenues. West Germany, the most prosperous member state, pays the heaviest contribution—by 1979 this had increased to around £3,000m. The U K's contribution was around £2,000m, approximately the same as France. By far the largest allocation of Community funds is given to agriculture (*see* Chapter I V). In comparison, the allocation to other common policies is extremely small with the remaining 10 per cent or so of the total Budget being spent on E E C administration.

Index

Details of some other Macdonald & Evans
publications on related subjects can be found
on the following pages.

For a full list of titles and prices write for the
FREE Macdonald & Evans Business Studies
catalogue available from Department BP1,
Macdonald & Evans Ltd., Estover Road,
Plymouth PL6 7PZ

The British Isles
W.M. SIMMONS
Part of the New Certificate Geography series, this systematic study of the British Isles departs from the traditional regional approach in which repetition of detail may obscure the over-all pattern of the national economy. This title will be of great value to those studying for "O" Level, CSE and similar examinations. "This book is a solid work and . . . has much to offer the younger students." *Journal of the Scottish Association of Geography Teachers*

A Geography of Agriculture
P.A.R. NEWBURY
This book adopts a systematic approach, by which specific regional studies are placed within a general theoretical framework. The studies, which are representative of each of the main world agricultural systems, have been prepared from the author's own fieldwork or from contributions from practising farmers and agricultural authorities. The final chapter contains guidance on the collection and presentation of field data. Designed specifically for students of geography, economic geography and agriculture in sixth forms, universities and colleges, it will also be of considerable interest to practising agriculturists all over the world. One of the "Aspect" Geographies series.

Geography for Business Studies
H. ROBINSON
This book caters primarily for students studying geography for National Certificate and Diploma examinations and the various papers in economic and commercial geography set by many professional bodies. Sixth-form students will also find it a comprehensive introduction to the subject. Includes sections on the energy crisis and retail trading.

A Geography of Manufacturing
H.R. JARRETT
This book is designed as a guide for those studying for the first time the geography of manufacturing industry as a discipline in its own right. Part One deals with location theory. Part Two contains studies of selected industries and Part Three gives a summing-up and reviews certain urgent problems of large-scale industrialisation. This title is part of the "Aspect" Geographies series.

Human Geography
H. ROBINSON
This HANDBOOK gives the student starting a course in human geography a basic understanding of world problems, and covers the topics commonly found in most "O" and "A" Level syllabuses. It will also be a most useful text for BEC courses in geography and economic geography. Includes material on early steps in human progress, basic concepts of demography and the political geography of the oceans.

A Geography of Transport
C.G. BAMFORD & H. ROBINSON
This book will meet the needs of students taking the examinations of the Institute of Transport, transport options for Higher National Certificates and Diplomas, and first-year degree courses, and will be of value to anyone with interests in geography, economics and planning. The text deals with the principles of transport, its nature and problems, and its economics and role in planning and tourism, as well as giving a detailed account of transport throughout the world, region by region. One of the "Aspect" Geographies series. "I strongly recommend this book to those who are commencing their professional transport studies, and to all those in the varied activities in industry, commerce, civil service and local government, and to elected representatives, who have a need to obtain an overall view of some of the fundamental matters pertaining to transport so as to enable them to be better informed for their problem-solving tasks." *Chartered Institute of Transport Journal*